The Most Dangerous Man in America?

The Most Dangerous Man in America?

PAT ROBERTSON AND THE RISE OF THE
CHRISTIAN COALITION

Robert Boston

Prometheus Books

59 John Glenn Drive
Amherst, New York 14228-2197

Published 1996 by Prometheus Books

00 99 98 97 96   5 4 3 2 1

Library of Congress Cataloging-in-Publication Data

Boston, Rob, 1962–
    The most dangerous man in America? : Pat Robertson and the rise of the Christian Coalition / Robert Boston.
        p.   cm.
    Includes index.
    ISBN 1–57392–053–3 (pbk. : alk. paper)
    1. Robertson, Pat. 2. Christian Coalition. 3. Conservatism—Religious aspects—Christianity—Controversial literature. 4. United States—Politics and government—1993–   I. Title.
BV3785.R595B67   1996
269'.2'092—dc20
[B]   96–4169
                                                                                        CIP

Printed in the United States of America on acid-free paper

To my wife, Carol, a real example of "family values."

Contents

8   THE MOST DANGEROUS MAN IN AMERICA?

Acknowledgments

My primary debt of gratitude is to the staff of Americans United for Separation of Church and State. It has been my privilege for the past eight years to work with one of the finest staffs in the world of Washington public policy/advocacy organizations.

These years have been a period of growth and challenges for Americans United. The Religious Right's surge and the emergence of Pat Robertson as leader of this movement have challenged Americans United and frequently stretched our resources to the limit. Although a good deal smaller than the Christian Coalition and lacking a money-generating TV network, Americans United has managed to keep out in front of the debate and become a leading voice of opposition to the Religious Right.

Specifically on the Americans United staff, I extend my thanks to Joseph L. Conn, director of communications and editor of *Church & State*. A veritable walking encyclopedia about the Religious Right and church-state separation, Joe's guidance and suggestions were essential to this book. It has been my privilege to work for and learn from him.

I also thank AU Executive Director Barry W. Lynn, who had the vision to understand the importance of this project and gave me the time to do it. Barry, who is both a minister and an attorney, has spent his adult life defending the Bill of Rights. He has personally debated many leading Religious Right figures, including Pat Robertson. I am in awe of Barry's knowledge and skill and the depth of his commitment.

I also thank Ellen Chatterton, former research associate at Americans United. Ellen took the time to watch several hours of "700 Club" broadcasts to double-check quotes and facts. She assisted with fact-checking in other ways, all of which I deeply appreciate. Thanks also to Susan Hansen, editorial department staff assistant, who provided essential computer technical support services to me during this process.

To the rest of the Americans United staff, too numerous to mention, I extend my thanks. I also appreciate the assistance and encouragement of our allies in this struggle in Washington and elsewhere. Many fine organizations monitor, respond to, and oppose the Religious Right. Some are religious in nature, while others are not. All do excellent work and research. The Baptist Joint Committee on Public Affairs, for example, gave me access to some interesting information about Robertson. The BJC keeps alive the Baptist tradition of religious liberty through the separation of church and state, a notion that is sadly neglected by some Baptists today. Its director, the Rev. James Dunn, is a true champion of religious freedom through the separation of church and state.

Also in Washington, the staff of People for the American Way has been producing top-quality research about Robertson for many years. I used some of their materials here and acknowledge my debt. Outside the Beltway, I thank Skipp Porteous of the Institute for First Amendment Studies in Great Barrington, Massachusetts. Skipp, a former fundamentalist minister who once had Religious Right sympathies himself, has seen up close the dangers of what Robertson and the Religious Right are trying to do. Skipp graciously confirmed some information for me and once took the trouble to duplicate both an audio- and a videotape. I also found useful *The Religious Right: The Assault on Tolerance & Pluralism in America,* a top-notch exposé on the Religious Right written by David Cantor, senior research analyst with the Anti-Defamation League in New York.

Lastly, the support and encouragement provided by my wife, Carol, was vital throughout the process. Her understanding of my need to occasionally keep long hours made the project go smoother. Also, supreme thanks to my daughter, Claire, whose bright smile and laughter never failed to lift my spirits at the end of a long, hard day. Claire was not even two years old at the time I wrote this book, but it was because of the wonderful way in which she changed and enriched my life that I learned up close why so much of what the Religious Right spews out about "family values" is nonsense.

A final word: although I relied on a number of resources and sources in compiling this book, I am ultimately responsible for its contents, including any possible errors.

Robert Boston
December 1995

Introduction

Why Should We Care About Pat Robertson?

In George Orwell's nightmarish novel of totalitarianism, *1984*, a pivotal scene involves the torture of dissenter Winston Smith by a government agent known as O'Brien. O'Brien attempts to convince Smith that whatever "Big Brother"—the one-party government—says is true, regardless of what contrary evidence, no matter how strong, may indicate.

O'Brien holds up four fingers and asks, "How many fingers am I holding up, Winston?"

Smith replies, "Four."

"And if the Party says that it is not four but five—then how many?" continues O'Brien.

Although Smith at first continues to insist that the answer is four, under torture he eventually breaks down and whimpers, "I suppose there are four. I would see five if I could. I am trying to see five."

In the world of TV preacher and ultraconservative political activist Pat Robertson, it isn't necessary to resort to torture to see five fingers. In Robertson's world, truth changes simply because Robertson says it does. This amazing ability to bend truth like taffy is what enables Robertson to literally change his story on controversial topics from week to week and day to day. It permits Robertson, for example, to denounce separation of church and state one day as a constitutional myth foisted on the American people by Communists in the former Soviet Union and then barely weeks later insist with a straight face that he has always supported the doctrine of church-state separation and have one of his employees claim that in America it should be "complete and inviolable."

Then, even more incredibly, Robertson can go back to the original story just weeks after that and again assert that church-state separation is an invention of liberal, God-hating Supreme Court justices.

Likewise, Robertson's insistence that whatever he says is true at the moment allows him to insist one day that he does not support the notion that the United States should be officially a "Christian nation" and just weeks after that laud the president of Zambia for proclaiming his country a "Christian nation" and salute that action as a model for the United States and the world.

In Robertson's universe, up can become down, black can become white, and two plus two can equal four, five, or even twenty-eight, if that's what Robertson says. What's more, anyone who dares to criticize him, to point out the inconsistencies, to cry "The emperor has no clothes!" is labeled a religious bigot, an anti-Christian fanatic, or an enemy of God.

That last weapon is a potent one, and may be the single best explanation for how Robertson continues to get away with changing facts and his story whenever the mood suits him. Although Robertson is no longer an ordained minister, he still carries around him an aura of "a man of God." Millions of Americans believe he enjoys some sort of divine favor. To their way of thinking, to criticize Robertson is to criticize God.

But millions of other Americans hold a different view of Robertson. To them he is a greedy televangelist, power hungry and possibly megalomaniacal. Having failed in his effort to become president of the United States in 1988, Robertson is determined to make himself into a political kingmaker. (After all, if you can't be king yourself, the next best thing is not "vice-king," but having the ability to name the next king, thus making him beholden to you for certain political favors.) Robertson, these critics are convinced, seeks to make the United States a fundamentalist Christian version of Iran with himself installed as chief ayatollah.

To these millions of Americans, the real story about Robertson is not that he claims on TV that God uses him to heal goiters or even that he has amassed a corporate fortune that staggers the imagination. It's not that he runs his own graduate-level university or Religious Right law firm. Yes, these things are all important and are vital components of the Pat Robertson story, but the real story—or perhaps the real threat—behind Pat Robertson is the fact that he currently holds the Republican party in a headlock and is making great progress toward his theocratic goals.

The attention of most Americans is not stirred when Robertson says he has expelled demons from a woman in Dubuque or claims to have healed a man of stomach ailments in Tulsa. They do perk up when forces under his command take over the local GOP or seize control of the school board. They do pay attention when Robertson's minions, taking their orders from Virginia Beach, rally to demand organized prayer in public schools, a ban on the teaching of evolution, or tax funding for private religious academies.

But there is a third view of Robertson, and this is perhaps the most important one. Millions of other Americans—probably the majority of people—hold an alternative view of the man. Imagine a face with a blank stare asking, "Who?" or, alternatively, picture a dismissive wave of the hand and a voice asserting, "You mean that TV preacher? Who cares about those types anymore?"

Most Americans neither love Robertson nor loathe him. They don't think about him at all. If asked, they might recall that he once ran for president and didn't do very well. They may run into his beaming persona on television every now and then while cruising channels and pause for a minute and smile while Robertson prays for a woman named Betty in St. Paul who, right now, at this moment, is having her financial burdens lifted. To these people, Robertson is just another one of those guys who preaches on TV, and no one takes them seriously any more, right? These folks have probably never heard of the Christian Coalition, Robertson's political unit with a $25 million annual budget. They don't know that the Christian Coalition claims to have 1.7 million members and 1,600 local affiliates and chapters in all fifty states. They don't know that Robertson has a master plan for the nation that he has outlined in books and that his agenda is radical and dangerous to the personal freedom and religious liberty of every American. They aren't aware that Robertson has embraced anti-Semitic conspiracy theories of history so bizarre they would make Oliver Stone blush. (And they don't know that Robertson has, of course, denied this.)

Thus, there are three ways of looking at Pat Robertson: love him, be suspicious of him, or don't think about him at all. This book is designed primarily for people in the latter two camps. On one hand, it is for people who don't know much about Robertson, what he believes and what he wants to do to this country; on the other, it is for people who already know Robertson is a menace but want evidence backing this claim.

This is not a biography of Robertson. Although some biographical material will be included, it is not my purpose to survey Robertson's life, examine his influences, and relate charming anecdotes from his past. Instead, this book is designed to be a warning. Consider it a fire alarm, ringing loudly and warning of immediate danger—that an intolerant extremist now comes perilously close to holding the reins of American politics. It is an examination of his views, his inconsistencies and hypocrisy, and, frankly, his power.

I will make no special effort to change the minds of those who are convinced that Robertson is especially favored by God. To quote George Orwell again, "There are some people whom you simply cannot answer." I recall a conversation with a woman who, after listening to me deliver a lecture on Robertson and the Christian Coalition, demanded to know why Robertson was such a menace. "After all," she said, "he feeds many people through Operation Blessing."

"I have no quarrel with his humanitarian work," I replied. "It is his political activity that concerns me."

"But," the woman sputtered, "a person who helps so many people must be a true man of God!"

I was tempted to reply, "Remember, even Rasputin was able to stop the tsar's son from bleeding once or twice."

The fact is that millions of Americans are convinced that Robertson has a true link with God. Some of his supporters may accuse me of doing Satan's work in trying to expose Robertson. They may accuse me of trying to blacken the reputation of a man who is working to rebuild America's moral foundations. They may assert that I am an agent of the "radical left" who believes religious conservatives have no place in politics. Let them have their say. If this book engenders a fierce response, it will only be because it speaks the truth.

I should also stress here that I mean nothing in this book to be critical of conservative, Bible-believing Christianity. Millions of Americans belong to conservative denominations, and the majority of them do not look to Robertson as a leader. In fact, many disagree with his stands and tactics, and some are speaking out, such as Ron Sider of Evangelicals for Social Action and the Rev. Tony Campolo, a minister who has criticized the Religious Right's mean-spirited attacks against President Clinton. In 1995 two groups of prominent Christians issued separate statements criticizing the Religious Right for its intemperate rhetoric and for coopting the very term "Christian." These groups, Cry for Renewal and the Maston Colloquium, put out forceful statements stressing the point that the Bible and Christianity are not the exclusive property of the Religious Right. I agree and wish to stress again that my criticism is of Robertson's political goals, not his theology.

(I would also like to point out that in this book, I frequently refer to Robertson as a "fundamentalist." Technically, he is a charismatic, or Pentecostal, Christian. Miles of theological ground exist between fundamentalist Christians and Pentecostals, but for the layperson's sake, I have used the more common terminology.)

The staff of Americans United for Separation of Church and State, my employer, has been monitoring Robertson for more than fifteen years now. We have watched his broadcasts on "The 700 Club"; we have collected books, pamphlets, and other materials produced by his various ministries and political and legal groups. We have on file articles about him that appeared in the secular and religious press. We did not do this because we are paranoid. We did it because we realized, even years ago when Robertson dwelt in the shadow of Jerry Falwell, that his views were extremely hazardous to religious freedom and that, should he ever come to prominence, he would be a formidable character to deal with. My own interest in Robertson predates my employment at Americans United. As a young college student in the early 1980s, I remember my concern over the mounting power of the Religious Right. I remember reading controversial books, some of which had been banned by sectarian pressure groups in earlier times, wondering if I would be able to do that if the Religious Right ever came to power. I remember the spirited give and take of university life—both inside the classroom and out—and feeling that that was too precious to give up for anyone who claims to have revealed political or religious truth.

It was with pleasure that I joined the Americans United staff in 1987 and began studying and writing about the Religious Right as assistant editor of AU's *Church & State* magazine. Those were heady days. Robertson's presidential campaign was in full swing, and he was featured in the newspapers nearly every day.

When the campaign collapsed, most members of the national media lost interest in Robertson. Many reporters just assumed that he went back to his television pulpit. Meanwhile, Robertson was quietly amassing money and building a political empire designed to carry him into the next century. Americans United continued sounding the alarm, and *Church & State* magazine, under the careful eye of Managing Editor Joseph L. Conn, began publishing regular reports on Robertson's political activities.

As Robertson steadily rose to power, Jerry Falwell and his Moral Majority sank lower and lower. Still AU's concerns escalated. By the late 1980s it was clear that the Moral Majority was dead and that the Religious Right had a new leader—Pat Robertson. In the wake of Robertson's candidacy, with the rise of the Christian Coalition, those of us on the AU staff knew we had been wise to keep a close eye on the smiling evangelist from Virginia Beach.

I should say a few words about the title of this book. I remember a few years ago seeing an American Civil Liberties Union (ACLU) fundraising letter that showed photos of Pat Robertson alongside his top lieutenants Ralph Reed and Jay Sekulow, under the headline, "The Most Dangerous Men in America?" While I believe Reed and Sekulow are dangerous, I don't believe either can hold a candle to Robertson in that department. After all, he's had a lot more experience—and he signs *their* paychecks.

Robertson displayed the ACLU mailing during one of his many fundraising telethons. He was not offended by it; if anything, he seemed pleased to have been so singled out by his archnemesis. I remember him waving the letter about, grinning widely, hoping to stir up enough outrage among the faithful that they would go get the checkbook.

Despite rhetorical flourishes it may have employed, the ACLU was right. Robertson *is* dangerous. This book is an effort to explain why. Robertson may very well find it offensive—or amusing—to be the subject of such an exposé. But for those with an open mind, such a detailed examination of his views is essential. This is a man, after all, who wants to play a role in all of our lives and, if current trends continue, will be in a position to make decisions that have the potential to affect all Americans. We have a duty to hold him accountable for the things he has said and done.

Some may complain that I have been too forceful. Robertson supporters may accuse me of penning a "hatchet job." I disagree on both counts. Robertson is so powerful that any response to him *should* be forceful. I believe it is time for those of us who support meaningful religious liberty, diversity, equal rights, public education free from sectarian control, and church-state separation to stand up to the zealots of the radical Religious Right and face them toe to toe, eyeball to eyeball. Let us stand up to the radical forces that would trash our secular democracy and knock down the wall of separation of church and state wherever they operate.

Let us take them on in the political sphere, from the local school board around the block to the halls of Congress in Washington, D.C. Let us engage them in the court of public opinion, through debates, the media, and other appropriate avenues. Let our religious leaders respond to them with vigor. And, above all, let us rip a page out of the Religious Right's own play book and organize, organize, organize.

If we are to "do battle" with the radical Religious Right, then let us be well armed. A good place to start is with a solid dose of the truth about the most prominent leader of the radical Religious Right today. That's what this book is about. It is not an attack on Pat Robertson. It is an attack on what he would do to this country. My hope is to arm the reader with something to say the next time he or she encounters anyone who says, "Pat Robertson's not an extremist!" or, worse yet, "Pat Robertson—that TV preacher? Who cares about those guys anymore? Aren't they harmless?"

What you will read in this book is well documented. It is fully referenced. In many cases, the words come straight from Robertson's own mouth, from his writings, or from publications produced by his organizations. In other cases, they come from the mouths of his top associates, people Robertson has personally hired to run various segments of his religious-political empire, people like Ralph Reed and Jay Sekulow. Robertson always has a ready excuse for some of his more extreme statements, but they ring hollow after just a short while.

I would also point out that it is not my intention in writing this book to imply that Robertson and the Christian Coalition are the only Religious Right forces menacing church-state separation and religious freedom today. I wish that were the case, but sadly it is not.

Dr. James Dobson's radio empire, Focus on the Family, is growing rapidly, is just as political, and attacks church-state separation with equal force. Other Religious Right leaders include the Rev. D. James Kennedy of Coral Ridge Ministries; Beverly LaHaye of Concerned Women for America; the Focus on the Family spinoff dubbed the Family Research Council, headed by Gary Bauer; John Whitehead's Rutherford Institute; Kevin Hasson's Becket Fund; the Free Congress Foundation of Paul Weyrich; and many, many others. Even the Rev. Jerry Falwell is still on the scene, though admittedly on the fringes.

All of these groups espouse theocracy or church-state union to some degree, and all pose a grave threat to our freedoms. I have chosen to focus on Robertson because he is the most powerful of the lot and the first to build a truly effective, nationwide, political machine.

Lastly, I implore the reader to indulge me for a few personal observations. I expect that publication of this book will result in personal attacks against me by Robertson's devotees. They may charge that I hold some sort of personal grudge against Robertson or have an axe to grind because I belong to one of the many groups he frequently attacks.

In fact, I am in many respects exactly the type of person Robertson and his ultraconservative counterparts seek to win over to their side. I am firmly entrenched in the middle class, with a house in the suburbs and two modest economy cars. I am married and a father.

It was the birth of my daughter about twenty months ago (at this writing) that convinced me more than ever that not only are Robertson and the Religious Right wrong about so many things, they are offensively wrong. According to Robertson, I am not "pro-family," because I disagree with him on a number of political issues. Yet, as any parent can tell you, "family values" or the definition of "pro-family" are not measured by where one stands on the death penalty, gun control, or prayer in schools. "Family values" spring from concrete actions and behaviors. I have never felt so "pro-family" as when my wife and I arose at 2:30 A.M. to comfort our infant daughter, or when we put aside so many aspects of our social and professional lives for the opportunity to shepherd a new life into the world.

Family values are found among conservatives, liberals, and the apolitical. They are found among Christians, Jews, Buddhists, atheists, and others. They are not the exclusive property of Robertson or his minions. In fact, the Christian Coalition and groups like it have distorted the definition of "family values" by appending to it a whole host of irrelevant political issues that have nothing to do with one's ability to be "pro-family." It is time those of us on the flipside of this issue from Robertson took those words—"family values" and "pro-family"—back from the radical Religious Right. The Religious Right does not own them, and, in fact, members and leaders of that movement often behave in ways that are alien to the true meaning of "family values."

For that reason alone, it was important to write this book.

Brace yourself, because you are about to enter the world of Pat Robertson. It may be said that up is down, that black is white, or even that two plus two equals twenty-eight. But through it all remember that the number of fingers O'Brien is holding up—no matter what Big Brother says, no matter what the party says, and no matter what Pat Robertson says—is still four.

1

Beginnings

"There is nothing wrong with being successful financially, but you must be careful not to make riches and honor your god. . . . If a man is humble before God and learns to fear the Lord, he will be granted riches, honor and life as a result. . . . In God's eyes, the successful person is the one who lives within the kingdom and by its rules. Worldly possessions are of secondary importance."
—Pat Robertson, *Answers to 200 of Life's Most Probing Questions*

Pat Robertson's ministry hasn't always been political. When Robertson first entered religious broadcasting in the early 1960s, he was convinced that the best way to change the world was through spiritual means. Although he first began flirting with politics in the late 1970s, as recently as 1980 Robertson was still sending mixed signals about the political system. In September of 1980 Robertson wrote in a newsletter titled *Pat Robertson's Perspective*, "Christians should be wary of placing their hopes in non-Christian men and in programs of secular political parties. Even the best of men fail and find themselves rendered ineffective by today's systems."[1]

On New Year's Day, 1980, he warned Christian Broadcasting Network employees that the behavior of sinners cannot be changed by law. "You'd be better to try to save those people and lead them to Jesus," he said. "You'd be better to try to tell all of these people how to get saved."

But politics ran in Robertson's blood, so it's not surprising that after a period of wavering, he eventually jumped into politics head first. Today he runs what is arguably the most political religious ministry in the nation, and, despite his unusual views, he is a key player in the Republican party.

Robertson is the scion of a well-to-do and political Virginia family. His father, A. Willis Robertson, a conservative Democrat, served as a U.S. congressman and senator from 1932 to 1966: fourteen years in the House of Representatives and twenty in the Senate.

Robertson was born on March 22, 1930, and named Marion Gordon. As a child he was nicknamed "Pat" in honor of a family friend. He attended public schools in his hometown of Lexington, Virginia, and Washington, D.C., but finished his last years at a private high school in Chattanooga, Tennessee. Robertson completed his undergraduate work at Washington and Lee University, majoring in history and graduating with honors.

Following a stint in the Marines during the Korean War, Robertson enrolled in Yale Law School in 1952. After graduating, however, he was unable to pass the bar exam and decided to try his hand at a number of business ventures in New York City.[2] These were not successful, and Robertson despaired. In his autobiography, *Shout It from the Housetops,* he writes that during this period he fell so low that he even contemplated suicide.[3]

Robertson was not particularly interested in religion during this period of his life. At Washington and Lee he had a reputation for indulging in drink, cards, and women, a reputation that followed him to Yale. In 1954, while still a law school student, Robertson married Adelia (Dede) Elmer. Elmer was pregnant at the time, and ten weeks after the wedding their first child, Timothy, was born. (The circumstances surrounding Timothy's birth became a point of controversy during Robertson's 1988 quest for the presidency when it was revealed that Robertson had lied about the date of his wedding to cover up the fact that Dede was pregnant at the time of their wedding.)[4]

Robertson's interest in fundamentalist Christianity can be traced to his mother, Gladys, an intensely religious woman who became convinced that her son was living in a spiritual void. In 1956 Gladys Robertson introduced Pat to Cornelius Vanderbreggen, a Philadelphia minister. Robertson adopted some of Vanderbreggen's theology and subsequently enrolled in the New York Theological Seminary. While there he came in contact with "charismatic" Christians who spoke in tongues and believed in the gifts of the Holy Spirit, such as healing and prophecy. Robertson reports that a Korean woman, Su Nae Chu, nicknamed "the tongues woman," first introduced him to the charismatic prayer style.

Robertson graduated in 1959 and two years later in Virginia was ordained a Southern Baptist minister, although he never pastored a church. This is not surprising since the Southern Baptist Convention does not hold speaking in tongues, faith healing, and other charismatic "gifts" as theologically valid. Indeed, Robertson would have been hard pressed to find a Southern Baptist church that would have tolerated such activities.

Robertson's immersion into Pentecostal theology was not always smooth. Shortly after he became "born again," Robertson announced to Dede that he planned to leave for a month-long religious retreat in Canada. As Robertson describes the situation, the family was desperately poor; furthermore, Dede was seven months pregnant.

Not surprisingly, Robertson's wife exploded. "Pat, I've tried to adjust to this 'saved' jag you're on, but you've become a fanatic," she said. "All you do is read that Bible all day and sit around and talk to Jesus. I'm a nurse. I recognize schizoid tendencies when I see them, and I think you're sick.

It's just not normal for a man to walk out on his wife and leave her with a small child when she's expecting a baby any minute—while he goes off into the woods to talk to God. God doesn't tell people to do things like that. At least, my God doesn't."[5]

Robertson refused to abandon his plans to attend the retreat. When Dede wrote to him in Canada begging him to return home to his family, Robertson sent back a note reading, "I can't leave. God will take care of you."Eventually, Dede, who was raised a Roman Catholic, also had a conversion experience, ending any potential conflicts over religious disagreements.

Robertson's career in broadcasting began not long after he received his seminary degree. In 1960 he purchased a small UHF television station in Portsmouth, Virginia, and chartered the Christian Broadcasting Network (CBN). In *Shout It from the Housetops* Robertson reports that he never made a business move without first consulting with the Almighty. Robertson says that before purchasing the UHF station he fasted for a week. On the second day of the fast, he received a clear message. "Then, deep in my heart, I heard him speaking to me about the television ministry," Robertson writes (along with co-author Jamie Buckingham). "Go and possess the station. It is yours."[6]

Robertson relocated to Virginia's Tidewater area with some hesitation. In his autobiography he reports that the region was "literally a spiritual wasteland" that for years had been "in the grip of demon power."[7]

With considerable bluster, Robertson confronted the owner of the deserted station with the announcement, "I'm Pat Robertson. God has sent me here to buy your television station." Thanks to God's good business sense, Robertson got the station, WYAH, and its equipment for a song—$37,000. This became the cornerstone for his television empire. Robertson reports that he had three dollars in the bank when he arranged to buy the station. In *Housetops* Robertson notes that he received some money to complete the transaction from friends and sympathetic local residents who got wind of what he was doing.

From the beginning, fundraising appeals played an important role on the Christian Broadcasting Network. During the station's first telethon in the fall of 1963, Robertson asked 700 viewers to pledge to send the ministry $10 every month, thus enabling the station to meet its $7,000 per month budget. These original contributors became known as "The 700 Club."

Money was a persistent problem in those early days. At times, the lack of funds nearly drove Robertson to despair. At one point, he reports, his spirits were lifted by his mother, who had a vision that, in light of Robertson's later success at money raising, proved to be nothing short of remarkable.

"On February 7, I was in prayer up here in Lexington," she told Robertson over the phone. "And I saw a vision. I've had only two other visions before. This time I had been on my knees praying for you when I saw heaven opening. I saw you kneeling in prayer with your arms outstretched toward heaven. And as you prayed, I saw a packet of bank notes floating down out of heaven into your hands. I looked closely and saw that they were made up of large denominations. I didn't know how much money it was, I just knew it was a lot; and it was as if you were kneeling under the open windows of heaven, and God was pouring out his wealth upon you."[8]

In *Shout It from the Housetops* Robertson repeatedly insists that Satan tried to derail his TV ministry. Several times he mentions that Virginia Beach was home to the Edgar Cayce Foundation, an early New Age group that espoused the doctrine of reincarnation. Robertson insists that many people in the mainline churches were caught up in Cayce's movement. "People were calling in from all over Tidewater pleading with us to pray because their loved ones were being caught up in séances and occult groups," he writes. "The whole area was rife with Satan's power."[9]

Robertson also explains how "Satan" sought to destabilize

his ministry by sowing dissension among the staff at WYAH and "infiltrating our organization with all sorts of strange people." As Robertson fought off the Dark One's evil offensives, he also struggled with getting a radio station on the air. Robertson considered buying the cheapest transmitter on the market, but God would have none of it, going so far as to recommend radio equipment by brand names. "Pat, I want you to have an RCA transmitter," God insisted.[10]

(Robertson has also had at least one conversation with Satan. In *Shout It from the Housetops* he relates that Satan spoke to him while he was in Canada at the retreat. While lying on a cot, Robertson heard Satan say, "Jesus is just playing you for a sucker, Robertson." Satan went on to say that Robertson would surely end up in hell when he died for having blasphemed the Holy Spirit while in college. Robertson replied, "Devil, it may be. But I still know that Jesus is my savior. Even in hell I'll praise him."[11])

In September of 1965 Robertson hired Jim and Tammy Bakker to coordinate children's programming at WYAH. The Bakkers' puppet routine, Robertson says, "drew kids to their meetings in droves." During a telethon later that year, Jim Bakker came on the air and with tears streaming down his face begged for contributions to keep the Christian Broadcasting Network alive. Money rolled in. "By 2:30 A.M. we had raised $105,000, and we finally signed off the air," writes Robertson. "We had no further plans but to go home and praise God."[12]

Those early days in broadcasting apparently taught Robertson much. He has never abandoned the successful formula that kept WYAH alive. At his Christian Broadcast Network frequent telethons featuring emotionally charged appeals warning of imminent disaster to the ministry unless checks are sent immediately are CBN staples today. CBN now has an endowment of $1 billion and Robertson is a multimillionaire, but he is never shy about asking for more.

By the late 1960s, CBN began expanding. Robertson purchased a UHF station in Atlanta and was given five radio stations in New York. The nature of this donation is rather vague, as Robertson mentions it in *Shout It from the Housetops*, but provides no details. He does mention, though, that the combined values of the five stations equaled $600,000.

CBN's 1966 telethon was so successful that Robertson decided to launch a nightly program. This was the birth of "The 700 Club," a show named in honor of Robertson's original group of contributors. Originally, the program did not have a regular host. Early shows were often hosted by Jim Bakker. It aired at 10 P.M. but had no definite ending time. There was no script. Notes Robertson, "If God said sing, we sang. If he said give an invitation, we gave it. If he said interview a guest, we interviewed the guest." It must have been a far cry from the highly polished, carefully scripted "700 Club" of today.

By 1975, CBN reached an estimated 110 million homes through cable. With the ministry growing rapidly, Robertson began dabbling in politics. In 1978 he supported G. Connoly Phillips, who unsuccessfully sought a U.S. Senate seat representing Virginia. In 1979, he made the following interesting observation to the liberal *Sojourners* magazine: "There is only one job in the United States and the world, I suppose, that would give me any more opportunity to do good for my fellow man. That would be the presidency."[13]

By 1980 Robertson was attending Religious Right rallies and exhorting conservative Christians to get involved in politics. At the April 1980 "Washington for Jesus" rally he exclaimed, "We have enough votes to run the country. And when the people say, 'We've had enough,' we are going to take over."[14]

In 1981 Robertson formed his first political group, the Freedom Council. The group's mandate called for it to "encourage, train, and equip Americans to exercise their civil [sic] responsibility to actively participate in government." According to the *New York Times*, Robertson poured $8.5 million of CBN's money into the Freedom Council, a move of dubious legality that sparked an IRS investigation.[15] By 1985, according to the Anti-Defamation League, he was already contemplating a run for the presidency, and the Freedom Council became the basis for that jump into politics. (Under the Internal Revenue Service Code, nonprofit organizations like CBN are restricted in the amount of political activity in which they may engage. They also are not permitted to turn their assets over to groups that have political activity as a chief focus.)

The early and mid-1980s were heady times for the Religious Right. The movement enjoyed close ties to President Ronald Reagan and the Republican majority in the Senate. Most people, when they think about the Religious Right of the 1980s, tend to associate the movement with the Rev. Jerry Falwell and the Moral Majority. It's true that Falwell was the primary figure and leading spokesperson for the Religious Right throughout most of the 1980s. But even as Falwell hogged the limelight, a number of smaller and lesser-known figures continued to operate on the fringes. Pat Robertson was one of these. While some of the more peripheral figures, such as TV preacher James Robison, later stepped away from right-wing politics, Robertson stayed with it. As the 1980s progressed, Falwell became less and less important while Robertson's star continued to rise. In 1989, Falwell shut down the Moral Majority entirely.

Why did this happen? Most observers of the Religious Right believe Falwell made a tactical error. While the Moral Majority had state chapters and tried to cultivate a grassroots presence, it remained largely a mailing list with Falwell as chief beneficiary. It also tended to focus most of its energy on Washington—Congress and the White House.

In 1986 the Democrats regained control of the Senate, dealing the Moral Majority a serious blow. The group lost more prestige when it became apparent that President Reagan had no intention of going all out for the group's social issues agenda. Reagan introduced a school prayer amendment, but it failed to gain the necessary super-majority to pass the Senate. Reagan took a number of steps to oppose abortion by issuing various executive orders, but the medical procedure remained legal, and a constitutional amendment to ban nearly all abortions went nowhere. On another front, the Religious Right's goal of securing federal aid for private sectarian schools also died in Congress. After eight years of Reagan, who was supposedly a champion of the Religious Right's causes, the Moral Majority had little to show for the work it had done. Disenchanted movement activists began asserting that the Moral Majority had made a mistake zeroing in on Washington. The way to change the United States, they said, is to pay more attention to state and local politics.

Pat Robertson was already preaching this message. In preparation for his 1988 presidential run, he had already laid the groundwork for unprecedented grassroots work by ultra-conservative fundamentalists. Robertson had the money, brains, and national presence to make it happen. It was only natural, then, that Robertson would assume the mantle that Falwell allowed to slip from his grasp.

Today Robertson presides over state-of-the-art, multimillion-dollar broadcast studios at the CBN complex in Virginia Beach. He owns the Family Channel, the nation's seventh largest cable network, which broadcasts "The 700 Club" daily. His far-flung business dealings have made Robertson a millionaire many times over. He owns a graduate-level college, Regent University, and presides over the Christian Coalition, arguably the single most influential political organization in the country today. Robertson hobnobs with presidents, senators, and heads of state and is eagerly courted by rising stars in the GOP.

Meanwhile in Lynchburg, Virginia, Falwell must struggle to keep his school, Liberty University, from sinking into bankruptcy. He no longer has a significant national organization and is rarely quoted in the media. Falwell's "Old Time Gospel Hour" occasionally appears on low-power UHF stations around the country, but it is clearly not the money generator it once was. To make a living, Falwell has been reduced to selling scurrilous videotapes that accuse President Bill Clinton of being a cocaine addict. Even fellow conservatives have denounced him for engaging in such mean-spirited character assassination.[16]

Robertson is up and Falwell is down, and that situation is not likely to change. Robertson's Christian Coalition, fronted by the benign-looking political whiz kid Ralph Reed, is the clear vehicle of choice that millions of fundamentalist Christians use to mobilize in far-right politics. As the Christian Coalition grows, Robertson has even tried to distance himself from the group. Lately he has taken to referring to himself as an "elder statesman" and claims that Reed is really running the show day to day.

Reed's title is executive director, but Robertson remains president of the Christian Coalition, as well as one of its four national directors. Two of the other three directors, the Rev. Billy McCormack and Dick Weinhold, are close Robertson associates. The third is Robertson's son Gordon. Reed was hand-picked by Robertson to run the group. Despite the talk, the Christian Coalition remains Pat Robertson's organization, and it is Robertson, not Reed, who sets the policy.

The shift of focus from Robertson to Reed is part of a careful strategy by the Christian Coalition to make itself appear moderate and nonthreatening to the average American. Robertson has a paper trail several hundred miles long. In his lengthy career, he has uttered countless extremist statements and levied numerous baseless charges against his perceived enemies. The point is, Robertson scares people; Reed, who is invariably described as being "baby faced" or accused of resembling a choir boy, does not. So Reed is the smiling, nicely groomed young man who stands before the cameras while just behind the curtain lurks the sinister persona of Pat Robertson.

It's not hard to rip open that curtain. All one must do is go back into the public record and do a little digging. Even a cursory dig unearths a plethora of extremist statements and untruths unleashed by Robertson. Of course, Robertson says they are taken out of context. They are not. Robertson says he didn't say them. He did, and in many cases on television. Robertson says throwing this stuff up in his face is an example of "anti-Christian bigotry." It's not.

Robertson has chosen to enter the political fray. He has stepped forward with a highly controversial agenda wrapped in divisive rhetoric. He has engaged in name-calling and smearing those who disagree with him on political questions. And yet, when he receives return fire—as he inevitably will and, quite frankly, should—he wails, moans, and whines as if his alleged status as a "man of God" should somehow shield him from the public spotlight.

For better or worse, that's not the way American politics works. It's a rough-and-tumble world out there. Robertson's own group, the Christian Coalition, has become a master of dirty politics. Why should the organization be surprised when its opponents refuse to be intimidated?

Any group that espouses theocracy—as the Christian Coalition surely does, though again, Robertson and Reed repeatedly swear it isn't so—should expect criticism and plenty of spirited opposition. Robertson has the right to believe whatever he wants theologically, but when he calls for writing those personal theological views into the secular legal code for all to follow, it's time to take off the gloves.

Pat Robertson would like to play an important role in all of our lives. It is fair, then, for us to hold him accountable and demand to know what type of man he really is. Robertson says he is not an extremist. Does the record back that up? I believe it does not. Has Robertson said extreme things about religious freedom, separation of church and state, and the rights of religious minorities? I believe he has. Is there reason to doubt his sincerity when he says today that he's harmless? I believe there is.

For a man who made his fortune in broadcasting, Robertson seems to have a difficult time grasping the idea that words have meaning. Comments made on national television or set down in books cannot be ignored or dismissed just days or weeks later. During his 1988 presidential campaign, Robertson seemed to have an especially difficult time realizing that, as a national figure, people were paying attention to what he had to say. Looking back on that campaign now, one sees that it is a gold mine of extremism and gaffes.

The next chapter examines the campaign in more detail.

Notes

1. Quoted in David Cantor, *The Religious Right: The Assault on Tolerance & Pluralism in America,* 2d ed. (New York: Anti-Defamation League, 1994).

2. T. R. Reid, "Robertson's Bid Powered by Faith, Self-Assurance," *Washington Post* (September 11, 1987).

3. Pat Robertson and Jamie Buckingham, *Shout It from the Housetops* (Planfield, N.J.: Logos International, 1972), p. 3.

4. "Pat Robertson Having to Face Facts of His Life," *Atlanta Constitution* (October 8, 1987).

5. Robertson and Buckingham, *Shout It from the Housetops*, p. 18.

6. Ibid., p. 85.

7. Ibid., p. 89.

8. Ibid., pp. 107–108.

9. Ibid., p. 164.

10. Ibid., p. 165.

11. Ibid., p. 23.

12. Ibid., p. 173.

13. Quoted in *The Religious Right: The Assault on Tolerance & Pluralism in America,* p. 16.

14. Ibid.

15. Wayne King, "Pat Robertson: A Candidate of Contradictions," *New York Times* (February 29, 1988).

16. Laurie Goodstein, "Evangelical Leader Petitions to Rebut Anti-Clinton Tapes," *Washington Post* (January 27, 1995).

2

President Pat?

"Of course, you always have to consider what the Lord wants. If He were to say, 'Run for president,' then obviously any man of God would have to obey. The whole thing would depend on what He wanted."
> —Pat Robertson, interview with the
> *Saturday Evening Post*, March 1985.

"With the Lord behind him, he can't lose."
> —Robertson supporter Shirley Tippin,
> commenting on his plan to run for president

When Pat Robertson officially announced, on October 1, 1987, that he would be a candidate for president of the United States, it was a surprise to practically no one. Robertson had begun laying the groundwork for his run years in advance; at a September 17, 1986, rally he promised to enter the race if three million Americans signed petitions asking him to run. "If, by September 17, 1987, one year from today, three million registered voters have signed petitions telling me that they will pray, that they will work, that they will give toward my election, then I will run," Robertson declared.

The petition drive was more than just a political stunt. When the time came to formally enter the race, Robertson had amassed an enormous mailing list that he was already using to solicit contributions. By the time he officially jumped in, Robertson had raised $11 million, just below the amount raised by then-Vice President George Bush, the front-runner. It was an impressive feat for a man who had never run for— let alone held—public office.

It's hard to say exactly when Robertson first got the idea of seeking the Republican nomination. What is known is that he began undertaking exploratory work as early as 1985. Late that year he convened a closed-door meeting of Religious Right leaders in Alexandria, Virginia, to gauge their reaction to the idea. Attendees included the Rev. Jerry Falwell, at that time head of the Moral Majority; the Rev. Charles Stanley, president of the Southern Baptist Convention; the Rev. D. James Kennedy of Coral Ridge Ministries; Ben Armstrong, head of the National Religious Broadcasters; and Bill Bright of Campus Crusade for Christ.

Jerry R. Curry, a retired military officer who worked with the Freedom Council, a Robertson-founded political group for born-again Christians, later told a reporter with the *Washington Times* that Robertson called the meeting to ask the ministers for "their wise counsel and understanding and experience regarding whether or not he should consider running for president."[1]

Reagan's second term was barely under way when rumors began circulating that Robertson was planning a bid for the White House. Asked to comment on the question by the *Saturday Evening Post*, Robertson was coy. "Of course, I've heard that rumor before; I don't live in a vacuum," he said. "But I've never taken it seriously. Good heavens, I've got the best job in the world right now. I would be crazy to want to change it. I enjoy what I do—and I love it—and on top of that, I'm serving the Lord."[2]

Evidence indicates that at the time he granted the interview, Robertson had already made up his mind to run. According to syndicated columnist Michael J. McManus, Robertson channeled $8.5 million in CBN funds to the Freedom Council from 1984 through 1986, which could indicate that Robertson was toying with the idea as early as the end of Ronald Reagan's first term. Although Robertson insisted the Freedom Council was founded to encourage conservative Christians to participate in the political process, the organization soon began functioning as a de facto "Robertson for President" unit. (The IRS investigated this money transfer, but Robertson disbanded the group in the fall of 1986 before the matter was resolved.) In Michigan, McManus reports, Robertson hired Marlene Elwell to run the Freedom Council's state affiliate. Elwell remarked, "The time for education is over. The time for action is now."[3] Elwell later became Midwest coordinator for Robertson's campaign.

On April 5, 1988, NBC's "Nightly News" interviewed Dick Minard, a former Freedom Council official, who said, "The entire process was to create a launching pad for Pat Robertson's bid for the presidency. I was a conduit . . . in spreading his work and his charade . . . to hundreds of people around the country to get involved in the Freedom Council, for a legitimate cause that turns out wasn't a legitimate cause." Curry, who resigned in April of 1986 told NBC, "You have to come to the conclusion that more and more you are becoming, whether you want to or not, a cover of some kind for Pat Robertson's campaign. I felt we were crossing the line, and I was just uncomfortable with it."[4]

McManus used the Freedom of Information Act to receive copies of the Freedom Council's tax returns for 1983–86. He reported, "What I found was peculiar. The report for 1983 only had zeros. The IRS got no report for 1984 at all. And the 1985 report said [the Council's] aim was to write and give out 'nonpartisan materials encouraging public participation in the democratic process.' But of a $5 million budget, only $10,193 was for publications. The rest went for a massive staff that mobilized thousands of Christians at churches to become Republican delegates. Result: He has taken over [Michigan's] Republican Party."[5]

(McManus has been a frequent critic of Robertson over the years. But anyone who believes that this is because he is a member of the "liberal media" should think again. McManus, an Episcopalian, holds conservative views on many issues.)

The Michigan branch of the Freedom Council recruited precinct delegate candidates for congressional districts, working through local fundamentalist churches. Normally seen as low-level slots, precinct delegates were very important to Robertson because eventually the people who held those positions selected Michigan's delegates to the 1988 Republican Party National Convention. Robertson's organizational strengths in Michigan caught Bush off guard and also surprised GOP contenders Jack Kemp (former Secretary of Housing and Urban Development) and Sen. Robert Dole (R-Kan.). Robertson claimed to have recruited 4,500 supporters from ultraconservative churches in Michigan, an achievement he hailed in a fundraising letter headlined, "THE CHRISTIANS HAVE WON!"

The major candidates failed to take Robertson seriously early on, but they soon learned from that mistake. In caucuses and straw polls, Robertson did very well because of his well-placed state organizations and the determination of his supporters. For a brief period of time early in the campaign, he actually looked like a contender. Robertson eagerly fed this image because it boosted his fundraising efforts. In a very short time, of course, the campaign crashed and burned, but by then Robertson had reaped numerous benefits from his excursion into electoral politics—benefits he continues to reap today.

Robertson claimed divine sanction for his run more than once. At the September 1986 rally, he declared, "What is God's will for me in this? Let me assure you I know God's will for me."[6] But even a stamp of approval from the Almighty, it seems, couldn't help Robertson on Super Tuesday.

Speaking at a fundamentalist church in Bedford, New Hampshire, in February of 1988, Robertson was even more forward. "This is where God wanted me to be. . . . Here I am in New Hampshire, before a major primary. I assure you that I am going to be the next president of the United States."[7]

According to Robertson, the campaign was God's idea. In the mid-1980s, he claimed, God began urging him to throw his hat in the ring. "I had everything you could ask for," he said, "but God had something else for me to do. I heard the Lord saying, 'I have something else for you to do. I want you to run for president of the United States.' "[8]

With God overseeing the campaign, Robertson was not surprised at his early success in Iowa. "I didn't think that the One who has never failed me was going to fail me now."[9]

For a divinely inspired event, Robertson's campaign had plenty of rocky moments. Even for a modern political campaign it was marked by a number of cheap political stunts and transparently staged events that more often than not exploded in the candidate's face. Robertson claimed to have God's backing, but his campaign was certainly less than divine. Adding to the volatile mixture were an increasingly large number of gaffes and misstatements by Robertson and embarrassing revelations about his personal life. Robertson seemed to think that as a "man of God" he would receive softer treatment from the news media. For a communications magnate and public figure, he seemed genuinely unprepared for the tough scrutiny he received. As a result, Robertson spent much of the campaign complaining that reporters were out to get him.

Just days after Robertson announced his candidacy, the *Wall Street Journal* broke a story reporting that Robertson had been lying about the date of his wedding for years in an effort to conceal the fact that his wife was more than seven months pregnant when the ceremony occurred. The *Journal* reported that Robertson and his wife were married on August 27, 1954, in a secret ceremony before a justice of the peace without the knowledge of their parents. As late as the summer of 1987 Robertson was still misleading the press about the matter. He told the *Washington Post* that he and his wife were married on March 22, Robertson's birthday. Asked to explain the discrepancy, Robertson's rather lamely replied that he and his wife have always considered March 22 their wedding anniversary because "our son was conceived on that day."[10] He also excused his premarital sex by pointing out that it took place before he became "born again."

Robertson was outraged that the media called him on his deception, telling reporters in Philadelphia October 8, "It is outrageous to pry into a man's past and try to do damage to a man's wife and children under the guise of journalism." (One wonders if Robertson believes the same standard should have been applied to President Bill Clinton, a frequent target for the Religious Right's character assassination squad.)

At about that same time, other discrepancies in Robertson's record came to light. The *Washington Post* reported that Robertson had claimed to be a member of the board of directors of the United Virginia Bank, when in fact he only served on a community advisory board. He also claimed on his resume to have done graduate study at the University of London, when in fact he once took an introductory summer arts course for visiting Americans there. (Robertson later corrected his resume.) The *Dallas Morning News* noted that Robertson had variously described his IQ as 159, 139 and 137—which would qualify him as a genius—and that his 1986 book *America's Dates with Destiny* says he is a "Yale-educated tax lawyer," although he never passed the bar.

Revelations about Robertson's war record also dogged his campaign. In his campaign literature Robertson claimed to be a combat veteran of the Korean War. In fact, he served three miles from the front in a headquarters function ferrying codes to Japan and never saw combat.

Former GOP congressman Pete McCloskey of California,

who served in the same unit as Robertson, claimed that Robertson had relied on his father's influence to get him out of combat duty. Robertson was so rankled by the charge that he sued McCloskey and Representative Andy Jacobs, an Indiana Democrat who also circulated the charges, for $35 million.

McCloskey insisted that Robertson was on a ship headed for combat until his father used his influence to have him removed. According to McCloskey, Robertson later boasted that he had used his father to "get him out of combat duty."[11]

The libel suit turned out to be an embarrassment to Robertson. During depositions, Paul Brosman, Jr., a retired university professor who served with Robertson in Korea, backed up McCloskey's claim and went even further, asserting that the televangelist had consorted with prostitutes and had sexually harassed a Korean cleaning girl who worked in the barracks. Brosman's deposition asserted that Robertson once feared he had contracted gonorrhea from a prostitute and was "very relieved" when he discovered the problem was a urinary tract infection. Brosman added that he had never personally seen Robertson with a prostitute and said some of his remarks were based on "scuttlebutt" he heard from others.[12]

The trial also established that Robertson's father did indeed send a number of letters about his son, on Senate stationary, to Marine officials. In one the elder Robertson expressed concern that his son had not been adequately trained to be a combat officer.[13]

McCloskey's lawyers also revealed that Robertson had used a freelance journalist to gather information to use against the congressman. The reporter, John Hasbrouck, had occasionally done pieces for the Christian Broadcasting Network but represented himself to McCloskey as a reporter for "Worldwide News Service." The *New York Times* reported that Hasbrouck interviewed McCloskey on videotape without telling the congressman he was working for Robertson. Robertson admitted in a deposition that he told Hasbrouck what questions to ask then reviewed the hour-long tape before deciding to sue McCloskey. The *New York Times* also reported that Robertson asked Iran-Contra figure Oliver L. North, then a White House security aide, to help him locate military records to boost his case. North put Robertson in touch with a Marine general in the Pentagon who provided copies of his service record.[14]

In the end, Robertson dropped the lawsuit, claiming that the trial date, which was set for March 8, the day of the "Super Tuesday" primaries, was too inconvenient. Robertson groused that U.S. District Judge Joyce Hens Green "presented me with one of the most unfair choices I have ever had to make" when she set the trial date. When Robertson dropped his suit the court required him to pay some of McCloskey's court costs, though not his legal fees.

The case hurt Robertson in another way: it led to a spate of stories in the press recounting other instances of the TV preacher's dishonesty. In one of the most shocking examples, the *Washington Post* reported that in the summer of 1987 Robertson insisted that CBN's "financial affairs have been completely open and on the record." In fact, CBN refused to join the Evangelical Council for Financial Accountability, an oversight group that provides voluntary standards for financial disclosure. (Robertson finally got around to signing up CBN for the ECFA in 1995, but only after most of his most profitable business ventures were spun off from CBN and the National Religious Broadcasters threatened to expel any members that were not accredited by the agency.)

The *Washington Post* reported that on December 15, 1985, Robertson insisted on NBC's "Meet the Press" that CBN had released a public financial statement. In fact, no such statement existed, and Robertson was forced to order one quickly drawn up. The document was not published until 1986 but was back-dated with a 1985 copyright.[15]

Information about Robertson's personal finances also revealed some contradictions. In April of 1987 Robertson issued a "Statement of Stewardship" stating that his 1986 CBN salary was $60,000. In a sworn deposition, he later admitted to receiving considerably more—$104,000. The *Washington Post* questioned Robertson and his staff repeatedly but was unable to get a figure of what CBN really paid him.[16]

Several reporters also scoured old Robertson books and in one of them, *Answers to 200 of Life's Most Probing Questions,* found this gem: "Lying is a deliberate attempt to deceive by use of any form of untruth. . . . A person who falsifies his achievements or age is lying. A person who covers up or exaggerates facts is lying."[17] Reported the *Post*: "Political aides said Robertson gets livid when asked about such misstatements. As a television evangelist, Robertson is accustomed to an adoring and unquestioning reception from his followers. On the campaign trail, he has been stunned to find how 'rough' the political world can be."[18]

As Robertson traveled the country prior to his official announcement that he would be a candidate, his stock speech contained what Michael McManus charged was another well-rehearsed piece of political theater. During the speech, someone in the crowd would yell out, "Are you going to run for president?" Robertson would reply something like, "I'm not sure. Do you want me to run?" Deafening cries of "YES!" would shake the podium. McManus says the questioners were Freedom Council plants.

Even the day Robertson officially threw his hat into the ring was stormy. Robertson decided to make the announcement in the Bedford-Stuyvesant neighborhood of Brooklyn, where he and his wife lived for three months in 1959. He chose the gritty, heavily African-American enclave in an effort to portray himself as a champion of the underclass, telling reporters he was seeking the presidency "because I have a commitment to the cities of the United States and to the poor of this nation."[19] But the image of a multimillionaire who favors abolishing the social safety net positioning himself as a champion of the poor was too much for some people to bear. Robertson's event was crashed by a crowd of two hundred vocal protesters, and he was forced to shout to be heard. Even the introduction went poorly. Former NFL star Rosie Grier introduced the candidate as "Pat Robinson."

Representative Major Owens, a Democrat who has represented the area in Congress for thirteen years, was not impressed by Robertson's political theater. "I consider him a menace," Owens said. "This is a political stunt. There's really no affinity or concern for the issues important to the black community."[20]

The protesters didn't faze Robertson or his supporters, however. Despite all that had come out about the candidate, his band of hard-core followers remained loyal, brushing it all off as a smear campaign orchestrated by the liberal media. (Again, it is highly ironic that many of these same people today are willing to swallow any bit of pernicious gossip about Clinton, the Democrats, or liberals paraded about in the right-wing media or put forth by talk radio hate-mongers like Rush Limbaugh.)

In Iowa, Robertson backers brushed off suggestions that their man had lied for changing his wedding date, and some of them engaged in incredible acts of self-delusion to keep the pristine image of their hero intact. Remarked John Miller, Robertson's Iowa field director, "Pat Robertson wasn't necessarily trying to cover up a story. He was just trying to keep it quiet for the protection of his family."[21] The logic of Robertson loyalists works like this: what would be considered a lie by anyone else becomes a pro-family act if it is uttered by Robertson.

At the time he made the announcement in Brooklyn, Robertson was riding high. Just two weeks before, he had come in first in a straw poll in Iowa, embarrassing Bush, who took third behind Dole. While Bush tried to brush off the poll as "just a scrimmage," his political team was clearly shaken. Robertson's people, meanwhile, gloated over the victory. "I have mixed emotions over Saturday's results," a sarcastic Marlene Elwell remarked. "My heart ached for the vice president, and I felt pain."[22] (Later, in the actual caucus, Robertson came in second, behind Dole but again ahead of Bush, taking about 25 percent of the vote.)

Although Robertson eventually mended fences with Bush once the vice president secured the nomination, earlier the two camps verged on open warfare. In August of 1987 Robertson bitterly accused Bush strategist Lee Atwater of unleashing "dirty tricks" against his campaign, although he admitted he could not prove it. Robertson said the "dirty tricks" included Bush campaign workers phoning Robertson supporters around the country and telling them Robertson would appear at rallies that the candidate in fact had no intention of attending.

Robertson continued to make allegations against the Bush campaign. After Robertson came in last in the New Hampshire primary, his staff was certain Bush was to blame. Robertson also accused Bush backers of leaking details about the Jimmy Swaggart sex scandal to the media, hoping to embarrass Robertson. No evidence was offered, and Bush dismissed the allegations as "crazy" and "absurd."

Ironically, at the same time he was making these charges, Robertson's own people were engaging in bona fide "dirty tricks" against another GOP hopeful, Jack Kemp, who noted that just one day before the Iowa caucus, thousands of flyers accusing him of being pro-pornography appeared in church parking lots all over the state. The flyers bore the name of a group called the "Christian Connection." Syndicated columnist Michael McManus did some digging and found that Dan Scalfe, director of Robertson's campaign in Illinois, had worked as a "volunteer" with the Christian Connection. McManus also learned that Scalfe changed the positions of other GOP hopefuls in a document called "The Biblical Scorecard" that purported to list where the candidates stood on various social issues. Kemp's opposition to pornography was left out entirely. McManus also located six Iowa pastors who reported that Robertson staffers had asked them to circulate the document. The pastors regarded it as a smear campaign and refused.[23]

Kemp was livid. In one speech he blasted Robertson by name and demanded that he abide by the Ninth Commandment: "Thou shall not bear false witness."

Robertson's candidacy was a short-lived affair, but he managed to stick his foot in his mouth several times during his campaign. At a Republican debate in New Hampshire in February of 1988, he insisted that the Soviet Union had stationed nuclear missiles in Cuba. This claim came as quite a surprise to the staff of President Ronald Reagan, who issued a statement pointing out that all of the nuclear missiles in Cuba were removed after the 1962 missile crisis. Backpedaling furiously, Robertson later insisted that he only meant to imply that there "may be" missiles in Cuba and said "I have no idea" whether they contain nuclear warheads, but reporters continued to dog him about the matter. Robertson grew angry and while touring a gun factory in Rochester, New Hampshire, he picked up an unloaded rifle and mockingly pointed it at the reporters, saying, "We like NBC; you don't understand."[24] The implication seemed to be that Robertson didn't want to hurt anyone, but he would defend himself if necessary.

Less than two weeks later a second Robertson foray into foreign affairs sparked controversy. This time the candidate claimed that CBN knew the location of several American hostages being held in Lebanon and implied that the Reagan administration could have known, too, if staffers had only watched CBN news reports. "We identified in our news department at CBN the location of those hostages in Lebanon very shortly after they were taken. And they were in a position where they could have been rescued," Robertson said during an Atlanta news conference. "They were in Beirut, and they could have been freed."[25]

President Reagan later commented, "It'd be very strange if he actually did have information as to the location of those hostages. . . . If he thought he knew, he kept it to himself." Later, Robertson's own Beirut bureau chief denied ever having any information about the location of the hostages.

Facing increasing criticism from the White House and other GOP contenders, Robertson fell back on his standard tactic of accusing others of manufacturing the controversy. He called the hostage remark "a throwaway line" and said he found it "hard to understand why there has been such an incredible flap."

Robertson must have sensed that voters would perceive him as weak in the area of foreign policy, so on several occasions he tried to talk tough. Unfortunately for Robertson, his efforts to play global Dirty Harry usually just ended up making him sound like a loose cannon. At a news conference in Van Nuys, California, in February of 1987, Robertson called on the U.S. government to form "hit squads" to assassinate terrorists. Government-sponsored assassination, Robertson asserted, "may not appeal to our Anglo-Saxon sense of justice, but it certainly is an appropriate response to war. And this is war. If they're going to commit assassinations as an act of war, then we have every right to retaliate with that discreet type of response."[26]

While the Republican party emerged intact from all of the infighting, for a time it appeared that Robertson's presence in the campaign might lead to some sort of GOP fissure. His candidacy energized hard-right evangelicals all over the country, with tens of thousands of them pouring into the party and seizing local leadership slots.

This didn't always go down too well. Old guard Republicans were understandably reluctant to give up to newcomers positions of power that some of them had held for decades, and political warfare erupted in some states. In South Carolina's Richland County, Bush partisans had to evoke obscure procedural rules to keep the party from being taken over by Robertson delegates. Robertson in turn angrily accused Bush of subverting the democratic process.

Some old-line Republicans in South Carolina could not hide their distaste for Robertson's backers. William B. Depass, Jr., chairman of the GOP convention in Richland County, attended a Robertson meeting and compared it to "a Nazi pep rally." "The group was whipped into a froth," Depass told the *New York Times*. "It was mob mentality. I've never seen a political meeting like this in my life. It was like holding up dog biscuits and having people bark for them."[27]

But Robertson had the last laugh in South Carolina. His followers organized and took 40 to 50 percent of the seats at the state GOP convention. "The Robertson forces came on like gangbusters," said John Courson, a Republican state senator. "It was like a hurricane coming in from the Caribbean. We were blindsided."[28]

Throughout the campaign, Robertson was dogged by accusations that as president he would use the power of government to enforce his narrow theological beliefs and abolish the separation of church and state. Robertson pretended to be mortified anytime this allegation was raised, but that never stopped him from making a number of extremist statements during the race.

One of his most shocking utterances occurred a full year before he officially became a candidate. At the time Robertson was viewed as likely to run, and found himself being sought out by reporters and editors. Meeting with a group of writers from the *Washington Post* in June of 1986, Robertson brazenly declared that "a Supreme Court ruling is not law" and asserted that Congress and the president don't have to obey Court rulings with which they disagree.

During the session, a *Post* staffer asked Robertson about *Roe* v. *Wade*, the 1973 high court decision that legalized abortion, referring to it as the "law of the land." "I take issue with your premise," Robertson replied. "A Supreme Court ruling is not the law of the United States. The law of the United States is the Constitution, treaties made in accordance with the Constitution, and laws duly enacted by the Congress and signed by the president. And any of those things I would uphold totally with all my strength, whether I agreed with them or not."

Later Robertson added, "I am bound by the laws of the

United States and all 50 states . . . [but] I am not bound by any case or any court to which I myself am not a party. . . . I don't think the Congress of the United States is subservient to the courts. . . . They can ignore a Supreme Court ruling if they so choose."[29]

Robertson's interpretation of the separation of powers is creative, to say the least. It is also dead wrong. While it's true of course that the Supreme Court does not have the power to make laws, it can, through the doctrine of judicial review, invalidate laws of Congress as well as state and local governments. This matter was settled nearly two hundred years ago in *Marbury* v. *Madison.* And the Court's decisions most certainly are binding on Congress and other legislative bodies, as well as on private citizens.

Robertson expounded on his unusual legal theory on the October 23, 1987, edition of "The 700 Club," remarking, "Supreme Court decisions are binding in the court systems . . . but in terms of general law, which binds every citizen, why should you and I be bound because of the ineptitude, if you will, or the skill of one or more defense lawyers, or the plaintiffs in any particular lawsuit?"

For someone who has a law degree, Robertson has on several occasions shown himself to be simply out of touch with the realities of modern courtroom jurisprudence. Bemoaning the Court's church-state decisions yet again on the December 10, 1990, broadcast of "The 700 Club," he complained, "They [advocates of church-state separation] scream, 'First Amendment.' Of course, the First Amendment, as you and I both know, is a restriction on Congress. . . . So it really doesn't have anything to do with what you say or what I say, one way or the other."

Years earlier, on the April 11, 1986, broadcast, Robertson said flatly about the First Amendment, "There is never in the Constitution at any point, anything that applies that to the states, none at all. The Supreme Court has done it over repeated attempts by Congress which have been beaten back to do such a thing."

Meeting with editors and reporters at the Atlanta *Journal and Constitution* during the summer of 1987, Robertson reiterated his belief that the Bill of Rights does not apply to the states. Newspaper staffers pressed Robertson to say whether as president he would appoint only judges who share that view—assuming he could find any. Robertson refused to answer.[30]

Robertson's insistence that the Bill of Rights doesn't apply to the states is simply incorrect. First-year law students are taught the history of how the First Amendment came to be binding on the states. Following the Civil War, Congress passed the Fourteenth Amendment, which "incorporates" the entire Bill of Rights and applies it to the states. Although the Supreme Court for many years stubbornly refused to recognize what Congress had done, by 1925 the Court began ruling that provisions of the Bill of Rights are binding on the states. This "incorporation" doctrine applied the religious liberty clauses of the First Amendment to the states in the 1940s in the cases *Cantwell* v. *Connecticut* and *Everson* v. *Board of Education*. Today, even the most radical right-wing activists on the Supreme Court, such as Chief Justice William H. Rehnquist and Justice Antonin Scalia, acknowledge that incorporation is a valid legal doctrine. For Robertson to say that the First Amendment applies only to Congress is either an example of abysmal ignorance or a deliberate attempt to mislead.

On another occasion, Robertson was challenged on his view that only Christians and Jews are fit to hold public office. On the January 11, 1985, edition of "The 700 Club," Robertson remarked, "Individual Christians are the only ones really—and Jewish people, those who trust the God of Abraham, Isaac, and Jacob—are the only ones that are qualified to have the reign, because hopefully, they will be governed by God and submit to him."

Robertson's co-host, Ben Kinchlow, tried to rescue him, asking, "Obviously you're not saying that there are no other people qualified to be in government or whatever if they aren't Christians or Jews."

Robertson replied, "Yeah, I'm saying that. I just said it. I think anybody whose mind and heart is not controlled by God Almighty is not qualified in the ultimate sense to be the judge of someone else. . . . No one is fit to govern other people unless first of all something governs him. And there is only one governor I know of that is suitable to be judge of all the universe, that's God Almighty. Yes, I did say that. You can quote me. I believe it."

In September of 1987, *Time* magazine confronted Robertson with the statement. He flatly denied it. "I never said that in my life. . . . I never said only Christians and Jews. I never said that." Unfortunately for Robertson, a copy of the tape soon turned up proving he was wrong and that he did indeed say that. It was turned over to *Time* by Edmund D. Cohen, a Philadelphia psychologist and Robertson critic.[31]

These days Robertson has returned to his original position in favor of religious tests for public office. In his conspiracy tome titled *The New World Order,* Robertson once again asserts that Christians and Jews are "better qualified to govern America" than Hindus, Muslims, or nonbelievers. The full quote reads, "You don't dare say America or Christianity is a better way of living. When I said during my presidential bid that I would only bring Christians and Jews into the government, I hit a firestorm. 'What do you mean?' the media challenged me. 'You're not going to bring atheists into the government? How dare you maintain that those who believe the Judeo-Christian values are better qualified to govern America than Hindus and Muslims?' My simple answer is, 'Yes, they are.' "[32] (Note how Robertson has cleverly reconstructed history to make it seem that he boldly proclaimed his belief that only Christians and Jews should hold public office during the campaign, when in fact he at first tried to deny that he had ever said such a thing.)

On a PBS "Firing Line" debate that aired in September of 1993, the Rev. Barry W. Lynn, executive director of Americans United for Separation of Church and State, challenged Robertson about this point, asking how restricting public office to Christians and Jews could be anything but "an example of naked religious bigotry." Robertson's reply was somewhat uninspired. "Would you want Muammar Qaddafi as secretary of defense? Would you like to have Ayatollah Khomeini in charge of Health and Human Services?" he asked through his seemingly permanent grin. (Religious tests for public office, by the way, are flatly barred by Article VI of the Constitution and were declared unconstitutional at the state and local level by the Supreme Court's 1961 case *Torcaso* v. *Watkins*.)

In 1986 Robertson made similar comments that offended even one fellow conservative. Appearing in Lansing, Michigan, he was asked if there are some issues Christians feel more strongly about than non-Christians. He replied, "I think patriotism, love of God, love of country, support of the traditional family. They [Christians] believe it would be good for our country if families were closer together. . . . I think they feel about them more strongly than others do."[33]

The remark prompted William J. Bennett, then Reagan administration education secretary, to include a thinly veiled reference to Robertson in a speech decrying such "invidious sectarianism." Robertson hit the roof. He sent Bennett a three-page letter, which was widely reported and excerpted in the media, seeking an apology. Queried Robertson in the letter, "What in heaven's name provoked you to lash out at a simple statement by a fellow Reagan supporter who merely said that 'maybe' evangelical Christian people supported Ronald Reagan's issues more strongly than others?" Again, note how Robertson has shifted what he said. Robertson did not tell the crowd in Michigan that evangelicals support Reagan's issue more than nonevangelicals; he said evangelicals love their country more and feel more strongly about families and God. That's quite a difference.

Bennett refused to back down and in a reply to Robertson he said, "Let me add, Pat, that I am troubled by anyone who celebrates electoral success by writing, 'The Christians have won,' or 'What a victory for the Kingdom!' I am not alone in sensing some ambiguity in your position on the role of religion in politics." The rift between Bennett and Robertson was only temporary, however. The ultraconservative Bennett, whom the Religious Right has touted as the ideal presidential candidate, has since appeared at Christian Coalition events and enjoys a close relationship with CC Executive Director Ralph Reed.

Aside from applying a religious test for public office, Robertson also said during the campaign that he would appoint only ultraconservatives to government posts. Addressing supporters in New Hampshire, he criticized President Reagan for naming Howard H. Baker, Jr., a moderate Republican, as chief of staff. "Over 100,000 people in government serve at the pleasure of the president," Robertson said. "I'm told that a good portion of them are Jimmy Carter appointees who are holdovers, and in the first week of my administration I intend to ask for the resignation of all of them."[34]

As usual, Robertson was playing fast and loose with the facts. There are nowhere near 100,000 government workers who serve at the behest of the president. In fact, the actual number of full-time positions a president is expected to fill is less than four thousand. Most government workers are career employees whose jobs are nonpartisan in nature. They stay in their slots even as administrations come and go. Robertson also offered no proof that Carter appointees were still serving in Reagan's administration, an assertion that is highly dubious, to say the least.

Realizing he had an image problem, Robertson attempted to redefine himself during the campaign. But his effort to portray himself as just a "religious broadcaster" and businessman fell flat on its face. Prior to entering the race, Robertson renounced his ordination as a Southern Baptist minister. He chafed at being called a television preacher, or worse, a televangelist. Biographical material produced about him during this period played down his ties to fundamentalist religion and attempted to recast Robertson as a conservative business tycoon. As *Des Moines Register* columnist Roger Simon pointed out, Robertson was happy to take votes from born-again Christians, but he "bristles when asked about religious matters."

But Americans didn't buy it. For years Robertson had been appearing on television, where he preached. To most people, this made Robertson a TV preacher. Thanks to sex and money scandals involving Jimmy Swaggart and Jim and Tammy Bakker, as well as the bizarre behavior of Oral Roberts, who in 1987 insisted that unless viewers sent him $8 million in contributions God would kill him, in the late 1980s that job description became equivalent to "used car salesman" or "carnival huckster" to most Americans; understandably, Robertson wanted no part of it.

Robertson was especially peeved because reporters continued to ask him about an incident in 1985 in which he claims to have diverted a hurricane from Virginia Beach through prayer. "I can't understand what's the big deal," Robertson snapped at Roger Simon. "Ninety-four percent of the [American] people believe in God. We're a very religious people. And I get asked by the press as if this is something weird. I don't see where it would be strange for a man to pray." Pressed further by Simon, an exasperated Robertson finally replied, "I've been ridiculed, laughed at, pilloried and pinioned. Right now, I got to win Iowa. I got to talk about national issues. I'll talk to you about the budget. I'll talk to you about national defense, about welfare, education, you name it, but enough of this."[35]

Although embarrassed by the incident, years later Robertson did not hesitate to return to the hurricane diversion business. In August of 1995 he took credit when Hurricane Felix, which had been menacing the East Coast, suddenly turned course and ran out of steam many miles offshore. A smug Robertson declared that the hurricane's about-face was the result of prayers he personally led on "The 700 Club." Robertson went on to say that since he began warding off hurricanes through prayer, not one had dared to approach Virginia Beach. "Lord, take the sting out of this Hurricane Felix!" Robertson prayed on television. "Take the sting out of it! And I ask you that it will peter out and that people will not come to grief, in the name of Jesus."

Two months after Hurricane Felix petered out, Hurricane Opal slammed into the Gulf Coast of Florida, killing fifteen and doing millions of dollars in property damage. One must wonder why Robertson did not also turn back this hurricane and thus prevent the appalling loss of life and property destruction. If he does indeed have this gift, why does he selfishly limit it to Virginia Beach? It's also worth noting that in 1985, after Robertson sent Hurricane Gloria away from Virginia Beach, it veered north and devastated Long Island, New York. It is fair to ask what good it does to pray a hurricane away if it just moves on to hurt someone else.

In 1985, Simon and other reporters were not questioning Robertson about the hurricane incident with the intent of embarrassing him. In fact, they were simply trying to get the candidate to explain how his direct pipeline to God might affect his presidency. Some reporters, for example, wondered in the opinion columns of various papers if Robertson would be able to divert Soviet missiles through prayer, just as he claims to turn back hurricanes. It may sound absurd at first, but the question is a fair one. If Robertson really does believe he could turn back missiles as well as hurricanes, that ability could very well influence his decision-making in foreign policy. Voters deserved a coherent answer to the question, but they never got it.

If anything, Robertson worked day and night to downplay his religious views. Robertson's pollsters had warned him to distance himself from his religious background. Public opinion surveys conducted for the campaign revealed that many people harbored deep reservations about voting for a preacher. The polls also indicated that most people knew little about Robertson's business background and lumped him in with the other televangelists. To get around the problem, the Robertson campaign planned commercials in Iowa and New Hampshire that depicted Robertson as a statesman, educator, and communicator. Remarked Constance Snapp, Robertson's communications director, "People don't understand the fact that he knows world leaders and he has been in the world's hotspots and knows them firsthand."[36]

Once again, Robertson attempted to pull a two-faced routine on the American public. To his already convinced television audience, Robertson wanted to be able to preserve his image as a religious broadcaster who enjoys special access to God, a man blessed with the ability to change the weather and see the future. To everyone else, he wanted to be pictured as some type of world leader and elder statesman. This time, Americans did not fall for it. The effort to recast Robertson as just a conservative businessman was a wash out. Reporters continued to dig up embarrassing episodes from his past. The day of the Iowa caucus, Robertson appeared on NBC's "Nightly News" broadcast, where anchor Tom Brokaw asked him, "When you were a television evangelist, you often said that you had God's advice on specific decisions that you had to make. Do you get His advice as well on specific political decisions?"

Again, it was a completely fair question, considering how often Robertson claims God advised him during his early career in broadcasting. If God were so interested in Robertson that He went so far as to recommend broadcasting equipment by brand name, it's not illogical to assume that the Almighty might be slipping Robertson some political pointers as well and would continue doing so if Robertson were to occupy the White House.

A clearly uncomfortable Robertson squirmed a bit then replied, "I'd like to point out to you, if you don't mind, I think it's the last time that I want to be called a television evangelist. I've been a TV broadcaster . . . and because I am a religious broadcaster, I've talked to people on major issues . . . and I really believe that henceforth the religious bigotry that question of yours implies is going to be a dead issue. I don't like it."

But Brokaw pressed on and restated the question. At that point, a mysterious audio breakdown rendered the candidate mute. A rumor circulated afterward that a Robertson staffer monitoring the broadcast disrupted it by kicking an audio cable. Robertson later told supporters, "If I'm asked that question one more time, I won't do another interview with NBC."[37]

After the Iowa caucus, Robertson's campaign began a rapid nose dive. He placed fifth in New Hampshire, and, although he bragged that an "invisible army" would carry him to victory in the Southern states on Super Tuesday, he fared quite poorly. In most states he took third place. Polling data later revealed that most self-described "born again Christians" who voted in GOP primaries backed Bush. Data also showed that the bulk of Robertson's supporters came from charismatic and Pentecostal backgrounds. The candidate had failed to make headway in Southern Baptist and conservative Catholic communities.

Robertson lost even in South Carolina, where his forces had organized so well. Robertson predicted he would win the primary, which was held three days before Super Tuesday, but he ended up with a poor third place and captured only 19 percent of the vote. Robertson failed to carry any of the state's forty-six counties.

The day after the primary Robertson remained defiant. "It ain't over till the fat lady sings," he quipped. "If this is not the one, I'll be back four years later."[38] But Robertson soon had to face political reality. On April 6 he announced that he was suspending active campaigning and conceded that Bush had the GOP nomination sewn up. He told reporters in Washington that he would remain active in the race as the campaign wound down to make sure Bush remained committed to the social issues Robertson championed. He left the presidential contest with nineteen delegates, having spent $23 million. During the campaign he received $10 million in federal matching funds—more than any other candidate up to that point.

Robertson left the race vowing to run again. Speaking at a fundamentalist church in Denver on April 3, 1988, he said:

"There is an enterprise the Lord set me on a year or so ago—running for president of the United States. Out of what seems to be defeat, we are laying the foundation for a great victory for this nation. It may not be in 1988 . . . but I am not going to quit." Robertson said he would run again in 1992, adding, "That is His plan for me and for this nation."[39]

Two interesting footnotes occurred in the wake of the campaign. As Robertson traipsed around the country seeking votes, he left CBN and "The 700 Club" in the hands of his son Tim, then thirty-three. Tim was made president of CBN and host of "The 700 Club." Unfortunately, Robertson's son lacked the star power viewers demanded. Without the senior Robertson at the helm, viewers abandoned the program in droves, and contributions fell off sharply—by as much as 56 percent according to some accounts. Pat Robertson had to return to the show and resume his role as host to shore up the sagging network. (To save CBN, Robertson laid off more than six hundred employees and slashed the budget by $34 million; he also upped the time spent on "The 700 Club" soliciting contributions from 20 percent to 44 percent.)[40] Clearly, returning to "The 700 Club" was not part of Robertson's original game plan. Seven months earlier, in the August 7, 1987, edition of *Christianity Today*, Tim Robertson boasted that his father's days as a TV talk show host were through, remarking, "Regardless of what Dad does with his political campaign—regardless of whether he runs or doesn't run—he's never, ever, ever going back to being Pat Robertson, host of a five-day-a-week Christian television program."[41]

More interesting fallout occurred nearly four years later when the Federal Elections Commission (FEC) released a detailed audit of the Robertson campaign. The FEC uncovered a laundry list of violations of federal campaign guidelines, including allegations that the campaign exceeded spending limits in Iowa and New Hampshire. Robertson's campaign was asked to reimburse the federal government to the tune of $380,000. (Robertson was also ordered to reimburse various news media organizations more than $100,000 for overcharging them for airline flights.)[42]

Other improprieties cited by the FEC include:

- The Robertson campaign leased a corporate jet from an arm of CBN and reimbursed the group for air flights at rates below the standard established by the FEC.
- Public policy organizations founded by Robertson set up a computer firm that later sold the campaign an IBM computer system at a rate considerably below fair market value.
- The campaign spent nearly $75,000 to send supporters to the Republican National Convention and attempted to count the money as a campaign expense, even though Robertson had been out of the race for at least three months by the time the convention occurred.
- Campaign contribution funds were improperly used to pay federal and local tax penalties.
- Americans for Robertson headquarters in Iowa and New Hampshire were claimed as "regional offices" even though most activities at them ceased after the Iowa caucus and New Hampshire primary.

These types of irregularities in a presidential campaign are not uncommon. What is unusual is the number of incidents Robertson racked up in such a short-lived political endeavor. Robertson was also accused of exceeding spending limits by a wide margin. "We're talking about very, very substantial amounts of money," said Commissioner John Warren McGarry during a March 26, 1992, FEC meeting in Washington to discuss the audit. "I'm not aware of any publicly funded presidential candidate exceeding both limits by that amount."[43]

But the most important result of Robertson's quest to become president was the creation of the Christian Coalition three years later. The campaign gave Robertson a list of three million petition signers and a core of dedicated activists who went on to form the basis of the Coalition.

Time magazine religion writer Richard Ostling called it correctly. Shortly after the Robertson campaign ended, Ostling gave a speech at Union Theological Seminary in which he predicted that Robertson's run would form the basis of a large social and political movement. Ostling said the media missed the real significance of Robertson's campaign.[44] In just four years the Christian Coalition grew to become one of the most important—perhaps the most important—pressure groups active in American politics, holding the Republican party in a virtual headlock. The Christian Coalition was launched in 1990 to "mobilize and train Christians for effective political action." As of this writing, it claims 1.7 million members and is said to be growing rapidly. Robertson's forces already control the GOP in eighteen states and enjoy great influence among most Republican presidential contenders. At the same time, the group is active in promoting congressional candidates and urging local members to run for school board.

What does Robertson hope to achieve through the Christian Coalition? What are his goals for the Republican party and American society? How does the group intend to achieve them? The next two chapters take a look at these important questions.

Notes

1. "Robertson, Religious Right Discuss 1988 Run for the White House," *Church & State* (January 1986).

2. Cory SerVaas and Maynard Good Stoddard, "CBN's Pat Robertson: White House Next?" *Saturday Evening Post* (March 1985).

3. Michael J. McManus, "Did CBN Finance Robertson's Campaign?" *Morning Call*, Allentown (Pa.) (February 13, 1988).

4. Charles R. Babcock, "Robertson Accused of Using Tax-Exempt Group for Politics," *Washington Post* (April 6, 1988).

5. Michael McManus, "Close Up Look at the Man Who Would Be President," *Muncie Star* (December 5, 1987).

6. "Robertson Moves Toward Presidential Crusade," *Church & State* (November 1986).

7. T. R. Reid, "Robertson Says God Guides White House Bid," *Washington Post* (February 15, 1988).

8. Ibid.

9. Ibid.

10. Darrell Turner, "Will Robertson's Followers Forgive and Forget?" Religious News Service (October 9, 1987).

11. William Bole, "Disputed War Record Becoming Robertson's 'Character Issue,' " Religious News Service (June 16, 1987).

12. Knight-Ridder News Service, "Pat Robertson Linked to Korean Prostitutes," *Atlanta Constitution* (December 4, 1987).

13. T. R. Reid, "Robertson's Honesty to Go on Trial," *Washington Post* (September 11, 1987).

14. Phil Gailey, "Robertson Used Journalist to Get Data for Libel Suit on War Record," *New York Times* (April 2, 1987) and Bill Peterson, "Robertson Hunts Data for Libel Suit," *Washington Post* (April 1, 1987).

15. T. R. Reid, "Robertson's Bid Powered By Faith, Self Assurance," *Washington Post* (September 11, 1987).

16. Ibid.

17. Pat Robertson, *Answers to 200 of Life's Most Probing Questions* (Nashville: Thomas Nelson Publishers, 1984), p. 207.

18. Reid, "Robertson's Bid Powered By Faith, Self-Assurance."

19. Steve Harvey, "Robertson Enters Presidential Race, Vows Aid to Poor," *Atlanta Constitution* (October 2, 1987).

20. Ibid.

21. David Yepsen and Kenneth Pins, "Robertson's Followers in Iowa Remain Faithful," *Des Moines Register* (October 9, 1987).

22. Ralph Z. Hallow, "Robertson Wins Iowa Poll; Dole Second, Bush Third," *Washington Times* (September 14, 1987).

23. Michael McManus, "What Dirty Tricks, Mr. Robertson?" *Muncie Star* (March 5, 1988).

24. Lloyd Grove, "Cuban Missile Fallout Dogs Robertson," *Washington Post* (February 16, 1988).

25. Charles R. Babcock, "Robertson: Knew Location of Hostages," *Washington Post* (February 25, 1988).

26. Ira Rifkin, "Pat Robertson Calls for U.S. 'Hit Squads' to Kill Terrorists," Religious News Service (February 6, 1987).

27. Phil Gailey, "A Bitter Struggle Splits South Carolina GOP," *New York Times* (April 6, 1987).

28. Paul Taylor, "Robertson Campaign Persists Amid Setbacks," *Washington Post* (March 31, 1987).

29. David S. Broder, "Robertson Says High Court Not Preeminent,"

Washington Post (June 27, 1986).

30. Tom Teepen, "Pat Robertson and Religious Freedom: Clipping the Establishment Clause," reprinted in *Church & State* (July-August 1987).

31. "Robertson's 'Good Forgettery,' *Charlotte Observer* (December 30, 1987).

32. Pat Robertson, *The New World Order* (Dallas: Word Publishing, 1991), p. 218.

33. "Robertson's 'Good Forgettery.' "

34. Wayne King, "Robertson Plans Washington Purge," *New York Times* (October 25, 1987).

35. Roger Simon, "What Robertson is Leaving Out," *Des Moines Register* (January 24, 1988).

36. Wayne King, "Robertson Plans an Ad Campaign to Enhance TV Minister's Image," *New York Times* (September 7, 1987).

37. Reported in "Pat Robertson's Born Again Campaign," *Church & State* (March 1988).

38. "Robertson Hangs In," *New York Times* (March 10, 1988).

39. "Robertson Hears Call to Run Again in '92," *Washington Times* (April 4, 1988).

40. John Taylor, "Pat Robertson's God, Inc.," *Esquire* (November 1994).

41. "Pat Robertson's Son Says Dad Will 'Never, Ever' Return to Hosting a Daily Christian Television Program," *Christianity Today* news release (July 27, 1987).

42. Rob Boston, "Hey Big Spender," *Church & State* (May 1992).

43. Ibid.

44. Albert J. Menendez, "Robertson's Invisible Army: Missing in Action," *Church & State* (April 1988).

3

The Two Faces of the
Christian Coalition

"If the Christian people work together, they can succeed during this decade in winning back control of the institutions that have been taken from them over the past 70 years. Expect confrontations that will be not only unpleasant but at times physically bloody. . . ."
—Pat Robertson, *Pat Robertson's Perspective*,
October/November 1992

In Roman mythology, the god known as Janus has two faces, one looking forward and one looking backward, in order to see simultaneously where he is going and where he has been. The Christian Coalition has two faces, too, though for a different reason. One face of the Christian Coalition is Pat Robertson's, who serves as the group's president. Robertson gives the Coalition its star power. Immediately recognizable to millions of followers, his beaming persona provides the charisma and personal connection that so many Christian Coalition members apparently long for.

But Robertson's face has a powerful downside. To many of the millions of Americans outside of the Religious Right who don't take "The 700 Club" seriously, Robertson's face is a portrait of extremism. When these people think of Robertson, they conjure up not the image of smiling pleasantries but rather the scowling mask of hate that dominated the 1992 Republican National Convention.

Therefore, the Coalition needs a second face. That face belongs to Ralph Reed. Young, telegenic, and inevitably described as "baby-faced," Reed is the CC's executive director. An ultraconservative, born-again wunderkind, Reed oversees the day-to-day operations of an organization that commands the attention of senators, representatives, and would-be presidents. It's a staggering responsibility for a thirty-four-year-old.

Together Robertson and Reed make up an unusual tag team that enables the Christian Coalition to present a bifurcated image to two very different audiences. For the true believers, Robertson offers up the red meat. His books, newsletters, speeches, and TV appearances are loaded with denunciations of the Enemy of the Day—"humanists," homosexuals, liberals, Bill and Hillary Clinton, and feminists are favorite targets. In Robertson's world, the United States is a once-great and once-Christian nation that has seen its strength sapped by atheists on the Supreme Court and socialists in government. He sees conspiracies everywhere, and in his view the country is constantly menaced by sinister forces that seek to undermine Christianity, decency, honor, and all that is good and proper.

Reed presents a kinder, gentler image. He markets the Christian Coalition as merely an organization of concerned Americans whose members favor morality and conservative principles in government. Reed insists that the Coalition is not on a moral crusade and asserts that the organization is just as concerned with balancing the federal budget as it is with abortion and school prayer.

The dichotomy is often difficult to sustain, because Robertson and Reed draw such different pictures of the Christian Coalition. Reed insists one day that the Coalition does not seek to make the United States an officially "Christian nation." Days later Robertson grouses on "The 700 Club" that America used to be a "Christian nation" and lauds the president of Zambia for officially declaring that country Christian and passing legislation to back up the declaration.

Reed says the Christian Coalition considers separation of church and state an "inviolable" concept. Robertson tells his followers there's no such thing in the Constitution and that Communists in the old Soviet Union cooked it all up.

So which is it? Who really speaks for the Christian Coalition? Is it Reed, the voice of moderation and the mask of pleasantness; or Robertson, the attack dog? The fact is that Robertson founded the group. Robertson is its president and sits on its tightly held board of directors. Reed was hired by and works for Robertson, not the other way around. While Robertson may give Reed a great deal of latitude in running the group's day-to-day operations, it would be naive to think that Reed actually sets the organization's agenda or policies. The Christian Coalition is Robertson's organization. If Reed were to resign tomorrow, Robertson would still be there running the show.

In his franker moments, Reed admits who really calls the shots at the Christian Coalition. During "The David Frost Special" that aired on PBS May 19, 1995, Frost demanded to know who runs the Coalition. Speaking of Robertson, Frost asked, "Who's the boss, though, you or him?" Reed quickly replied, "He is."

Although Reed has nowhere near the cult of personality that Robertson enjoys, his own legend has been growing in a steady, albeit modest, manner, especially with the national press corps. In 1995 he was the subject of flattering puff pieces in *Time* magazine and *People*. Stories about Reed in the national media usually emphasize his youth and boyish appearance, as if to suggest that a person possessing such qualities is incapable of also being a ruthless political hack or hard-ball player for the far right.

As the legend goes, Reed was precocious as a young child with an early interest in politics. In high school he beat a popular football player in an election for junior class president. As a student at the University of Georgia, he headed up the College Republicans and wrote far-right columns for the school newspaper, *The Red and Black.* Reed's career as a newspaper columnist ended after he was accused of plagiarizing portions of a column on Gandhi from a piece in *Commentary* magazine. Reed was not formally disciplined by the school, and today he says of the incident, "I didn't fully cite sources. It was a mistake I regret, but I think I'm a better person for it."[1]

Reed became a born-again Christian in 1983. Five years later he met Robertson at an inaugural dinner for George Bush in Washington. Reed and Robertson hit it off from the start, and Robertson asked Reed, who was then completing his doctoral studies at Emory University, to draw up a plan for a new conservative political organization. According to the *Georgia Alumni Record,* by September of 1989 Robertson was introducing Reed to people as the head of his new political group.

During the five years between his graduation in 1984 and his ascension to head of the Coalition in 1989, Reed engaged in some activities that he prefers to keep under wraps today. In 1984 Reed arrived in Raleigh, North Carolina, to work on Senator Jesse Helms's reelection campaign. Reed, then twenty-three, stayed behind after Helms's victory and began leading antiabortion protests in the area. According to the Raleigh *News and Observer,* Reed's presence energized the somewhat lethargic antiabortion movement in the Raleigh-Durham area. He chose as his target the Fleming Center, which provided abortions as well as a variety of other gynecological services and sex therapy. Clinic workers noted they had always had protesters, but Reed's leadership dramatically escalated the stakes. "I don't remember it getting bad until he showed up," Denise Moore, former head nurse at the clinic, told the newspaper. "It was scary—every single day."[2]

Another clinic worker, Denise Lowery, recalls, "We went

through Hell. When Reed was there, people were . . . threatening us, threatening our children, screaming obscenities at patients. They really carried it to an extreme." The clinic's owner had to install a security system and hire guards. Lowery reported that on March 18, 1985, she heard loud noises outside on the front porch of the clinic. When she opened the door, she found Reed sitting in a chair reading a Bible and surrounded by TV cameras. Ordered to leave, he refused. Lowery called the police. Reed still refused to leave and had to be carried away from the scene by law enforcement officers. "The whole time, he was quoting Scripture; he was screaming," Lowery remembers.

At Wake County Jail, Reed threatened a hunger strike but later that same day changed his mind and posted bond. The charges against Reed were eventually dismissed. (The *News and Observer* ran Reed's arrest mug shot on July 16, 1995. He is shown with the same boyish look on his face, every hair neatly in place, wearing a suit and tie.)

Such extreme tactics are an embarrassment to Reed today. Contacted by the *News and Observer*, Christian Coalition spokesman Mike Russell said Reed did not want to discuss that period of his life. "He doesn't have any desire to go on the record about that incident," Russell said. "It was a peaceful protest and civil disobedience. He doesn't want to re-address it. His efforts now are to raise concern about the sanctity of human life through policy and legislation. He's moved beyond that kind of tactic."[3]

Just as he would rather ignore his early history as an anti-abortion zealot, Reed would rather not spend time today trying to explain the numerous off-the-wall comments Robertson has uttered over the years. Reed gets perturbed when reporters cite Robertson's intolerant and extremist statements. Reed's usual tactic is to dodge the issue by claiming that the quote has been taken out of context or deny that Robertson ever said it. Reed has learned much at his master's feet. The good cop/bad cop routine Robertson and Reed seek to put over on the American people more often than not works. It is an amazing thing to hear Reed say one thing and Robertson the polar opposite just days later and have no one point out the contradiction. It has happened more than once, and because it is not widely known among the general public, so far the two have gotten away with it.

Perhaps the best example of the Robertson/Reed dichotomy concerns the issue of separation of church and state. Robertson has attacked this constitutional principle repeatedly over the years, going back at least as far as 1981. No other issue underscores so clearly Robertson's efforts to mislead the American public than does his stance on church-state separation. The First Amendment's religion provisions state, "Congress shall make no law respecting an establishment of religion, or prohibiting the free exercise thereof." The first part of this amendment is known as the "Establishment Clause," while the latter half is called the "Free Exercise Clause." Together, they provide for the constitutional doctrine of separation of church and state. Robertson has criticized the concept over and over again. Yet when challenged about it, Robertson has the audacity to insist that he supports the principle. Because this is such an important issue, it is necessary to examine it in some detail here. It is not my aim to be repetitious, but I believe a thorough airing of what Robertson has said about separation of church and state over the years is necessary. Once this is done, I believe any fair-minded reader will conclude that Robertson simply does not support the concept and that when Reed insists that the Christian Coalition does, he is, quite simply, not being truthful.

If it is indeed the case that Robertson does not support church-state separation, then let him come right out and say it. After all, other leaders of the Religious Right have done so. But Robertson knows that opposing church-state separation sounds extreme, so, as usual, he tries to have it both ways. His followers get one story, and the general public gets another. Reed is a major factor in perpetuating this deception.

With that thought in mind, here are comments Robertson has made about separation of church and state over the years:

- In October of 1981, Robertson's "700 Club" aired what amounted to a week-long attack on the separation of church and state. Titled "Seven Days Ablaze," the special broadcasts featured commentary by Robertson that asserted that church-state separation was not intended by the founding fathers and was foisted on the American people in recent times by the American Civil Liberties Union (ACLU) and the federal courts. Robertson called federal judges "unelected tyrants" and said the wall of separation between church and state is a myth promoted by the ACLU to "bring the United States into line with the Constitution, not of the United States, but of the USSR"—a tasteless attempt at red-baiting that Robertson has returned to time and time again. The telecast also included a segment called the "separation illusion" touting tuition tax credits for private schools, a scheme that would violate church-state separation by requiring Americans to pay the equivalent of a church tax.

  During the same week of broadcasts, Robertson called for a new constitutional amendment "over and above the First Amendment" to guarantee "religious liberty."[4] The following year, Robertson's first political group, the Freedom Council, announced it was working with Professor Charles Rice of Notre Dame University on the wording for the new amendment. (Although an ultraconservative Roman Catholic, Rice found common cause with the Robertson group. The Notre Dame professor once recommended that the pope be given the power to approve all aspects of "natural law"* binding on people and government.)

Webster's defines "natural law" as rules of conduct supposedly inherent in the relations between human beings and discoverable by reason; law based upon man's innate moral sense. Professor Rice advocated that the pope have final say on laws regarding moral issues.

- During a 1982 "Washington for Jesus" rally, Robertson addressed "America's Christian Heritage." He again claimed that separation of church and state comes from the Soviet Union and, in vague generalities, accused federal courts of trying to take away the religious rights of Christians. He waxed nostalgic for the days when every state "recognized Jesus Christ in its constitution."[5]
- Testifying before the Senate Judiciary Committee in favor of a school prayer amendment on August 18, 1982, Robertson tried once again to link church-state separation to communism. "We often hear of the constitutionally mandated 'separation of church and state,'" Robertson remarked. "Of course, as you know, that phrase appears nowhere in the Constitution or the Bill of Rights. . . . We do find this phrase in the constitution of another nation, however: 'The state shall be separate from the church, and the church from the school.' Those words are not in the Constitution of the United States, but that of the Union of Soviet Socialist Republics—an atheistic nation sworn to the destruction of the United States of America."[6]

  Robertson was so proud of this testimony that he had it printed up in a little booklet that he eagerly distributed. Yet years later, he tried to position himself as a defender and supporter of church-state separation—even though these negative comments about the principle were reprinted in the booklet and despite the fact that they became part of the official records of Congress and could easily be looked up by anyone.
- On October 2, 1984, Robertson told a "700 Club" audience, "There is nothing in the U.S. Constitution that sanctifies the separation of church and state."
- In an interview with the *Conservative Digest* in January of 1986, Robertson again pushed the red-baiting button, saying, "It's amazing that the Constitution of the United States says nothing about the separation of church and

state. That phrase does appear, however, in the Soviet Constitution, which says the state shall be separate from the church and the church from the school. People in the educational establishment, and in our judicial establishment, have attempted to impose the Soviet strictures on the United States and have done so very successfully, even though they are not part of our Constitution."[7]

- During the April 11, 1986, broadcast of "The 700 Club," Robertson said the following: "The First Amendment says Congress shall pass no law respecting an establishment of religion or prohibiting the free exercise thereof—nothing about a wall of separation, nothing about separation of church and state! Merely, Congress can't set up a national religion. End of story."

- Robertson has continued the antiseparation drumbeat in more recent times. Addressing a Christian Coalition "God and Country" rally in Greenville, South Carolina, in November of 1993, he attacked the "radical left," saying, "They have kept us in submission because they have talked about separation of church and state. There is no such thing in the Constitution. It's a lie of the left, and we're not going to take it anymore."[8]

- In March of 1994, Robertson's CBN offered viewers a "fact sheet" titled "Church & State: America's Myth of Separation." The one-page sheet recycled common Religious Right attacks against church-state separation.

- On January 22, 1995, Robertson lashed out against separation again. During a discussion of religion in public schools, "700 Club" cohost Ben Kinchlow asserted that some school officials are afraid to let students talk about religion because of the separation of church and state. An angry Robertson immediately interjected, "That was never in the Constitution. However much the liberals laugh at me for saying it, they know good and well it was never in the Constitution! Such language only appeared in the constitution of the communist Soviet Union."

This last outburst occurred just a few months after the Christian Coalition issued a booklet titled *Ten Myths about Pat Robertson and Religious Conservatives.* Despite the track record outlined here, the booklet has the audacity to assert, "Robertson repeatedly has stated his belief in the separation of church and state and the evil of an established church."[9]

Just three months before Robertson's latest attack on church-state separation, Reed had the gall to appear before a crowd at the National Press Club in Washington and insist, "We believe in a separation between church and state that is complete and inviolable."[10] Reed repeated the line before the Anti-Defamation League in Washington April 3, 1995, and said much the same thing during a speech to the American Jewish Committee in Washington May 5, 1995. Once again we see Robertson and Reed's good cop/bad cop routine. In late 1994 and into 1995, Reed told Jewish groups and others in Washington that the Coalition is all for separation of church and state, that it should be "complete" and "inviolable." Two hundred miles away in Virginia Beach, Robertson was on television blasting church-state separation as a Communist plot and denouncing it as a concept alien to the U.S. Constitution.

- On a taped segment that aired on "The 700 Club" on August 1, 1995, Robertson explained his understanding of the relationship between religion and government.

> There was no concept of separation between God and government in the New Testament or the Old Testament. . . . The concept that was before us in the Bible is that rulers are ministers of God, that the sword that they wield is not in vain, but they've been placed in authority by God to make sure that law and order prevails in our land and there is no anarchy.
>
> Now when atheism came in under what used to be called the Soviet Union a new constitution was written, which said the state shall be separate from the church and

the church from the school. . . . In the United States of America people have tried to apply that phrase from the Soviet Constitution to the schooling of children in America. Both of these constitutions are wrong. There is nothing that should indicate that God Almighty should be separated from the government nor that godly people should not hold office in government. . . . So there is nothing to indicate that there should be a separation.

Later in the same segment, Robertson admitted that perhaps the state-run churches of the Middle Ages hadn't been such a great idea, but even here his language was tepid. "I am not at all sure that is a good thing today, that we should have the official church linked in with the official government," he said. "I do think it is better, given the sinful state of our world, to keep the organizational church separate from the organizational government, but never a separation of the Bible, of God, of Jesus, of God's holy law, from the principles of governing our lands, wherever they happen to be."

Note the only type of "separation" Robertson would allow: The *organizational* church from the *organizational* government. Separating the organizational church from the organizational government would still leave room for mandatory religious exercises in public schools, required support for religious groups through taxation, religious tests for public office, government promotion of religion and many other things that would today be seen as excessive entanglement between religion and government. Essentially, he has denounced a state-established, official Church of the United States of America. And that's all. Robertson is saying that the church has no interest in running the Department of Motor Vehicles. Big deal. His scenario still leaves plenty of room for the civil legal code to be saturated with *his* narrow understanding and interpretation of the Bible and "God's holy law."

- Attacking the National Education Association during the 1995 meeting of the Christian Coalition in Washington, D.C., Robertson said, "I believe in a separation not between church and state, but between the educational institutions of America and the NEA."

Is there some example we can look at for godly government and the proper relationship between church and state? Try the Massachusetts Bay Colony! In *The New World Order* Robertson writes, "The founders of America—at Plymouth Rock and in the Massachusetts Colony—felt that they were organizing a society based on the Ten Commandments and the Sermon on the Mount. They perceived this new land as a successor to the nation of Israel, and they tried their best to model their institutions of governmental order after the Bible. In fact the man who interpreted the meaning of Scripture to them, the pastor, was given a higher place than the governor of the colony. These people built an incredible society because they exalted 'the mountain of the Lord's house' above the other mountains."[11]

In reality, as any history book will tell you, the Massachusetts Bay Colony was hardly an "incredible society." It was an intolerant theocracy where all society was ordered along sectarian lines. Ironically, anyone who dared to practice a Pentecostal theology like Robertson's would have been expelled or put to death in the Massachusetts colony. The community's religious leaders believed only one mode of religious worship was correct and pleasing to God and compelled conformity to it. To them, Pentecostal practices such as speaking in tongues and exuberant forms of worship would have been blasphemous or possibly inspired by Satan. The colony was certainly no model for religious liberty.

Aside from these attacks on church-state separation taken directly from Robertson's mouth, ample evidence from other sources strongly indicates that the TV preacher opposes the separation principle. For instance, every year the Christian Coalition invites David Barton, a notorious Religious Right propagandist from Texas, to speak at its conferences. Barton offers up a cut-and-paste revisionist "history" of the United States that asserts that separation of church and state was never intended and that the United States was founded to be a Christian nation. Barton wrote and self-published an entire book attacking separation of church and state called *The Myth of Separation*.[12] The book's back cover boldly asks, "Did you know that the separation of church and state is a myth?" Barton hates church-state separation so much that he has gone so far as to fabricate a quote from Thomas Jefferson disowning the concept.* One is forced to wonder why Robertson, that great friend of church-state separation, always finds a spot for Barton on the Christian Coalition program? (Barton was there again in 1995, just months after Reed insisted that the Christian Coalition is all for church-state separation.)

Robertson personally approves of Barton's work. During an October 25, 1995, appearance on "Janet Parshall's America," a syndicated Christian radio program, Robertson was asked about Barton's books. "I tell you, David Barton is a wonderful man," Robertson replied. "He has done extensive research on the history of America, and I admire him tremendously for his breadth of information."

Here are some other examples of "wall bashing" by Robertson forces:

- In 1994 the Maryland branch of the Christian Coalition advertised in its newsletter a booklet attacking separation of church and state. The publication, it was promised, "will forever demolish the myth of separation of church and state." Again, it is fair to ask, why does an organization that believes separation of church and state

---

*For details and a discussion of Barton's fabricated quote, see my book, *Why the Religious Right Is Wrong*.

to be "inviolable" and whose founder supports separation allow one of its affiliates to promote so eagerly a booklet like this?

- During the 1992 Colorado GOP convention, the state branch of the Christian Coalition issued a flyer stating, "The Separation of Church and State is (1) Not a teaching of the founding fathers; (2) Not an historical teaching; (3) Not a teaching of law (except in recent years); (4) Not a biblical teaching." The director of the Christian Coalition in Colorado went on to say in the flyer, "In summary, there should be absolutely no 'Separation of Church and State' in America."[13] Why would an organization that supports separation of church and state release such a document?

- In 1992 the American Center for Law and Justice, a legal group founded by Robertson, printed an article titled "TEAR DOWN THIS WALL!" in its *Law & Justice* newsletter. The article, written by ACLJ director Keith Fournier, compared the wall of separation between church and state to the Berlin Wall and demanded that it be demolished. Fournier insisted that religious liberty in the United States "has been hampered by this fictitious wall that was never intended by the founding fathers and one which militates against the First Amendment."[14] In the same newsletter, Robertson raged against the "so-called 'wall of separation' between church and state."

In the wake of a Supreme Court ruling in favor of the Equal Access Act in 1990, which allows students at public secondary schools to form student-run religious clubs during "non-instructional time," ACLJ attorney Jay Sekulow crowed, "Yes, the so-called 'wall of separation' between church and state has begun to crumble!"[15] Once again one must wonder why Robertson, as a champion of separation of church and state, allowed these things to happen.

(As a veteran of the talk radio circuit, I should mention how often I have been confronted by callers on the air who denounce separation of church and state as a "myth" or a "Communist idea." Many of these people are quick to identify themselves as Christian Coalition members.)

What does Robertson really believe? The evidence strongly indicates that Robertson doesn't support the separation of church and state; he never has, and he probably never will. It's true that sometimes Robertson makes public statements claiming to support church-state separation. Under fire in early 1995 for his bizarre views, Robertson penned an opinion piece for the *Wall Street Journal* in which he had the gall to state, "Despite claims to the contrary, I have never suggested or even imagined any type of political action to make America a 'Christian nation.' While it should never mean that religious ideals and ideas are to be excluded from political discourse, I agree that church and state should be separate because the separation of church and state is good for religion, religious institutions, and the religious liberty of believers."[16]

The *Wall Street Journal's* editorial page is one of the most conservative in the nation and the editors frequently print articles by Religious Right figures. It is fair to say it is dominated by right-wingers who apparently admire Robertson, but at least one of the newspaper's editors was not taken in by him. Albert R. Hunt, Washington executive editor of the *Wall Street Journal*, put it succinctly when he assailed "the dual role where Pat Robertson can rail against separation of church and state one day—a liberal shibboleth more consistent with the constitution of the old Soviet Union he has declared—while the next day Mr. Reed assures everyone how mainstream the movement's beliefs and values are." Hunt labeled the Robertson-Reed tag team "a good cop/bad cop routine . . . which was really about politics, not tolerance."[17] (Robertson's disavowal of the "Christian nation" concept is also untrue, as we will learn in an upcoming chapter.)

Hunt is right. As the numerous examples given above indicate, Robertson's claim is simply not true. It is clear that Robertson's infrequent expressions of support for church-state separation are examples of his "I-can-have-it-both-ways" strategies. Now every time a newspaper or magazine columnist points out that Robertson does not support the separation of church and state, one of his well-trained public relations people immediately sends in a letter insisting, "But Pat told the *Wall Street Journal* he supports separation!" Needless to say, they don't mention the laundry list of attacks Robertson has unleashed on church-state separation over the years.

Robertson's supporters tried just that in October of 1995 when Robertson was criticized by Senator Arlen Specter (R-Pa.) for his views on church-state relations. Specter, who was at that time a contender for the GOP presidential nomination, cited Robertson's attacks on church-state separation during debates and other public forums in the early days of the campaign. Robertson wrote him a three-page letter, dated October 12, 1995, insisting that he supports the separation of church and state. The letter was later released to the media by the Coalition's public relations machine.

In the letter, Robertson cited both the *Wall Street Journal* article and an April 10, 1991, appearance on "The Larry King Show" during which he spoke favorably of separation of church and state, saying it was better than the state-established churches of Europe. "I repeat: I believe that the institutional church should be separated from the institution of government," Robertson wrote to Specter. "I would, however, suggest that neither the Constitution of the United States nor the time-honored tradition of this great land dictates that God should be separated from the government or from those who hold public office." Robertson demanded that, "In the future I would ask that your comments about me reflect truth and knowledge."

But Specter, familiar with Robertson's spotty record on the separation of church and state, wrote back the next day to dispute the TV preacher's claims. In his letter, which was released to the media by his campaign, he cited Robertson's attack on separation of church and state as a "lie of the left" in South Carolina in 1993 and specifically asked him to repudiate that claim.

Wrote Specter, "Are you prepared to repudiate the statement attributed to you in the *Washington Times* article of November 26, 1993—either by denying that you made the statement which is attributed to you, or by admitting that you made the statement but now acknowledging that it is incorrect—that the constitutional doctrine of separation of church and state is a lie of the left?"

He received no answer.

Specter, of course, could have gone on. He could have asked Robertson to repudiate the several statements he has made linking church-state separation to Communists in the former Soviet Union, since this is perhaps Robertson's most reckless and offensive assertion about church-state separation.

Robertson's public relations agents deserve credit for the valiant try, but once again Robertson's track record is simply too overpowering to ignore. For nearly twenty years he has been insisting that separation of church and state isn't in the Constitution, that Communists invented the concept, and that the separation principle is a myth. At every turn he has advocated policies that would reduce the wall of separation to a pile of rubble, such as state-sanctioned prayer in public schools and vouchers. He has ridiculed and blasted U.S. Supreme Court rulings that uphold church-state separation. Members of his Christian Coalition tout David Barton, an extremist who makes his living attacking the wall of separation, and Robertson's ACLJ strives to undermine the wall in the courts.

This much is clear: Pat Robertson is no supporter of separation of church and state.

Other right-wing televangelists have come right out and admitted that they don't support the separation of church and state. They are at least honest about it. Why can't Robertson do the same? Amazingly, for all the ugly things he has said about Thomas Jefferson's wall, Robertson would like to be perceived as a defender of church-state separation, probably because he knows that most Americans support it. When Americans think of countries with no separation, brutal and repressive theocracies such as Iran or Geneva under John Calvin often spring to mind. Americans want none of that. Therefore, Robertson once again wants to have it both ways. He wants to rage militantly against that atheistic, Soviet-inspired wall of separation when he is trying to rally his faithful. But when he wants to charm the masses, separation of church and state is proclaimed by Ralph Reed as the greatest concept around.

The most startling thing about Robertson's track record on church-state separation is not how ugly it is, but how often he has gotten away with distorting his position. Robertson moans incessantly that the "liberal media" is out to get him, but relatively few publications have bothered to point out that he's trying to have it both ways. And Reed's eagerness to be on television is well known in Washington. Just before the 1995 Christian Coalition meeting, Reed agreed to appear on the Sunday morning news shows only if he had the stage to himself and no adversaries were on with him. All of the shows were so eager to have Reed's pearls of wisdom that they immediately caved in to his demands.

Some specialty publications have been laboring for years to expose Reed and Robertson. *Church & State* magazine, a publication of Americans United for Separation of Church and State, is an example. As early as 1985, *Church & State* pointed out in an article that Robertson has "called for scrapping the First Amendment, replacing the 'wall of separation' with constitutional provisions allowing more sectarian control of civil government."

Robertson was livid when he saw this and fired off a letter to *Church & State* threatening to sue for libel unless a retraction was printed. "I am a Southern Baptist, and I believe very strongly in the Southern Baptist position concerning church and state separation. I resist strongly the interferences of government in the affairs of our churches. I certainly do not favor sectarian control of civil government," Robertson wrote.[18]

Mindful that in libel cases truth is an absolute defense, *Church & State* ran Robertson's letter in its entirety with a response detailing several of the instances in which the televangelist attacked separation of church and state. No suit was filed, and nothing more was heard from Robertson.

Aside from his attacks on separation of church and state, Robertson has put forth extreme opinions on other matters pertaining to religious freedom. For example, one of the Religious Right's favorite themes is that the First Amendment guarantees freedom *of* religion, not freedom *from* religion. Right-wingers recite this phrase *ad nauseam*, apparently believing they have stumbled onto something clever. What the Religious Right fails to grasp is that freedom *of* religion and freedom *from* religion are two sides of the same coin, and that one cannot exist without the other. When a person exercises freedom *of* religion by, for instance, joining the Presbyterian church, that person is saying by extension that he or she does not want to be a Mormon or a Roman Catholic. That is, in a very real sense, a declaration of freedom *from* religion, at least those specific religions. But even in a more general sense, it is clear that the two concepts complement one another; they don't clash. Obviously, the whole idea of religious freedom would be meaningless if it did not also encompass the freedom to entirely reject religion as well.

Robertson latched onto the insipid "freedom of religion, not freedom from religion" comment in a June 2, 1994, essay in *USA Today*. He said it straight out: "The First Amendment guarantees freedom of religion, not freedom *from* religion." Some months later, George McEvoy, a columnist for the *Palm Beach Post* in Florida blasted House Speaker Newt Gingrich for picking up the same phrase while promoting a school prayer amendment and failing to understand that freedom of religion and freedom from religion are the same thing. McEvoy said the phrase "makes a nice bumper sticker, but not much sense." He also criticized "the Pat Robertsons and D. James Kennedys, all the narrow-minded leaders of the religious right [who] took Rep. Gingrich's statement as a call to turn this republic into a theocracy."[19]

Immediately Robertson associate Gene Kapp, vice president for public relations at CBN, wrote a letter to the *Palm Beach Post* calling Robertson "an ardent defender of the First Amendment" and insisting that, "The Rev. Robertson would defend Mr. McEvoy's precious 'freedom from religion.' " If Robertson believes "freedom from religion" is worthy of protection, then why did he belittle the concept in *USA Today* just six months earlier and suggest that it's not included in the First Amendment? Six months is an awfully short time to completely repudiate one's views! And, unfortunately for Kapp, Robertson's *Wall Street Journal* (April 12, 1995) commentary contains this gem: "We should never allow freedom of religion to become freedom from religion."

Aside from his unflattering comments about separation of church and state, Robertson has, over the years, made a number of extreme statements about various political issues. It must again be stressed that the vast majority of these comments were uttered as part of the public record. Robertson said them on "The 700 Club," published them in newsletters, or made them during speeches in public places. They are not clandestine quotes that reporters had to dig up. When presented with these comments today, Robertson always has an excuse ready. But after a while, his stories begin to wear thin. Chapters 5 and 6 examine some of these statements in detail, but for now it is important to take a deeper look at Robertson's political arm, the Christian Coalition, and its goals for America.

Notes

1. Gayle White, "New Kid on the Bloc," *Georgia Alumni Record* 74, no. 3 (June 1995).

2. Anne Saker, "Christian Leader Was Firebrand in Raleigh," Raleigh *News and Observer* (July 16, 1995).

3. Ibid.

4. Joseph Conn, "Christian 'Hornets' Plan to Sting First Amendment," *Church & State* (May 1982).

5. "Robertson Riled," Letters, *Church & State* (October 1985).

6. "Why I Favor A Prayer Amendment," Testimony of Dr. M.G. (Pat) Robertson before the Judiciary Committee, United States Senate, August 18, 1982.

7. Howard Phillips, "Pat Robertson Adds Perspective," *Conservative Digest* (January 1986).

8. Lee Bandy, "Top Christian Conservatives Urge More Political Vigilance," *The State*, Columbia, S.C. (November 13, 1993).

9. *10 Myths About Pat Robertson and Religious Conservatives: The Facts You Need to Counter the Radical Left*, Christian Coalition, Chesapeake, Va., undated.

10. "Robertson Attacks Church-State Separation During Fund-Raising Drive," *Church & State* (February 1995).

11. Pat Robertson, *The New World Order* (Dallas: Word Publishing, 1991), p. 246.

12. David Barton, *The Myth of Separation* (Aledo, Tex.: Wallbuilders Press, 1989).

13. Cited in Joseph L. Conn, "Robertson Roulette," *Church & State* (October 1992).

14. Keith A. Fournier, Esq., "TEAR DOWN THIS WALL!" *Law & Justice* (Winter 1992.)

15. *CASE Notes*, newsletter of Christian Advocates Serving Evangelism (July 1990).

16. Pat Robertson, "I Have Kept My Vow," *Christian American* (May/June 1995; reprinted from April 12, 1995, *Wall Street Journal*).

17. Albert R. Hunt, "The Christian Coalition's Good Cop/Bad Cop Routine," *Wall Street Journal* (April 6, 1995).

18. "Robertson Riled," *Church & State* (October 1985).

19. George McEvoy, "Freedom to Ignore Religion, Too," *Palm Beach Post* (November 23, 1994).

4

The Christian Coalition: On the Road to Victory?

"We at the Christian Coalition are raising an army who cares. We are training people to be effective—to be elected to school boards, to city councils, to state legislatures and to key positions in political parties. . . . By the end of this decade, if we work and give and organize and train, THE CHRISTIAN COALITION WILL BE THE MOST POWERFUL POLITICAL ORGANIZATION IN AMERICA."
                           —Pat Robertson, July 4, 1991, fundraising letter[1]

On May 17, 1995, Ralph Reed stood in the ornate Mansfield Room of the U.S. Capitol Building's Senate wing to unveil the Christian Coalition's ten-point "Contract with the American Family." Reed was flanked by powerful members of Congress, including House Speaker Newt Gingrich and Texas Senator and presidential hopeful Phil Gramm. Later, Reed and leaders from the Coalition's state affiliates met privately with Senator Robert Dole, the GOP presidential front-runner.

Strangely enough, Pat Robertson was nowhere in sight. In fact, he wasn't even on the same continent. Reed ran the show, telling attendees that Robertson was in Zaire on a "humanitarian" mission helping victims of the Ebola virus. In fact, as the

Washington Post noted later, Robertson was in Zaire trying to end an international boycott against dictator Mobutu Sese Seko.*

Because of Robertson's habit of making extreme statements, there has of late been a move to put some distance between him and the Christian Coalition. Robertson has referred to himself as something of an "elder statesman" for the group, implying that he is not intimately involved in its day-to-day operations. To say the least, this is a dubious claim. Robertson is president of the Christian Coalition and serves as one of the organization's four directors. The other three are Robertson's son, Gordon; Dick Weinhold, a Texas man who is a long-time Robertson associate; and the Rev. Billy McCormack of Louisiana, also a close Robertson associate. This four-man team means that the organization remains under Robertson's control.

Robertson credits McCormack with urging him to form the Christian Coalition. A long-time conservative operative in Louisiana and minister in Shreveport, McCormack and his Religious Right forces led a successful effort within the Louisiana GOP to block moderate Republicans who sought to denounce former Klansman and neo-Nazi David Duke during his ascendence in politics in that state. The Louisiana GOP, which has been under the control of the Religious Right since 1988, also refused to investigate charges that Duke was selling *Mein Kampf* and other hate literature from his office as a state legislator.[2]

Further insight into the workings of McCormack's mind can be gained from comments he made to the *Los Angeles Times* during an interview published on November 14, 1990. Criticizing the ACLU McCormack said, "I'd like for you to take—but your paper might not allow you to do it—and that is to take the Jewish element in the ACLU which is trying to drive Christianity out of the public place, and I'd like to see

---

*Zaire became the target of an international boycott because of Mobutu's dismal record on human rights and antidemocratic policies. Nevertheless, Robertson, who has business interests in Zaire, has lobbied to have it lifted. See chapter 7 for more information.

you do something objective there. Because the ACLU is made up of a tremendous amount of Jewish attorneys."[3]

Robertson has guided the Christian Coalition to where it stands today. With a membership that, the organization claims, approaches two million, activists affiliated with the group are estimated to hold sway over the Republican party in eighteen states and have a significant voice in thirteen others, with an eye toward running all fifty state GOP units eventually. The organization already holds the GOP in a virtual headlock, and serious contenders for the presidency are forced to kowtow to Robertson and Reed.

(It should be pointed out that the Coalition's membership claims have been disputed. The November/December 1995 issue of the *Christian American,* the Coalition's flagship publication, ran a postal statement showing an average circulation of 418,428 for the period of October 1, 1994, to October 1, 1995. Since the group claims 1.7 million members, one is left to wonder why 1.3 million of them do not receive the group's primary communication vehicle.)

The group escalated to a powerful position in a remarkably short period of time. Formation of the Christian Coalition was announced in October of 1989. Promotional literature proclaimed that the group would "mobilize and train Christians for effective political action." Continued a Coalition brochure, "At long last, a grass roots coalition of Evangelicals, conservative Catholics, and their allies has formed to make government and the media responsive to our concerns. It's high time we realize the strength that comes through unity."

Despite the talk about bringing Catholics into the Coalition, the group remains heavily weighted with evangelical Protestants, many of whom are charismatics of Robertson's stripe. A survey of subscribers conducted by the Coalition's own *Christian American* newspaper in 1994 found that Catholics accounted for only 5 percent of the Coalition's membership. Twenty-three percent were Baptists, 9 percent were Assemblies of God, 10 percent were from other Pentecostal churches, and 35 percent were from "nondenominational" churches. Only 14 percent claimed membership in mainline denominations such as Lutherans, Presbyterians, or Methodists. In 1995, the Coalition surveyed its members and claimed that the number of Catholics was up to 16 percent.

Reed and Robertson occasionally claim Jewish support, but the same survey found that Jewish members account for only 2 percent of the group, and observers believe most of them are "Messianic Jews," that is, Jewish converts to Christianity. Robertson actively supports ministries that seek to convert Jews to fundamentalist Christianity.

Reed often brags about how well educated Christian Coalition members are, but again his own 1995 survey tells a different story. The majority of members, 56 percent, have either a high school degree or vocational school certificate. Thirty-two percent graduated from college or have an advanced degree. Nine percent didn't graduate from high school.

The Coalition also claims growing African-American support and always goes out of its way to see to it that prominent black conservatives such as radio talk show host Armstrong Williams and antiwelfare activist Star Parker are on the platform during Coalition conferences. But again, the number of black attendees at Christian Coalition events has been small, and it isn't likely to escalate soon, given Robertson's ultraconservative views. (African Americans account for only 3 percent of the Coalition's membership, according to the organization's 1995 poll.)

Robertson launched the group with modest goals. The Coalition, it was announced in the group's early promotional literature, would work to criminalize abortion, pass a school prayer amendment, increase the presence of religious symbols in public life, and protest "films and TV programs that defame our Lord and caricature His servants."

Looking at this list today, one is struck by two things: the overt religiosity of the goals sought, and the Coalition's honesty in saying forthrightly that it would pursue them. At some point along the way, Robertson and Reed discovered that harping continually on social issues such as abortion, prayer in public schools, and censorship made a lot of people nervous. Just two years after the group's founding Reed began insisting that the Coalition is a broadly focused group equally concerned about issues such as balancing the federal budget and ending the deficit. The Christian Coalition's early promotional material, however, does not highlight these economic issues, pushing instead the hot-button social concerns that so many Robertson followers are obsessed about. Robertson's grassroots troops were not drawn into the Christian Coalition with promises that the group would seek to add a Balanced Budget Amendment to the Constitution. The bait instead was school prayer, creationism, an abortion ban, opposition to gay rights, and a host of other favorite right-wing social concerns.

One of the Coalition's first public activities concerned religion in public schools—always a good rallying point for the Religious Right. Reed tried to literally make a federal case out of a relatively minor church-state flap in the Coalition's backyard of Chesapeake, Virginia. The controversy centered around a public school's use of a brochure put out by religious groups that advises teens to abstain from premarital sex. The brochure, *Dating and Your Right to Choose,* asserted that "God has given each person a priceless gift, but many people carelessly give it away." It also noted that "God condemns the sin of fornication." After local ACLU officials raised concerns about the pamphlet, school officials agreed that it was inappropriate. They told local reporters the issue was moot, since they had already planned to stop using the brochure. Nevertheless, Reed hit the roof. "We've got a war chest of over six figures," he blustered, "and we're willing to take it all the way to the Supreme Court if necessary." Reed also asserted, "This could be a test case for the whole country" and blasted the ACLU for promoting a "radical liberal agenda."[4]

Here was a perfect issue for the fledgling Coalition to exploit. Three of the right-wing's favorite villains were present: public schools, sex education, and the ACLU. It didn't matter that the case never went into any court, let alone all the way to the Supreme Court. Reed had scored his first public relations victory and the Coalition began to make its name known.

At the time the incident occurred, April of 1990, the Christian Coalition claimed twenty-five thousand members. Reed told *Christianity Today* that he hoped to have 150,000 by the end of the year. He also freely admitted that the organization was mining the Robertson presidential petition lists to build members. (Solicitation of this type is permitted, as long as a fair price is paid for the lists.)

Early on, Reed may have been a little too forthcoming. In the same *Christianity Today* interview, he expressed his hope that the Christian Coalition would field five thousand candidates at all levels by the year 2000. "We think the Lord is going to give us this nation back one precinct at a time, one neighborhood at a time, and one state at a time," he said.[5] Shortly afterward, Reed said nearly the identical thing during an interview with the *Los Angeles Times*, remarking, "What Christians have got to do is to take back this country, one precinct at a time, one neighborhood at a time and one state at a time. . . . I honestly believe that in my lifetime we will see a country once again governed by Christians . . . and Christian values."[6] Public relations professionals talk about sending a consistent message. Reed has apparently adopted this tactic for Christian Coalition use. In interviews in different newspapers given at around the same time, Reed often says things that are similar if not identical. It's clear he adopts a message for the week or month and stays with it. His "one precinct at a time message" was used more than once, but it backfired.

Reed may have intended the line as merely a clever quip, but critics of the group latched onto it. Years later it returned to haunt him and was cited as evidence by Christian Coalition critics, who charged that the group has a takeover mentality. In October of 1994, a reporter asked Reed about the comment during an appearance at the National Press Club. Apparently taking a cue from Robertson, Reed denied he had ever made the statement. "I don't know that I ever made that statement," he said. "It does not accurately reflect my views."[7]

To accept Reed's denial, however, one would first have to buy the notion that Reed was misquoted by two separate reporters on different occasions, both of whom just happened to misquote him over the exact same statement. Reed asks for too much.

In the early days of the Coalition, Reed pursued a hardline, "take no prisoners" strategy. He was especially fond of military metaphors. In a March 22, 1992, interview with the *Los Angeles Times,* Reed used a bluntness he would never rely on today.

The Christian Coalition had been accused of fronting "stealth candidates"—political hopefuls who run on secular issues like budgets and taxes without revealing their radical social issues agenda. Reed defended the tactic, calling it "just good strategy" and went on to say, "It's like guerrilla warfare. If you reveal your location, all it does is allow your opponent to improve his artillery bearings. It's better to move quietly, with stealth, under cover of night. You've got two choices: You can wear cammies [camouflage outfits] and shimmy along on your belly, or you can put on a red coat and stand up for everyone to see. It comes down to whether you want to be the British Army in the Revolutionary War or the Viet Cong. History tells us which tactic was more effective."[8]

Finally, in a November 9, 1991, interview with the *Virginian-Pilot,* Reed uttered a comment about the Christian Coalition's stealth election tactics that has since become infamous: "I want to be invisible," he said. "I paint my face and travel at night. You don't know it's over until you're in a body bag. You don't know until election night." This "body bag" quote has also haunted him many times since because Christian Coalition's critics have used the quip as evidence of the organization's extremism.

After Bill Clinton defeated George Bush in the 1992 presidential contest, some Republicans began blaming the Religious Right's harsh rhetoric for the GOP setback. They charged that Pat Robertson and Pat Buchanan had frightened voters with their mean-spirited speeches at the Republican National Convention.

Political analysts today still disagree on to what extent the rhetoric of the "two Pats" damaged the Republicans in 1992. Most believe the majority of voters abandoned Bush because the economy had turned sour. Nevertheless, Reed decided it was time for a change in tactics. He announced that henceforth he would stop using military metaphors and would instead substitute weather and sports metaphors. Suddenly, Reed was talking about tsunamis and home runs instead of guerrilla warfare. He sent a six-page letter to Coalition activists recommending that the warfare imagery be axed, but not all Christian Coalition activists got the message. When the group formed a chapter in Caddo Parish, Louisiana, chairman Dan Perkins told the Shreveport *Times*, "If they [local activists] are not properly trained, they're like soldiers going into battle who don't even know how to load their weapons, much less fire them. We'll teach people how to load and fire their weapons."[9]

In his 1994 book, *Politically Incorrect*, Reed tries to put a positive spin on the abandonment of warfare images. "Early in my service at the Christian Coalition," he writes, "I occasionally used military metaphors to describe our efforts to encourage people of faith to get involved as citizens. A few appeared in print. Political adversaries lifted these phrases out of context and repeated them in an attempt to harm us. At first I was angry at them for distorting my words. But I learned an important lesson. I realized that I bore a special responsibility to speak in a way that reflected God's character and love. Those of us who bear His name have a unique obligation to choose words that represent our Lord in a way that reaches others and makes knowledge acceptable."[10]

You see, then, it was all a plot by Reed's enemies to make

him look bad. His phrases were simply distorted; taken out of context. The innocent choir boy of the far right certainly hadn't done anything wrong.

Unfortunately for Reed, his explanation doesn't square with reality. What really happened is probably something like this: Reed made a number of extremist statements of a violent nature. He told them to reporters, knowing full well they would appear in print. When they did, either he or Robertson looked them over and realized the statements made Reed sound like a fanatic. Unable to retract them, he simply tried to blame it all on his enemies. It's one of the oldest tricks in the book. But no foe of the Christian Coalition made Reed use those words. No one "lifted them out of context." No one had to. The context was bad enough, and it spoke loudly about what Reed wants to achieve and how he wants to achieve it.

Like Robertson, Reed suffers from convenient memory lapses. During the Christian Coalition's 1991 "Road to Victory" conference in Virginia Beach, he bragged about how the organization one year earlier had helped North Carolina Senator Jesse Helms come from behind to defeat Democratic challenger Harvey Gantt. Reed told attendees that Helms called Robertson a week before the election asking for help. "I had access to the internal tracking, and I knew [Helms] was down by eight points," Reed said. "So Pat called me up and said, 'We've got to kick into action.' Bottom line is . . . five days later we put three-quarters of a million voter's guides in churches across the state of North Carolina, and Jesse Helms was re-elected by one hundred thousand votes out of 2.2 million cast."[11] But in 1994 when the Federal Election Commission announced it was investigating the affair, Reed changed his story. He told the *Charlotte Observer* that he could not remember Helms asking Robertson for help and claimed that conservative Christians decided to get involved on their own.[12] Like Robertson, Reed seems to believe that people will swallow any version of events he concocts, if he just says it often enough and with sufficient force. That may be the case with the legions of followers who hang on every word Robertson and Reed utter, but millions of other Americans can see the plain evidence and should understand that Reed is simply not being truthful.

The Christian Coalition's involvement in partisan politics has long been a sore point. The group's critics say the Coalition has clearly stepped over the line of permissible activity. As a nonprofit group, the Coalition is not allowed to have partisan politicking as its principal activity. The Coalition holds a nonprofit status that gives it some wiggle room. The group may be political, as long as political activity does not constitute more than 49 percent of its activities. Critics, however, believe that 100 percent of the group's work is political. The Christian Coalition is essentially an arm of the ultraconservative wing of the Republican party. It exists to elect ultraconservative Republicans to public office. It is the equivalent of a political action committee (PAC), and it ought to be required to pay taxes and report lists of donors, just as every other political action committee in the country must do. The fact that the Christian Coalition holds a tax-exempt status while representing one of the most extreme factions of the GOP is nothing short of a first-class scandal.

Anyone who doubts that the Coalition is an arm of the GOP need only look at the group's origins. It was founded in part with a $64,000 contribution from the Republican Senatorial Committee in October of 1990. The RSC is hardly in the business of forming nonpartisan political organizations.

The Christian Coalition's endorsement of the Republican party filters right down to the local level. At a May 1995 Coalition conference for activists interesting in running for school board slots, attendees were exhorted to target heavily GOP precincts. "Start with very top precincts with 70 percent Republican," Tim Phillips, a strategist for U.S. Representative Robert Goodlatte (R-Va.), told the crowd. "[Only take] precincts that are most Republican year after year."[13]

Phillips also recommended some "stealth" tactics to find

the "hard-core people"—the most conservative Republicans. He suggested inventing a phony polling firm, in his parlance a "generic name for a survey phoning group," and asking loaded questions about abortion, school prayer, gay people, and the National Education Association. Respondents giving the most right-wing views are later targeted for calls on election day to remind them to vote.[14]

When Republican leaders, led by Newt Gingrich, unveiled their "Contract with America" prior to the 1994 midterm elections, Reed was quick to add the Christian Coalition's endorsement. He pledged that the group would spend $1 million promoting the contract planks. Gingrich later returned the favor by appearing at the Capitol Hill press conference announcing the Coalition's ten-point "Contract with the American Family." The Coalition said it would spend $2 million promoting its legislative agenda, and Gingrich promised a floor vote on each item. Some of the Coalition's "Contract" was designed to be noncontroversial, but other planks were reactionary—such as the call for a new Religious Right-drafted First Amendment and the demand that "parents," that is, right-wing, fundamentalist Christians, be given veto power over public school curriculum.

During the health-care debate of 1993 and 1994, Reed and the Coalition consistently sided with ultraconservatives who labored day and night to sink the reform plan. Although many Christians interpret their faith as a mandate to help the needy and the sick, Reed takes a different view. He told the *Virginian-Pilot* that "Christians" oppose paying for mental health care and drug treatment programs because they rarely need those services. "Church-going families are less prone to use these programs—services they don't want or need," he said.[15] The Coalition's hostility toward health care should surprise no one. In a 1993 CBN pamphlet titled "Freedom from Demon Bondage," we are informed that many mental afflictions, such as split personalities, paranoia, anxiety, and "mental distress," may actually be the result of demon possession.

In 1995 the Christian Coalition was so desperate to help right-wingers in Congress pass a provision banning lobbying by nonprofit groups that receive federal money, it joined forces with the National Beer Wholesalers. The Coalition's target was Planned Parenthood; the beer wholesalers were gunning for "anti-alcohol" groups that they say have it in for them. The unholy alliance targeted the House Appropriations Committee and decided to split the work. "We divided up the list," said David K. Rehr, the beer wholesalers' vice president for government affairs. "In what districts did beer wholesalers have good contacts with the members? In what districts did the Christian Coalition have good contacts with the members? They'd have Christian Coalition members calling the districts, and we'd have beer wholesalers and their employees calling as well."[16]

A poll the Christian Coalition itself commissioned in 1995 lays bare the facts about the group's alleged "nonpartisanship": 68 percent of Coalition members identified themselves as Republicans; 20 percent said they were independents and a mere 5 percent claimed to be Democrats. (Ninety-five percent of the Coalition members polled said they planned to vote against President Clinton.) At a seminar on how to work within the Democratic party, held during the Christian Coalition's 1995 "Road to Victory" conference, less than a dozen people showed up. By contrast, a similar session focusing on gaining power through the GOP attracted a packed room of attendees.

Any doubts about the Coalition's ties to the GOP are dispelled by examining its fundraising mail. Robertson's letters are routinely loaded with bitter attacks on Democrats, usually described as "the far left," "radicals" or "liberals." Republicans are regularly praised, no matter what sins they may have committed.

In the summer of 1995 the Christian Coalition sent to members a four-page fundraising appeal begging for a regular contribution of $20 per month to join the "Christian Patriots." In an emotional appeal, Robertson declared that he was moved to form the patriots group because in the wake of the 1994 elections, "I'm concerned that Christian voters—flush with victory—will now become complacent . . . believing America is safe from the Clinton administration's liberal agenda." Robertson assured readers that "the Left will now fight even harder to regain the ground they lost last year."[17]

"The Left" can only do wrong, but conservatives who toe Robertson's line on social issues can be forgiven for virtually any transgression. Noted the letter, "You've probably already seen the incredible attacks being launched against pro-family leaders in Congress like Newt Gingrich—in which their statements are being taken out of context and distorted by the liberal news media."

At the same time Robertson was extolling Gingrich as a "pro-family leader," *Vanity Fair* magazine was publishing a piece on the speaker of the house chronicling his long history of marital infidelity. The article reported that throughout his first run for the House in 1974, Gingrich was having an affair with a young campaign volunteer. This was merely the first of his many extramarital relationships. Although his first wife worked to put Gingrich through several years of college, he abandoned her in the spring of 1980 and took up with Marrianne Ginther, yet another young campaign aide, whom he later married.

Gingrich left his first wife, Jackie, at an especially bad time. She was recovering from a bout with cancer and had survived several operations. She was recovering from one when Gingrich showed up to discuss the terms of the divorce. He later refused to pay Jackie's bills, leaving her nearly destitute. Remarked one of Gingrich's ex-lovers, "He's morally dishonest. He has gone too far believing that 'I'm beyond the law.' He should be stopped before it's too late."[18]

I bring this up not to smear Gingrich, but to point out the blatant hypocrisy of the Christian Coalition in anointing such an individual as a "pro-family leader." Gingrich seems to have been just as active on the extramarital front as the right-wing alleges President Clinton has been, yet the Coalition has conveniently ignored Gingrich's activities for only one reason: Gingrich pushes its moral agenda. Clinton doesn't, so he is ripped to shreds at every turn. If any Democratic House member were guilty of half of the things Gingrich has done, the Christian Coalition would spread that news far and wide. About Gingrich's bedroom antics they are mum.

Much of the Christian Coalition's support for Republicans isn't even subtle. In the May/June 1995 issue of *Christian American*, an article about Coalition activity in the states notes that in Florida, Representative Dan Webster, the House minority leader "is an unabashed born-again Christian and a strong advocate of religious conservative causes." Notes the piece, "If Florida Republicans are able to pick up just four more seats the 1996 elections, Representative Webster will be Florida's first Republican Speaker in a century." This is clearly an endorsement of GOP candidates.

The same roundup noted that Georgia still has a Democratic governor, Zell Miller, and quotes a political science professor who asserts that Miller and state Democrats will have to watch their step because, "They know the Christian Coalition and other groups are watching their every move."[19]

During the Coalition's 1995 "Road to Victory" conference in Washington, which I personally attended, several Republican office-seekers were endorsed. During a meeting of the South Carolina Christian Coalition caucus I attended, state director Roberta Combs introduced a GOP congressional candidate and said, "We do not endorse candidates but work with candidates as individuals"—a distinction without much difference when it comes to politics.

Combs began discussing South Carolina's fifth congressional district, saying in reference to the Democrat who holds the seat, "He needs to go." She then introduced Larry Bigham, a Republican running for the slot. "He's going to be our next congressman in the Fifth District," Combs told the 100-plus attendees.

Bigham challenged incumbent Democrat John M. Spratt, Jr., in 1994, but lost in a close race. He told the crowd that his appearance before the caucus September 9, 1995, constituted an official announcement of his candidacy in 1996.

Bigham noted that Spratt scored only 29 percent on the Christian Coalition's Congressional Scorecard.* "Larry Bigham will score 100 on your scorecard," he declared. "I need your help. I need your support. Roberta has given me her personal support." Continued Bigham, "With your help, we can defeat John Spratt. John Spratt is a nice guy, but John Spratt votes wrong." Before Bigham could finish, an indignant Coalition member called out, "If he votes wrong, that's not a nice guy!"

"In January of 1997," Bigham went on, "we will have a good Christian in office along with all the others." (Spratt, a Presbyterian, apparently does not fit the Coalition's definition of a "good Christian.")

Combs seemed well aware that her activities were of a questionable nature. I was present when twice she demanded that any reporters in attendance leave the room. On another occasion, when a man walked into the room carrying a camera tripod, Combs snapped, "Are you press?" In the interest of obtaining firsthand information about the Christian Coalition, I ignored these demands and stayed.

In other state Coalition caucuses I attended during the 1995 event, similar endorsements were handed down. In the Louisiana meeting, state director Sally Campbell pushed the gubernatorial candidacy of State Senator Mike Foster, a Republican. Campbell told attendees that she had met with Foster several times and that he promised her that if elected he would call a special session of the legislature to mandate a ballot initiative against gambling. Foster, Campbell reported, told her he couldn't be elected without the Christian Coalition's

---

*The Christian Coalition issues "scorecards" for national, state, and local officeholders that purport to say how incumbents voted on a variety of "pro-family" issues. Critics say that the scorecards are wildly distorted because they fail to give proper context for any of the votes.

help. (Foster went on to easily defeat a liberal Democrat in the general election.) Campbell related how she had made a television commercial on Foster's behalf in her capacity as Louisiana Christian Coalition director. When the national Christian Coalition got wind of the ad, she was forced to pull it.

To get around the national Coalition's alleged ban on straight political endorsements, Campbell recommended that Christian Coalition activists and officials go ahead and endorse but make certain the line "Affiliation given for identification purposes only" is included every time an endorsement of a candidate appears in print.

At the Wisconsin caucus of Coalition convention-goers, Scott West of Stevens Point, Wisconsin, stood up to thank the Coalition for supporting his unsuccessful congressional campaign against Democratic Representative David Obey the previous year. Carol Simmons, director of the Minnesota Christian Coalition, quickly interjected that what West "means to say" is that some Coalition members worked on his campaign as individuals, insisting that the organization does not endorse candidates. West wryly added that Coalition members are committed to the group's agenda twenty-four hours a day, but that some of them aided his campaign when they were not working for the Coalition.

A meeting of North Carolina Coalition members featured State Representative Robin Hayes, a Republican who discussed his religious beliefs, outlined a conservative legislative agenda, and asked for the support of individual Coalition members as he prepared to run for governor.

During the Texas Coalition caucus, "Christian Nation" advocate and Coalition activist David Barton crowed that three-fourths of the seventy-four candidates for public office "we supported" last year won. Barton said Religious Right activists in Texas are targeting the state Board of Education in 1996 and hope to win three seats.

Leaders of the Arizona caucus seemed especially concerned about media scrutiny. Guards were posted at the door with orders to remove anyone not personally approved by the caucus leader. During the session, Nathan Sproul, Arizona Coalition field director, urged attendees to become precinct committee chairs in the Republican party but not to let anyone know the Christian Coalition was behind the move. Sproul told the audience that the Coalition needs precinct committee chairs to attend the GOP National Convention to chose the presidential nominee.

Coalition leaders should have good reason to be concerned about the group's blatant GOP politicking. In South Carolina and in other states, the Christian Coalition is already the subject of an inquiry by the Federal Elections Commission over some of its activities. In South Carolina, three Coalition activists were ordered to appear in federal court for questioning. In addition, Combs was asked to provide various pieces of information such as letters and copies of checks.

The FEC is looking into Coalition activities in thirty-five states, based on a formal complaint filed by the Democratic National Committee on October 21, 1992. The Democrats charge that the group functioned as a political action committee but failed to follow federal law governing the reporting requirements for such entities.

Incredibly, despite the group's close identification with the most reactionary wing of the Republican party, Reed and Robertson continue to insist that the Christian Coalition is "nonpartisan." As the FEC investigation got under way, Coalition spokesman Mike Russell issued the following statement: "The information we distribute has been reviewed by the finest attorneys in the country, and it has met IRS specifications as being nonpartisan. We feel we're still in compliance with the law and feel like we'll be fully vindicated when this process is finished."[20]

Coalition leaders like Reed and Russell insist that the organization does not work on behalf of individual candidates but instead merely works to make sure fundamentalist Christians are informed about the issues and politically active.

To that end, the Coalition publishes "voter guides" that purport to give the candidates' views on a variety of issues. These guides are issued during every election, from presidential to local races. They are usually inaccurate and clearly biased in favor of the most reactionary right-winger in the race. Worse yet, they are frequently issued just days before an election, meaning that candidates whose views are distorted in them—as they frequently are—have no time to reply or try to set the record straight.

The guides do a great disservice to American politics by grossly oversimplifying complex political issues. The guides are set up so that each candidate is said to "support" or "oppose" certain issues. The Coalition insists that answers are taken from questionnaires or, in the case of incumbents, from actual votes. But this very set-up lends itself to distortions because no context is given for the unique circumstances surrounding each vote. For example, Coalition voter guides for members of U.S. Congress often contain a line, "Taxpayer Funding of Obscene Art." Virtually every politician who ever voted to keep the National Endowment for the Arts in the federal budget is listed as supporting "obscene art." In fact, the NEA awards grants to local agencies, which in turn are free to subsidize the arts projects of their choice. An extremely small percentage of the programs funded have been labeled "obscene" by the right-wing. In any case, when voting on the NEA's budget, no member of Congress was voting directly on "obscene art." Amendments have been offered by conservatives in Congress that would deny NEA funding to projects deemed "obscene" or "blasphemous," but many of these efforts were so poorly worded and vague that they were probably unconstitutional. When legislators voted against them, they were making a statement about the dangers of censorship; they were hardly casting a vote in favor of "obscene" art.

Other issues that appear on the guides are similarly distorted. One line item on the congressional guide for 1994 refers to "Banning Ownership of Legal Firearms." The use of the phrase "legal firearms" by the Coalition gives one the impression that Congress voted on a measure to send federal agents out to seize hunters' deer rifles and shotguns, as well as pistols used for self-defense. In reality, the vote in question concerned only assault weapons. The law was intended to get weapons of mass destruction out of the hands of drug dealers and the mentally unstable. This ban received the support of many Americans who do not favor a broad ban on all guns. Reading the Christian Coalition guide, however, one would think the ban was aimed at the rifle the average hunter uses during deer season.

One might also wonder what exactly makes gun ownership a "family values" issue. Reasonable people of good will differ on the question of gun control, of course, but the Christian Coalition implies that anyone who favors some controls on weapons—even on assault weapons—is "anti-family." This is grotesque. Many gun control advocates argue that protecting people from such weapons of terror is the real "pro-family values" position.

Similarly, the Coalition's "Family Values Voter Guide '92" for the presidential election listed among its issues "Increased Funding for SDI." The Strategic Defense Initiative is the euphemistic name for President Reagan's "Star Wars" missile defense system, a plan many scientists and military experts derided as a completely unfeasible. Again, people have different opinions on the viability of the system, but it is certainly not "anti-family" to suggest that the program funding be cut. Many Americans believe further SDI funding is akin to pouring money down a rat hole and urge that the dollars spent on it be diverted to other programs or simply not spent at all, a stance they argue is really "pro-family values."

Finally, sometimes positions listed for candidates are simply wrong. In 1994, U.S. Representative Andy Jacobs, an Indiana Democrat, was listed as opposing the balanced budget amendment on a Christian Coalition voter guide. Jacobs was amazed because he has favored the amendment since 1976. He called the guide "highly inaccurate" and the product of a "deceit brigade." "I am beginning to believe that the far right is completely un-inhibited by the truth," Jacobs said. "In a civilized world, you would like to think that Christian, God-fearing people would not lie or bear false witness against their neighbors."[21]

Jacobs was especially annoyed that he was listed as giving "no response" to a question about term limits. This leads a reader of the guide to assume that he had personally answered the questions on a Coalition survey. In fact, Jacobs never saw a questionnaire from the group and is certain no one on his staff did either, despite the Coalition's claim on each guide that surveys were sent by "certified mail or facsimile machine." This tactic of listing "no response" on guides for Democrats and liberals is a common Coalition smear tactic.

Aside from skewed voter guides, the Christian Coalition employs other strategies to let its people know for whom to vote. Sometimes they just tell them. At the group's 1994 conference in Washington, Paul Weyrich of the Free Congress Foundation showed up at a caucus of the Pennsylvania Christian Coalition and implored members to vote for Peg Luksik, an independent, far-right extremist running for governor. Weyrich was distressed because both the Democrat and Republican running held prochoice views. "Peg Luksik is totally pro-life and pro-family and needs our help," Weyrich said. "We are not professional Republicans. We must say to the Republicans, 'We do not support every piece of garbage you send our way.'"[22] (Luksik, a fringe candidate who travels across the state spreading horror stories about outcome-based education,* ended up receiving 13 percent of the vote.)

---

*"Outcome-based education" (OBE) is a frequent target for Religious Right attacks. OBE requires students to prove their mastery over subject matter, usually through some type of demonstration as opposed to a written test, before moving on to more advanced study. The program places a strong emphasis on techniques designed to help students achieve the desired result at the end of study, hence the term "outcome-based." It has been used in public schools in various forms for nearly 25 years.

The Christian Coalition's annual "Road to Victory" conferences are clearly partisan events. At the group's first meeting in 1991 in Virginia Beach, Ralph Reed explained how the groups used a telephone "voter ID" program to turn out the most conservative voters in Virginia Beach. Volunteers would call voters in selected precincts, claim to be conducting an informal survey for the Christian Coalition, and ask two questions: "Did you vote for Dukakis or Bush?" and "Are you a Republican or a Democrat?"

Said Reed, "If they answered, 'Dukakis, Democrat' that was the end of the survey. We didn't even write them down. We don't want to communicate with them. We don't even want them to know there's an election going on. I'm serious. We don't want them to know."[23] Voters who indicated they were Republicans were asked two additional questions: "Do you favor restrictions on abortion?" and "What is the most important issue facing Virginia Beach?" Files were created on each person contacted, and before the election, voters received a personal letter from the Coalition's favored candidate specifically earmarked to address the issue the voter identified as the most important facing Virginia Beach.

The letters made no mention of controversial social issues such as abortion, and Reed pointed out that many of the Republicans the Coalition talked to in the Virginia Beach area said they were prochoice. They still received computer-generated letters from the Coalition's candidates. Quipped Reed, "I'll take the votes of the proabortion Republicans." Thanks to Reed's tactics, prochoice GOP backers did not even know they were voting for Coalition-backed candidates who oppose legal abortion.

At the same conference, Reed explained that on election day 1991 he personally went down to a heavily trafficked polling place and conducted exit polling, telling voters he was with an "independent, outside organization." When he saw that the Republican was losing, Reed activated a Coalition phone tree to turn out the vote, reversing the tide.

How can the Coalition do such partisan work? Reed explained it like this: "We also control the Second District Republican party. So many of our people who were doing this voter ID were also (Republican) precinct captains. . . . So if they shared some of this voter ID information . . . we really didn't care."[24]

At its meetings, the Coalition tries to put on a face of non-partisanship, but the speakers list and attendees make a mockery of the effort. At the 1991 meeting, a series of briefings was held to explain how to become a delegate to the Republican National Convention depending upon what region of the country the attendee lived in. A single caucus was held on becoming a delegate to the Democratic Convention, but no one showed up.

During the 1993 "Road to Victory" conference, one speaker got a little carried away. Max C. Karrer recounted how the Florida Coalition helped a Republican win a seat in the state legislature using computerized membership lists from conservative churches to build a "Christian voter data base." The group then sold the list to the right-wing candidate for a nominal fee.

Observed Karrer, "We were not allowed to give them away, so we charged him five dollars—but we printed labels for him of the Christian voters, which enabled him to put out direct mailings to the Christian voter, that he would not necessarily do to the general public. . . . You want to talk about stealth campaigns—it was quietly done, and they [the opposition] didn't realize they were in trouble until it was too late. . . . We didn't give our list to anybody. What we will do is print labels for some people. That we will do. I sold him the labels. I didn't give them to him. It's legal then, see. For five dollars!

"Politicians in our section think we have a bigger data voter base than we do. But we don't change that perception, we don't tell them. They come to us now. When someone wants to run for office, they come to the Christian Coalition. . . . It gives you . . . tremendous lobbying power with the legislator because they think you have this huge bloc of votes that you can swing, though you can't necessarily."[25]

Karrer's speech is further evidence that the Christian Coalition is essentially a wing of the GOP, despite their denial of this. However, he may have been too forthcoming. A reporter from *The Freedom Writer*, a newsletter that monitors the Religious Right, was present during the session and taped Karrer's comments. They later appeared in *The Freedom Writer* and in *Church & State*.[26]

Speakers at Christian Coalition events are routinely drawn from the most conservative wing of the GOP. Speakers and attendees in 1991 included then Vice President Dan Quayle; Senator Jesse Helms; Representative Robert Dornan (R-Calif.); former Representative William Dannemeyer (R-Calif.); Religious Right leaders Phyllis Schlafly (Eagle Forum) and Gary Bauer, head of the Family Research Council, a Washington-based Religious Right group founded by James Dobson's Focus on the Family; and George Grant, a Christian Reconstructionist.* Reagan-era Education Secretary William Bennett and Iran-Contra figure Colonel Oliver North showed up for the 1992 event. In 1995, Pat Buchanan delivered the major address during the Coalition banquet, which was hosted by North. A long list of right-wing luminaries appeared at the event. At the 1995 event, only two Democratic politicians were featured speakers: former Pennsylvania Governor Robert Casey, an antiabortion zealot; and Representative Charles Stenholm of Texas, a conservative Democrat who more often than not votes with the GOP.

The first two Christian Coalition conferences were held in Virginia Beach. Both were supposedly closed to "outsiders"— non-Coalition members, but in both years the gatherings were attended by Coalition critics determined to expose the orga-

---

*Christian Reconstructionism is the most extreme manifestation of the Religious Right. Its adherents argue that U.S. civil law should be based on the Old Testament's harsh legal code. In their view, the government should treat adultery, blasphemy, fornication, and a long list of other things as crimes, with sentences ranging from imprisonment and flogging to mutilation and death.

nization. In 1991 and 1992, Frederick Clarkson, a writer and researcher who tracks the Religious Right, slipped into Christian Coalition meetings and wrote about them for *Church & State* magazine.

Partly because of this infiltration, the Coalition threw open its doors most of the way in 1993, when it moved the conference to Washington. Even today, however, state caucuses and breakout sessions can be closed to the media if the speakers want it that way, and many do. It is not uncommon at a Coalition state meeting for the first question asked to be, "Are there any media here?" If so, out they go.

During the first two years, Coalition leaders made the mistake of assuming that they were addressing uniformly friendly audiences and became a little too frank. Guy Rodgers, the Coalition's former field director, advised attendees in 1991 not to worry if the group's goals sounded extreme to most Americans. Voter turnout, he said, is so low that getting conservatives to the polls is all that matters. "We don't have to worry about convincing a majority of Americans to agree with us," Rodgers said. "Most of them are staying home and watching 'Falcon Crest.' " Rodgers went on to outline the group's "15 percent solution": In the average election, only 60 percent of all adults eligible to vote are actually registered. Of that number, only half cast ballots. Therefore, 15 percent of all eligible voters determine the outcome. "In low-turnout elections—city council, state legislature, county commissions— the percentage of eligible voters who determines who wins can be as low as 6 or 7 percent," Rodgers added.[27]

Alongside this endorsement of stealth tactics, the Coalition continued to promote a partisan agenda at its annual meetings. As the 1992 election approached, one man stood up at the Virginia Beach gathering and announced, "It is impossible for a Christian to vote for a Democrat." His comments met with thunderous applause and laughter.[28]

Perhaps sensing that this type of overt partisanship was hurting the group's image, Ralph Reed invited Democratic

Party National Chairman David Wilhelm to speak at the group's 1993 meeting in Washington. Wilhelm delivered a forceful address, taking the Coalition to task for suggesting that those who oppose its policies are anti-Christian. Amid catcalls, jeers, and boos, Wilhelm said, "I believe you can be a good Christian and support a woman's right to choose. I believe, as a majority of Americans do, that it should be a matter between a woman and her conscience, not a woman and her senator." Members of the audience began shouting "no!" and several called out, "It's murder!"[29]

Reed was livid. But ironically, he did not blame the unruly display on the members of the Christian Coalition who had generated it. Apparently, they are unable to tolerate an opposing view for even half an hour. He blamed Wilhelm. "We gave David Wilhelm a golden opportunity to build bridges with people of faith," Reed told the *Washington Times*. "We are disappointed that he chose not to. We tried to be even-handed, but we were rejected."[30] Reed got it backwards. Wilhelm came and gave an honest speech that reflected Democratic party principles. The party believes abortion ought to be legal, and Wilhelm said that. Wilhelm did not reject the Christian Coalition; the Christian Coalition rejected him.

With a Democrat in the White House, the rhetoric at the group's 1993, 1994, and 1995 conventions reached a fever pitch. Bill and Hillary Clinton were repeatedly attacked, and the speakers list included figures from the most extreme camps of the far-right, including GOP pundit and presidential aspirant Pat Buchanan, radio talk show host G. Gordon Liddy, and televangelist D. James Kennedy. Although the Christian Coalition claims to be a "prolife" organization, at the 1993 conference, attendees could purchase T-shirts bearing the messages "I Accelerate for Liberals" and "Nuke the Liberal Media." One woman from Illinois explained to *Church & State* magazine that she prays for the death of the movement's enemies, saying, "We need to pray that they be converted or removed. It's very biblical."

As the 1994 elections approached and it became apparent

from polls that the Republican party would gain seats, then-Representative Gingrich could not control himself. In commenting to NBC's Tom Brokaw on the recent arrest of Susan Smith, a South Carolina woman who became the focus of national attention after she murdered her two children by locking them in a car and pushing it into a lake, Gingrich claimed that her actions were due to liberalism. More Republicans, Gingrich asserted, would mean fewer Susan Smiths. A few weeks later a letter written by Smith's stepfather, Beverly Russell, Union County chairman for the Christian Coalition and state GOP official, made public the fact that Russell had started molesting her when she was sixteen and had resumed the sexual relationship shortly before Smith murdered her sons. On July 28, 1995, the *New York Times* reported that Russell, who has never been charged with the crime, testified to the molestation at Smith's murder trial. (Elsewhere, it was reported that Smith recalled her father molesting her one night in 1987 after he had returned home from posting "Pat Robertson for President" signs all over town.) Perhaps for the first time in his life, Gingrich remained silent.

The Coalition took credit for the GOP's sweeping gains in the 1994 midterm elections. The day after the elections, November 9, Reed appeared on "The 700 Club" and proclaimed that twenty-eight of the forty-eight new members of Congress were "conservative, religious, pro-family" candidates. Reed said the Coalition had distributed thirty-three million voter's guides during the election. He also claimed that participation by "born-again evangelicals" had soared to 33 percent in the election and that conservative evangelicals contributed 6 percent to the average Republican office seeker. "If the Republican candidate won with less than 53 percent of the vote, these voters provided the margin of victory," he said.[31]

Gushed Robertson, "It's an awesome win, Ralph, and much credit to you and all the members of the Christian Coalition and others who worked so hard."

With the 1994 elections behind him, Reed began focusing

on 1996. Wielding the group's increasing power in the GOP, Reed promptly issued a warning to party leaders that both the presidential and vice-presidential nominee must be antiabortion. His comments came as speculation increased that a moderate Republican, such as New Jersey Governor Christine Todd Whitman or Massachusetts Governor William Weld, who are both prochoice, might balance the GOP ticket as the party's nominee for vice president in 1996. Religious Right activists such as the Rev. Jerry Falwell and James Dobson of Focus on the Family* began making noise that if that happened, they would bolt the GOP in favor of a third party.

"There are still those who claim to be our leaders, and even those who aspire to be our president, who state that the social issues must ride at the back of the bus, and that innocent human life simply doesn't matter," Reed told a gathering of the Conservative Political Action Conference in Washington on February 10, 1995. "And they even propose that they balance the ticket in 1996 by choosing someone who is liberal on human life. Let me be sincere today. Prolife and pro-family voters, one-third of the electorate, will not support a party that retreats from its noble and historic defense of traditional values and which has a national ticket or a platform that does not share Ronald Reagan's belief in the sanctity of human life."[32]

At the time he made the comments, Reed and the Christian Coalition were under fire from other Religious Right leaders for supposedly backing down on core issues such as abortion and homosexuality. Seeking to shore up that vital constituency, Reed decided to talk tough. Although he later denied that his words were meant to be a threat, the meaning is plain enough, and the comment was not lost on Republican presidential hopefuls like Senator Robert Dole.

---

*Dobson runs Focus on the Family, a radio ministry based in Colorado Springs. Although Dobson claims the group's purpose is to support "traditional families," he and his subordinates frequently attack separation of church and state and work with other Religious Right organizations to advance the far-right's political agenda.

Dole at first seemed unwilling to knuckle under. For instance, he defended the Republican party's decision to select Whitman to give the GOP response to Clinton's 1995 State of the Union message. He told the *Washington Times*, "Some of the prolife people were calling in and complaining about it. I said, 'Well, Jiminy, you can't have everything.' "[33] But soon Dole was crowing about his 100 percent Christian Coalition approval rating and publicly pledging fealty to the group's repressive antiabortion agenda.

To groups like the Christian Coalition, the very idea that the Republican party has a prochoice contingent is anathema. Whitman, who became a rising star in the Republican party when she upset incumbent Democrat Jim Florio in the 1993 gubernatorial race, is a frequent target of the Religious Right's wrath. Although Whitman is conservative on many issues— she favors private school vouchers and takes a conservative line on taxes, for example—the New Jersey governor supports legal abortion, and that fact alone is enough to make her a public enemy to the Religious Right.

The Religious Right continues to hold the Republican party in a headlock over the abortion issue even though numerous polls have indicated that many Republicans are prochoice. In the wake of Bush's defeat, party leaders began pushing a "big tent" philosophy that said the conservative movement is broad enough to encompass a variety of viewpoints on the issue. But with the party forced to kowtow to the Religious Right, the space in the tent reserved for prochoice Republicans has been getting smaller and smaller. As the irrepressible Jerry Falwell once quipped, "If the Republicans decide to invite the gays, feminists, and abortionists into their BIG TENT, then I predict that millions of religious conservatives, including this writer, will be looking for a NEW TENT."[34]

At this writing, the 1996 presidential race had yet to heat up, and it was too early to tell if the Christian Coalition and other Religious Right groups would make good on their threat to require the GOP to field a solidly antiabortion ticket, or whether this issue would even be relevant to many voters. Many Americans apparently believe that abortion will remain legal because the Supreme Court, even after twelve years of conservative appointments, has failed to overturn *Roe* v. *Wade.* What they fail to understand is how close the Court has come to doing so. In fact, *Roe* v. *Wade* would probably be history now if Reagan and Bush hadn't accidentally put a few moderates on the court. A few more appointees by an antiabortion president could shift the balance. If that happens, the civil war the Republicans have managed to stave off for so long between Religious Right activists and moderates may finally erupt. If it does, it's a safe bet that the Christian Coalition will be in the thick of it, working out in front and surely behind the scenes. It is, after all, a "nonpartisan" organization.

As part of the research for this book, I attended the Christian Coalition's 1995 "Road to Victory" conference in Washington, D.C. I would like to conclude this chapter with some personal reflections about what I saw and experienced.

Every year, activists who support church-state separation sign up for the meeting and issue reports about what went on. To me, it always sounded too incredible to believe. I thought it was important to see it for myself. I'm glad I did. Although much of what I saw and heard sickened, angered, or just plain disgusted me, I now know it was vital that I see it "up close and personal." The written word cannot convey what it is like to attend a Road to Victory conference.

Several things struck me about the meeting: its overwhelming atmosphere of paranoia and siege mentality; its naked partisan overtones; and its utter lack of compassion, charity, and decency. At the event, speaker after speaker hammered home the same themes: "Conservative Christians are under attack. We are under siege. We face annihilation. Only we can save the country. If we fail, all we value and treasure will be taken away from us. The American family will be destroyed; indeed, the entire American republic may collapse."

Conference attendees, I decided, must feel surrounded by

an alien culture that, far from being benign, is out to deliberately subvert their values and seduce their children. Is it any wonder such folks embrace fanaticism? They are convinced that only a nation whose people embrace far-right politics wedded to an exceedingly narrow interpretation of the Scriptures can turn things around. And the Christian Coalition will do whatever it takes to make that happen—even if it means trashing the Constitution and advocating theocracy.

Such an atmosphere quite naturally leads to paranoia. It's not surprising, therefore, that Christian Coalition members believe that sinister forces—be they the "liberal media," secular humanists, the United Nations, Planned Parenthood, the American Civil Liberties Union, the "radical left," liberals, Democrats, or university professors—are out to get them. Some go so far as to assert that these various forces have combined to form a type of evil cabal that works behind the scenes pulling the strings of American society. I realize that conspiracy theories are popular these days, but at the Christian Coalition they are accepted de facto—no evidence required—and if you don't believe in them, well, you're the oddball for failing to see the obvious.

Several speakers shamelessly fed this siege mentality. One, failed Supreme Court candidate Robert Bork, asserted that the Court, through its decisions upholding separation of church and state, has in fact established the religion of secular humanism. Bork's views are so radical that in 1987 the Senate refused to confirm his nomination to the Court. He has since augmented his salary at the American Enterprise Institute by traveling the right wing's rubber chicken circuit of speaking engagements, telling his tale of woe to anyone who will listen.*

In a weary, pedantic tone, Bork ridiculed Supreme Court justices who dare to disagree with his bizarre and rigid inter-

---

*Bork called his judicial philosophy "strict construction" and claimed it reflected what the Founding Fathers thought about the Constitution. But critics charged that Bork had misread the Founders and that his reading of the Constitution was extremely narrow, failing to take into account the numerous changes in American society since the eighteenth century.

pretation of the Constitution, insisting that they are part of a plot by "liberal elites" to subvert American culture and instill moral relativism. There again was that conspiracy theory thinking. At any minute I expected Bork to whip out a chart explaining the Illuminati's role in all of this. He didn't, but the crowd ate it up anyway. Apparently not aware that he was addressing a group that calls itself "nonpartisan," Bork asserted that the only way to fix things is to elect Republicans and kick Clinton out of the White House. If Clinton is reelected, he said, all hope is lost. The crowd alternated between booing and cheering: booing at the mention of Clinton's name, and cheering the prospect of his defeat.

The Christian Coalition, of course, is about as nonpartisan as the conservative *National Review.* Attacks on President Clinton and the First Lady were a mainstay of the conference. Nearly every time Clinton's name was mentioned, the crowd reacted with boos and hisses. At some closed-door state caucuses, Coalition officials issued flat-out endorsements of GOP candidates for Congress and gubernatorial races, a practice Coalition Executive Director Ralph Reed insists is forbidden. At other events, Coalition members were trained in how to organize their "neighborhoods," that is, their political precincts. One speaker recommended visiting the neighbors, telling them you just want to say hello but in actuality scoping out their politics. If they turn out to be godless liberals, flee. If they're right wing, go home and make a file card about them as the first step toward bringing them into the Christian Coalition's political machine.

But perhaps the ugliest feature of the Road to Victory was that, in its haste to embrace every far-right Republican proposal to come down the pike, no matter how paleolithic, the group jettisoned its very last shred of moral compassion—if it ever had any to begin with.

The poor took an especially harsh beating. According to Star Parker, a black ultraconservative who routinely speaks for the far right, the poor are responsible for their own plight. Badly mangling one of Jesus' parables, she insisted that the way to help the poor is to take their meager resources and turn them over to the rich, who will use them to create jobs. "Trickle down does work," Parker insisted, failing to understand that the poor need more than a trickle in the America of the 1990s.

Parker contends that she lived on welfare for three years about fourteen years ago. She asserts that at that time, welfare mothers in Los Angeles routinely sold food stamps for cash, dumped their kids in government-run day care centers, and spent the day on the beach taking drugs before heading back to their palatial apartments with fireplaces, jacuzzis, and sub-terranean parking. Welfare mothers, Parker asserted, should be assigned to upscale families who will receive tax breaks for taking them in. "You start giving a real hefty tax relief to fam-ilies that will take in that welfare person and their children for a year or two until they get themselves together and you tell that girl, 'Listen, here's what you're going to do. You're going to take this name and address and you're going over to their house and you better do what they say. And if you don't do what they tell you for the next year and a half, we're going to take your kids, we're going to put them in an orphanage and we're going to put you in jail for child abuse.' " If that sounds like modern-day serfdom to you, it's not; it's the Religious Right's version of "family values."

If welfare mothers continue having children, the answer is not to educate them or provide them with birth control. The answer is to deny any additional benefits for the children. (Perhaps the Religious Right believes the problem will be solved once the children starve to death.)

As for crime, Parker has a guaranteed solution: "Where's the electric chair!" she shrieked. She recommended building a giant warehouse prison in East St. Louis, Illinois, where con-victs will be sent until their number comes up. Accelerating the pace of executions would help, too, she added. Although much of Parker's speech was incoherent (paraphrasing here does more justice than her own words), she received a wildly enthusiastic reception from the crowd. She was repeatedly interrupted with loud applause and, on conclusion, she received a prolonged standing ovation with cheers and whistles. Based on the crowd reaction, I would not hesitate to rate her as one of the most popular speakers at the Coalition's 1995 conference.

Make no mistake, issues like welfare and crime do vex the American public. Reasonable people of good will differ on what ought to be done. It certainly is not unreasonable to call for overhauling welfare or advocating a "get tough" policy on crime. But the type of simplistic, mean-spirited rhetoric offered by Parker and other Coalition speakers adds absolutely nothing useful to the national dialogue on these issues. Not one thing. Yet the 4,000 plus crowd repeatedly leapt to its feet and wildly cheered this dross.

As I stood there watching the crowd erupt into frenzy after frenzy, it struck me that the Christian Coalition has no answers beyond destruction and curtailment of rights. Problems with education? Abolish the Department of Education! In fact, abolish public education entirely! Don't like abortion? Make it illegal for everyone—even for victims of rape and incest and women carrying severely deformed fetuses that stand no chance of viability at birth. (Parker would make abortion illegal with no exceptions, because, as she pointed out, some people in the Bible were born as a result of rape.) The country's state of morals got you down? Make prayer and religious worship mandatory in public schools! Don't like the politicians? Declare America a Christian nation and impose religious tests for public office!

All of these extreme ideas and more were offered up by a parade of speakers, most of them limited to twenty minutes, who put forth soundbite solutions to our nation's serious problems. Sadly, every major Republican seeking the presidential nomination appeared at the event except Pennsylvania's Senator Arlen Specter (who wasn't invited but was occasionally ridiculed) and California's Governor Pete Wilson (who sent a telegram saying he was sorry he couldn't make it).

Finally, all of this folderol was wrapped in the rhetoric of "pro-family" values, the clear implication being that anyone who fails to embrace the Christian Coalition's narrow-minded political agenda is not "pro-family." Ideas such as censorship, mandatory prayer in schools, ending reproductive rights, and redistributing wealth to the rich were constantly referred to as "family-friendly."

In fact, many Americans would view the Coalition's agenda as a missile aimed at heart of the family. This, perhaps, is what is most offensive about the Christian Coalition. It dares to assume the mantle of "family values" *as defined politically*, when, as any parent can tell you, being "pro-family" has little to do with what lever one pulls inside the voting booth. "Family values" are not defined by whether one advocates a school prayer amendment or a tax cut. Rather, "family values" are defined by actions: mainly, are you willing to set aside many important aspects of your life and devote yourself to another life, helpless at first, who needs you to develop properly? On a more basic level, are you willing to get up four times a night for feedings, to spend your money on formula instead of that new CD player you've wanted, and crawl out of a warm bed at 3 A.M. on a cold winter's night because a little person in the next room just had a scary dream? And will you do these things willingly and consistently with a loving, not angry, approach? If so, you have "family values." And you can have them if you're Democrat, Republican, or Independent; liberal or conservative, Christian, Jew, atheist, or Hindu. That is a simple fact the Christian Coalition absolutely refuses to recognize.

Unfortunately for Reed and Robertson, all of the talk about "family values" isn't fooling anyone. More and more Americans realize that the Christian Coalition is an extremist organization, and the Road to Victory conference only served to prove it. Despite the much-flaunted, new, "moderate" Christian Coalition that we're told isn't obsessed with social issues, at this conference anyone who strayed from bashing legal abortion, gays, or the Clintons to talk about tax cuts and balancing the budget put the crowd to sleep. In fact, the throng reacted most vociferously to hot-button issues that are the

Coalition's bread and butter: screeds against abortion, demands that the Department of Education be abolished, attacks on our public school system, denunciations of liberalism, and paranoid invective about the United Nations and its aims at creating one world government. These are the issues that the Coalition obsesses over; these are the issues that pay Reed's salary, and he knows it.

As I left the meeting, I couldn't help but wonder what type of America the next generation will live in. Will President Reed or his hand-picked puppet have succeeded in putting the final provisions of the Bill of Rights through a paper shredder, all in the name of protecting family values and "saving the nation," or will enough Americans finally have stood up, shouted "Enough!" and pulled the country back from the precipice?

The answer, I submit, is up to the voters, activists, and defenders of church-state separation who are reading these words.

Notes

1. Quoted in David Cantor, *The Religious Right: The Assault on Tolerance & Pluralism in America*, 2d ed. (New York: Anti-Defamation League, 1994), p. 30.

2. Douglas Fox, ed., *The Emergence of David Duke and the Politics of Race* (Chapel Hill, N.C.: University of North Carolina Press, 1992), pp. 75–78.

3. Quoted in Cantor, *The Religious Right*.

4. Mark O'Keefe, "Robertson Group Vows Countersuit on Sex-Ed," *Virginian-Pilot* (April 11, 1990).

5. "Robertson Regroups 'Invisible Army' Into New Coalition," *Christianity Today* (April 23, 1990).

6. Cited in Religious News Service dispatch, May 15, 1990.

7. "Pat Robertson and History: A Pattern of Deception," *Church & State* (November 1994), p. 14.

8. Quoted in Cantor, *The Religious Right*.

9. David Westerfield, "Christians Find Their Voice," Shreveport *Times* (January 21, 1993).

10. Ralph Reed, *Politically Incorrect* (Dallas: Word Publishing, 1994), p. 68.

11. Frederick Clarkson, "The Christian Coalition: On the Road to Victory?" *Church & State* (January 1992).

12. John Monk, "Christian Group's Role in Helms Campaign Questioned," *Charlotte Observer* (June 7, 1994).

13. Hans Johnson, "School Board Crusade," *Church & State* (July / August 1995).

14. Ibid.

15. Mark O'Keefe, "Christian Coalition Aims to Sink Health Plan," *Virginian-Pilot* (February 16, 1994).

16. Jonathan Peterson, "Christian Group Adds Budget Items to Agenda," *Los Angeles Times* (October 30, 1995).

17. Christian Coalition undated fund-raising letter, received August 1995.

18. Gail Sheehy, "The Inner Quest of Newt Gingrich," *Vanity Fair* (September 1995).

19. D. J. Gribbin, "State Leaders Advance Cause," *Christian American* (May / June 1995).

20. Lee Bandy, "FEC Probes Christian Coalition," *The State*, Columbia, S.C. (September 30, 1994).

21. Joseph L. Conn, "Behind the Mask," *Church & State* (November 1994).

22. Ibid.

23. Clarkson, "The Christian Coalition."

24. Ibid.

25. "Stealth? Deception? You Decide." *The Freedom Writer* (April 1994).

26. See "Stealth? Deception? You Decide" and "Christian Coalition Claims 1,000,000 Members and 872 Local Chapters, But Critics Doubt It," *Church & State* (April 1994).

27. Clarkson, "The Christian Coalition."

28. Frederick Clarkson, "Inside the Covert Coalition," *Church & State* (November 1992).

29. Joseph L. Conn, "Detour on the Road to Victory?" *Church & State* (October 1993).

30. Thomas P. Edsall, "Democratic Party Chief's Fiery Words Stir Wrath as Christian Coalition Meets," *Washington Post* (September 11, 1993).

31. Joseph L. Conn, "Contract on the First Amendment?" *Church & State* (December 1994).

32. Joseph L. Conn, "Power Play," *Church & State* (April 1995).

33. Josette Shiner and Ralph Z. Hallow, "Dole Works at 'Reconnecting the Government to the People,' " *Washington Times* (February 3, 1995).

34. Jerry Falwell, "The Republican Party's Big Tent," *National Liberty Journal* (March 1995).

5

Pat Robertson's New World Order

"I know that this all sounds too much like a science fiction horror story, but the loss of United States sovereignty opens up the very real possibility that some day in the future a demonized madman like Hitler could seize control of a worldwide, homogenized government and then employ currently existing technology to turn the entire world into a giant prison."

—Pat Robertson, *The New World Order*

The previous two chapters looked at Pat Robertson's views on religious freedom and the separation of church and state and examined the rise of the Christian Coalition. By examining his own words—as uttered on "The 700 Club" and published in books, magazines, and other writings—my aim has been to illustrate the extreme views Robertson holds with respect to such important issues as church-state separation and religious freedom.

In Robertson's world, separation of church and state was invented by Communists in the Soviet Union, and ungodly humanists lurk behind every tree just waiting to brainwash innocent children in the public schools. Opinions this strange are quite shocking, and such views would strike many Americans as bizarre. But those opinions don't begin to scratch the surface of Robertson's highly unusual worldview.

To really get a look inside Robertson's mind, it is necessary to examine in some detail what he has had to say about a variety of issues, including non-Christian religions, the role of women in society, international affairs, public education, and marriage and family life, among others. I will sample some of Robertson's ideas on these issues in the next chapter. But before doing that, it is important to first take a look at what may rightfully be called Robertson's most famous (or infamous) book, *The New World Order*. In this tome Robertson outlines a centuries-old conspiracy theory of world history that does more than merely border on paranoia: the book plunges into it head first. Written in 1991, his book has quickly earned a spot as a classic of crackpot literature.

To sum up the central thrust of *The New World Order,* the volume postulates that for centuries a secret cabal of anti-Christian forces has manipulated governments and the world economy to enrich itself and consolidate control over the masses. The ultimate aim of this plot, Robertson asserts, is to usher in a "New World Order"—a one-world government under the auspices of the United Nations. Eventually, this government will fall under the sway of the Antichrist, sparking the apocalyptic battle of Armageddon. In this horrific showdown between good and evil, half of the world's population will be obliterated.

Who's responsible for betraying the United States to this sinister coterie of demon-inspired megalomaniacs? The culprits are the usual suspects of so much hoary conspiracy literature: Freemasons, the Illuminati, the Trilateral Commission, the Council on Foreign Affairs, the Federal Reserve, and mysterious "European bankers." Robertson lumps all of these forces into a collection of enemies he labels "The Establishment."

The Establishment has been busy during the past two hundred years. According to Robertson, this group and its agents engineered the assassination of President Abraham Lincoln, bankrolled the Russian Revolution, fostered world wars and U.S.-Soviet hostility and arranged the election of President Woodrow Wilson, knowing all along he would establish the Federal Reserve and the Internal Revenue Service.

The Establishment's meddling continues up to the present day. According to Robertson, both Democrats and Republicans serve this evil clique. He points out, for example, that former President George Bush served on the Trilateral Commission.*

Bush, according to Robertson, may not be demonic himself, he just unwittingly serves Satan. At one point in the book, Robertson wonders if it is possible that the ex-president was part of a succession of presidents, which also includes Jimmy Carter and Woodrow Wilson, who were "unknowingly and unwittingly carrying out the mission and mouthing the phrases of a tightly knit cabal whose goal is nothing less than a new order for the human race under the domination of Lucifer and his followers."[1] Bush, Carter, and Wilson weren't evil themselves, you see; Satan just led them around by the nose.

The New World Order is important because it outlines the plan by which Robertson has apparently been operating all of these years. While the book doesn't excuse his crude opinions on a number of important issues, it does help explain them. As one reads *The New World Order*, it becomes easier to understand how someone who holds such obviously paranoid views could easily adopt the siege mentality that Robertson so frequently spouts. As I said, it doesn't excuse it, but it does help explain it.

---

*The Trilateral Commission, the object of numerous conspiracy theories from both the right and left, does exist. Headquartered in New York, it was founded in 1973 by David Rockefeller, chairman of the Chase Manhattan Bank. His goal was to bring hundreds of leaders together from North America, Japan and Western Europe—hence the "tri" in trilateral—to discuss world problems. Several members of the presidential administrations of Jimmy Carter, Ronald Reagan and George Bush have been members of the group. Proponents of conspiracy theories frequently charge that the Trilateral Commission's true goal is the creation of one world government. For more information, see Cecil Adams, *More of the Straight Dope* (New York: Ballantine Books, 1988).

Before delving into his tome, it's necessary to discuss a few preliminary issues. First, Robertson is listed as the author of several books, but he apparently used ghost writers for many—if not all—of them. Aside from his autobiography, *Shout It from the Housetops,* which was discussed earlier in this book, Robertson is said to have authored numerous works, including *Beyond Reason,* an examination of the miracles he is alleged to have performed as a faith healer; *America's Dates with Destiny,* a look at what Robertson considers to be the pivotal dates of United States history; and *Answers to 200 of Life's Most Probing Questions,* in which Robertson employs a question-and-answer format to respond to such burning questions as "What do you think of long hair for a man?" "How can I lose weight?" and "Are credit cards associated with the mark of the Beast?"

It's difficult to know if Robertson actually wrote all or only portions of any of these books. He has been surprisingly frank in admitting that some were ghost-written. One of Robertson's ghost writers, Mel White, who wrote *America's Dates with Destiny,* later proved to be an embarrassment to Robertson when he came out of the closet, announced his homosexuality, and began publicly opposing Robertson's political agenda.

Unfortunately, it is unclear whether *The New World Order* was ghost-written or not. When the book became the subject of controversy a few years after it was published, Robertson defended it in the media as his own work. Appearing on CNN's "Evans & Novak" on April 15, 1995, he insisted he had written it himself. But later a letter from Robertson to one of his viewers in which he claimed that the book was ghost-written was forwarded to Americans United. He even identified the writer: James Black. This particular letter, on CBN letterhead and bearing Robertson's signature, is dated February 14, 1995. Once again, Robertson is guilty of spreading two contradictory stories. In February, he admits that *The New World Order* was ghost-written. Two months later he swears he wrote it himself.

In the end, it probably doesn't matter if *The New World*

Order was ghost-written. What's important is to determine if Robertson endorses the ideas that appear in the book and if they reflect his beliefs. On both counts the answer is yes, since Robertson was willing to allow his name to be on the cover and later claimed the book as his own. During the controversy over the book, Robertson never once stepped back from anything in it and defended the book vigorously. In fact, he denied that the tome embraces a conspiracy theory of history (even though the casual reader can see that it plainly does) and insisted that the book had no anti-Semitic overtones. I'll return to the issue of anti-Semitism later, but for now it's important to take a look at how this book came into being.

Although published in 1991, *The New World Order* failed to attract much attention in the general media at first. The religious media and some specialty publications that monitor the Religious Right did take note of it, however. Despite the fact that it was ignored by the mass media, the book sold well and for a while occupied a slot on the *New York Times* list of best sellers.

One of the few mass circulation publications to review the book early on was the *Wall Street Journal*. Satirist Joe Queenan had a field day with Robertson's conspiracy theories. Branding Robertson "a trailer-park David Letterman" with a "permanent village idiot's grin," Queenan dismissed the tome as a kooky, conspiracy-theory-laden jeremiad pieced together by a "paranoid pinhead with a deep distrust of democracy" in an "energetically crackpot style." Wrote Queenan, "*The New World Order* is a predictable compendium of the lunatic fringe's greatest hits. Included in its pages are the usual mad ramblings about European money powers (we know who *they* are) who hired John Wilkes Booth to knock off Abe Lincoln, the significance of the Masonic symbols on the $1 bill, the secret clout of the Council on Foreign Relations, the recall of General Douglas MacArthur, and the great granddaddy of both ultra-right-wing *and* ultra-left-wing conspiracy theories: the Trilateral Commission."[2]

Queenan's razor-sharp pen may have reduced Robertson

to a comic figure in print, but in real life many Americans were taking *The New World Order* seriously. Thankfully, a more serious examination of the ideas in the book appeared in *Church & State* magazine in June of 1992. In a two-page review, *Church & State* editor Joseph L. Conn dissected the book and sounded the alarm that it is in effect a blueprint for theocracy. Aside from being laced with conspiracy theories, the book, Conn charged, advocated restrictions on religious liberty, religious tests for public office, and curbs on freedom of the press. Also, it displayed an unswerving admiration for the harsh Puritan theocracy of colonial America. "All of this could be dismissed as harmless kookery if it came from one of the many obscure conspiracy mills, but Pat's tome made the *New York Times* best seller list," Conn wrote. "His publisher says 344,000 copies of the hardback are now in print, and the paperback edition, released in March, has already sold 134,000 copies. . . . When you combine this outreach with his nationwide television audience, Robertson's bully pulpit preaches his alarming theocratic message to a large congregation of Americans. In addition, his political, legal and educational divisions—as well as his personal wealth—are all growing steadily into an unholy empire. Americans who believe in religious liberty, church-state separation and our other constitutional freedoms have cause for concern."[3]

While organizations that monitor the Religious Right were quick to pick up on the significance of *The New World Order*, the mainstream media, with a few exceptions, continued to ignore the book for more than three years. That situation changed abruptly in February of 1995 when Michael Lind published a lengthy review of the tome in the *New York Review of Books*. Lind charged that Robertson's book was based on a laundry list of anti-Semitic sources, and he provided ample documentation to prove it. Suddenly, Robertson was forced to defend his work, and a firestorm quickly developed.

In the book, Lind points out, Robertson spins his conspiracy theory over centuries, tracing its origins to the creation of the

"Order of the Illuminati" in 1776 by Adam Weishaupt.*
Weishaupt, according to Robertson, used the Illuminati to in-
filtrate the Freemasons in Europe, thus bringing some of the
continent's most prestigious leaders into his plot. Robertson
asserts that wealthy Jews were admitted to membership in the
Freemasons for the first time in 1782, enabling them to under-
write Weishaupt's Illuminati takeover. Variations of the Illuminati conspiracy have surfaced in world history time and time
again, Robertson insists, engineering revolution in Russia, seizing control of the U.S. economy, and escalating the Cold War.

Central to the Establishment's goal to run the world was
its creation of the Federal Reserve in 1913. Robertson drafts
Paul Warburg and "the Rothschilds" as prime forces in this
power grab. These are names that reoccur time and again in
conspiracy theory literature as well as in the literature of anti-
Semitism. The Establishment, Robertson asserts, was always
happy to see global conflict because war forced nations to
borrow from "European bankers," increasing their wealth and
power. Many observers interpreted "European bankers" as a
euphemism for "Jewish bankers." Lind points out that
throughout his book, Robertson uses the adjective "German"
or "European" rather than "Jewish." This struck Lind as a
mere semantic dodge. "This does not necessarily mean
much," he observes, "since the adjective 'German' or 'European' frequently refers to Jews in the American literature of
anti-Semitism."[4] What's more important, Lind says, is to examine the sources Robertson used in compiling the book.
Robertson has often bragged that *The New World Order* is
based on an extensive bibliography. By this he means to imply

---

*The Illumnati, like the Trilateral Commission, is a frequent object of
obsession by conspiracy theory buffs. They maintain that the organization
is a shadowy cabal of elites founded in Europe in the eighteenth century
that has been secretly engineering world events, including sparking wars
and manipulating financial markets, ever since. Its goal is said to be one-
world government under the elites, known as the "illumined ones." According to Robertson, the Illuminati also seeks to destroy Christianity.

that the book was well researched and is in effect "scholarly"; and if a book is scholarly it must be true, right?

Not necessarily. Conspiracy theorists often cite one another's works in their books, and this is more or less what Robertson has done. Also, many of the books Robertson cites are of dubious quality. Several works cited in the bibliography have been identified as anti-Semitic tracts. They include *Secrets of the Federal Reserve* by Eustace Mullins and *Secret Societies and Subversive Movements* by Nesta H. Webster.

In a second piece for the *New York Review of Books,* Lind and writer Jacob Heilbrunn dissected Robertson's book and its sources even more thoroughly. Heilbrunn noted that two books by Webster—*Secret Societies* and *World Revolution*—"[b]oth portray Jews as sinister, conspiratorial forces." *Secret Societies,* he noted, contains chapters titled "The Jewish Cabalists" and "The Real Jewish Peril" and its appendix refers to "The 'Protocols' of the Elders of Zion," a notorious anti-Semitic forgery,[5] as if it were a credible source.

According to Heilbrunn and Lind, passages of *The New World Order* appear to have been lifted almost word for word from Webster's writings.[6] They also noted that Webster, like Robertson, denies being an anti-Semite. Nevertheless, the following Webster passage from the preface of *Secret Societies* is revealing: "[I]t will be noticed that anyone who attempts to expose the secret forces behind the revolutionary movement, whether he mentions Jews in this connection or even if he goes out of his way to exonerate them, will incur the hostility of the Jews and their friends and will still be described as 'anti-Semite.' The realization of this fact had led me particularly to include the Jews in the study of secret societies."[7]

A couple of excerpts from Webster's writings should prove helpful to the reader to decide for himself if Webster and, through his use of her work, Robertson, sounds like an anti-Semite. Heilbrunn cited the following:

- Referring to the French Revolution: "[I]t cannot be denied that the power of the Jews over the people was immensely increased by the overthrow of the monarchy and aristocracy."[8]

- Attempting to link Freemasonry to Jews: "Either Freemasonry is the cover under which the Jews, like the Illuminati, prefer to work, so that where cover is not available they are obliged to come out more into the open, or that Grand Orient Masonry is the directing power which employs Jews as agents in those countries where it cannot work on its own account."[9]

- Referring to Karl Marx: "Can we not see him, like some veteran Jewish rag-and-bone merchant, going over the accumulated debris of past social schemes, passing through his fingers the dry bones of dead philosophies, the shreds and tatters of worn-out doctrines, the dust and ashes of exploded theories, and with the practical cunning of the German and Hebrew brain shrewdly recognizing the use that might be made of all this lumber by skillfully welding it into one subversive whole?"[10]

- Warning of insidious forces: "There is another power at work, a power far older, that seeks to destroy all national spirit, all ordered government in every country, Germany included. What is this power? A large body of opinion replies: the Jewish power."[11]

- And finally, this gem: "The Jewish agitator is the tsetse fly carrying the poison germ of Bolshevism from the breeding-ground of Germany."[12]

These are some of the views of the individual Robertson cites as an authority in one of his most popular books. Robertson has yet to repudiate Webster or her writings, although he did later insist in a statement, "My book, *The New World Order*, does not embrace a conspiracy theory of history, and it certainly is not anti-Semitic."[13]

Commenting on the book, Ephraim Radner, a writer for the *Christian Century*, pointed out that it is highly unlikely that Robertson did not realize that Webster's writings were anti-Semitic. Radner, an Episcopal priest in Stamford, Connecticut, pointed out that Webster's anti-Semitism "has been well known by scholars for decades and is evident to any reader. Did Robertson not read the books he cites?" Radner also noted that a 1982 biography of Webster by Richard Gilman "conveniently gathers facts about her writings and commitments, and it includes some material that surely ought to have concerned Robertson."[14]

Michael Lind, noting that several prominent conservatives rushed to Robertson's defense following publication of his review of *The New World Order*, wondered, "It will be interesting to see how William F. Buckley, Jr., Midge Decter, James Bowman, Hilton Kramer, William Kristol, and Ralph Reed respond to the revelation that a principal source of the most comprehensive book by the leader of the Christian Coalition, cited approvingly as a scholarly authority by the Reverend Robertson, is an interwar conspiracy theorist who identified, behind half a dozen other conspiracies, the ultimate conspiracy: 'Jewish power.' "[15]

Of course, denunciations of Robertson from the right wing never came. Some leaders of the conservative movement in America may indeed be embarrassed by Robertson's views, but as long as Robertson controls a powerful bloc of votes, few dare speak out in public.

What are we to make of Robertson's defense of his book? First, it is simply absurd to claim that *The New World Order* does not embrace a conspiracy theory of history. Anyone who takes the time to read the book can see that it certainly does. In fact, that's the whole point of the book. Robertson's claim that the tome is not conspiracy literature is another example of his implicit claim that two plus two equals five. No matter how forcefully Robertson states his denial, the book speaks for itself. Notes Robertson in the book, "Authors who expose subversive secret organizations are usually ridiculed because, when asked for proof of the identity of participants in secret societies, they have to answer, 'That is impossible, since the names are secret.' But, invariably, there is a tiny secret core ring, a larger and slightly less secret middle ring, then a much broader and more public group. . . . Nevertheless, there is enough evidence and enough unexplained phenomena in the past two hundred years that clearly points to a hidden plan intended to establish the new world order. Looking back, it is possible to discover certain clear links."[16]

Likewise, Robertson's claim that the book must have merit because it landed on the best-seller list makes no sense. How a book sells is not an indication of its merit. The American public has a seemingly bottomless appetite for nonsense, as evidenced by the countless tomes about astrology, aliens from outer space, quack diets, and UFOs that have regularly graced best-seller lists over the years. Some books that sold millions have later been exposed as hoaxes. A slot on the best-seller list tells you exactly one thing about a book: that a lot of people bought it.

Robertson's book escaped critical review in most major publications, and apparently even the right-wing media, which can usually be counted on to fawn over just about anything slapped together by a conservative, preferred to ignore it. When the paperback edition of *The New World Order* appeared, the only glowing quote that could be found to grace its cover came from the *New American*, a magazine published by the John Birch Society. The *New American* lauded the tome, saying it "shines light on the invisible hand shaping U.S. government policies." It's not surprising that the Birchers, long fans of conspiracy theories themselves, found in Robertson a kindred spirit. What is surprising is that he had the poor judgment to trumpet it.

Robertson didn't spend a lot of time denying that the book espouses conspiracy theories. Rather, he devoted the brunt of his defense to deflecting the much more serious charge of anti-Semitism. This charge is more troubling, and also more difficult for Robertson. For years the TV preacher has been a strong supporter of Israel. When charges of anti-Semitism were raised against him, one of the first things Robertson did was to point to his years of support for Israel. Seeking to defuse the controversy, Robertson took a unique tack: His critics had it all wrong. *The New World Order*, you see, is actually a *defense* of Israel. "My primary objection was that a United Nations-driven foreign policy could ultimately be directed against the security interest of Israel," he wrote in a letter published in the *New York Times* on March 5, 1995. "For more than three decades I have consistently been one of the most reliable allies of the Jewish people and the state of Israel in the American evangelical community."

While Robertson has continually pursued political goals that trouble many American Jews, no one has doubted that his support for Israel is genuine. His support has been so strong, in fact, that after the controversy over *The New World Order* exploded, some Jews affiliated with the neoconservative movement were among the first to rush to Robertson's defense. Prominent Jewish conservative Norman Podhoretz went so far as to assert that yes, Robertson was guilty of anti-Semitism, but he absolved him of it, noting Robertson's long record of supporting Israel.[17] What these members of the Jewish community either don't know or choose to ignore for political reasons is why Robertson supports Israel. In Robertson's evangelical end-times scenario, Jews are simply pawns who help usher in the second coming of Christ. He believes that a mass conversion of Jews to Christianity will occur before Jesus returns to usher in the end of the world. In Robertson's view, the creation of the state of Israel was a necessary component in this eschatological drama. Thus, Robertson's support for Israel springs not from his view that Jews are worthy of respect as Jews or that Judaism has value outside of its ultimate use to Christianity; rather, it comes from his reading of the Bible and his unique spin on prophecy.

Preaching about this subject on the July 6, 1995, airing of "The 700 Club," Robertson explained his belief that the Jews' refusal to accept Jesus Christ when He was sent to earth opened up a wonderful opportunity for the Gentiles. "When they [the Jews] return to faith, it will be the equivalent of the resurrection of the dead," Robertson said. "Some people think that a certain sign of the return of Jesus Christ on earth will be the restoration of the Jewish people to an understanding of God's full revelation in Christ, their messiah."

Evidence of Robertson's dichotomous approach to Jesus is readily available. Robertson has no problem working simultaneously to support Israel and underwriting efforts designed to convince Jews to convert to fundamentalist Christianity. In fact, CBN publishes a pamphlet called "Hear, O Israel," which aims to convert Jews. Unlike some leaders of the Religious Right, Robertson has not been so crass as to suggest that Jews are bound for hell or to assert that God does not hear their prayers, but it's obvious from the proselytizing activities of CBN that he would prefer that Jews become "completed"— that is, converted to born-again Christianity.

In fact, Robertson has been a supporter of so-called Messianic Judaism. Also known as "Hebrew Christianity," this movement actively works to convert Jews to fundamentalist Christianity. However, the movement retains some trappings of Judaism. Its houses of worship, for instance, are called "synagogues" and Jewish holidays are celebrated, though in a Christian fashion. Robertson's "700 Club" has profiled Messianic Jews in a favorable light. Jay Sekulow, the lead attorney of Robertson's legal arm, the American Center for Law and Justice, is a member of the movement and was once featured in a book published by Jews for Jesus, the leading Hebrew Christian group. The Robertson-owned Founders Inn in Virginia Beach has hosted a gathering of Messianic Jews.

Not surprisingly, the effort to claim that one can simultaneously be a Jew and a Christian infuriates many Jews. Some Jewish leaders have accused Hebrew Christians of preying on vulnerable segments of the Jewish community—Russian immigrants, college freshmen, and elderly people. "I have much greater respect for straight-out missionary groups that say, 'We're Christian and here's our message,'" Rabbi James Rudin of the American Jewish Committee told *New York* magazine. "It's the deception and the targeting that I'm furious

about. . . . Accepting Jesus moves you out of the house of Israel, out of the Jewish people. This is an argument that was
settled almost two thousand years ago. At a certain point, the
Nazarenes, who were the early Jewish followers of Jesus, left
Judaism and formed their own religion, which is what we
know as Christianity. You can't change two thousand years of
history. . . . If Robertson is using his empire to foster something that aims for the spiritual extinction of Judaism, then
he's no friend of the Jewish people."[18]

Other Jewish leaders interviewed by the magazine were
equally blunt, accusing Messianic Jews of seeking to destroy Judaism. "What they are attempting is spiritual genocide," said
Philip Abramowitz of the Jewish Community Relations Council
of New York. "They want to see Judaism destroyed as an entity."

Israel's own government has not been taken in by the Messianic Jews. It rightly considers them what they are—Christians. In 1989, the Israeli Supreme Court ruled that Messianic
Jews are not entitled to automatic citizenship in Israel, because they are not Jews. The case was brought by a South
African couple who sought to settle in Israel under the country's 1950 law that grants citizenship to Jews all over the
world. Messianic Jews, observed the court, "do not belong to
the Jewish nation and have no right to force themselves on it.
Those who believe in Jesus are, in fact, Christians."

These facts apparently made no difference to the handful
of conservative Jews who defend Robertson. However, as the
controversy over the book played out, *New York Times* columnist Frank Rich raised an important point. If Robertson's ravings had been uttered by just about anyone else, they would
have been denounced immediately from the left and the right.
To prove his point, Rich quoted from a February 26, 1995,
speech delivered by controversial Nation of Islam leader
Louis Farrakhan in Chicago, during which Farrakhan ranted
about "international bankers" fostering wars in order to line
their own pockets. "*The New World Order* and Mr. Farrakhan's
tirade have the same pedigree," Rich observed. "Among its

'original historical sources,' Mr. Robertson's bibliography does not include either Paul Warburg's papers or books, but it does list Nesta Webster's *Secret Societies,* a notorious anti-Semitic tract from the 1920s. Our two most prominent extremists of the 1990s are both dipping into the same well of pseudo-history that once served Father Coughlin and Henry Ford.*
. . . Is Pat Robertson anti-Semitic? He says not. But that doesn't alter the fact that his book disseminates old anti-Semitic conspiracy theories, however encoded."[19]

Thus Farrakhan is acknowledged as an anti-Semite and promptly criticized for his ludicrous ravings, while similar comments by Robertson are ignored. How can this double standard be justified? It's mainly due to the fact that Farrakhan doesn't represent votes for the right wing. Robertson does, and thus has been awarded a lifetime license to say whatever he pleases, with the proviso that any criticism ever lodged against him for his comments, no matter how off the wall they may be, will be ridiculed as religious bigotry.

In Robertson's other writings, he makes a distinction between "liberal Jews" (who are bad) and Jews who agree with him on political questions (who are good). In *The New Millennium* he excoriates liberal Jews and charges, "A sad irony of the last 40 years, though, is the fact that the liberal Jewish population in America has been intent on diminishing Christian influence in the public life of America. They believe that Christianity is a threat to Judaism, and many recite the terrors of the Holocaust as evidence of the Christian 'blood libel' against the Jews." Elsewhere in the book, Robertson becomes <u>even more offensive when</u> he asserts that Jews who dare to

---

*Known as the "radio priest," Father Charles E. Coughlin began broadcasting sermons in Detroit in 1926. By the early 1930s his "sermons" had become political jeremiads that were increasingly critical of President Franklin D. Roosevelt. In 1934 Coughlin formed an opposition group, the National Union for Social Justice, and by 1937 his broadcasts were increasingly steeped in fascism and ladened with anti-Semitic conspiracy theories. Coughlin became a Nazi sympathizer and leading apologist for Adolph Hitler and the Third Reich, and his movement collapsed after the start of World War II.

disagree with him on political questions are no longer truly religious people. "[T]he Liberal Jews," he writes, "have actually forsaken Biblical faith in God, and made a religion of political liberalism."[20] Here Robertson is doing to Jews exactly what he has done to liberal and moderate Christians—insisting they are not people of faith, because they fail to accept his political agenda. Could anything be more offensive?

The not-so-subtle implication is that Jews who support the separation of church and state are intent on "diminishing Christian influence" in American life. Rubbish. Many Jews support church-state separation for the same reason many Christians do—it is good for religion and for government. As a religious minority, Jews do have more at stake, especially in questions of religion in public education. Jews who have children in the public schools do not want them to be proselytized by teachers or school officials or pressured to give up their faith and convert to Christianity. This is a reasonable request, and it is their constitutional right. You can bet that if the situation were reversed, and Robertson's children or grandchildren were left with no choice but to attend public schools saturated with Judaism, Islam, or any other faith, he would be the first to utter howls of protest.

Further proof of Robertson's disdain for Judaism and other non-Christian religions is found in a 1992 letter he wrote to Frank Banko, a Wyoming, Michigan, man who designed a poster promoting peace among world religions. The poster contains the slogan, "There will be peace on Earth when there is peace among the world religions" in seventeen languages accompanied by the symbols of various faiths. Banko sent a copy of the poster to Robertson. Robertson wrote back, "There can be no unity between Christianity and the other religions listed, because they do not believe that Jesus Christ is 'the truth' and the *only* way to be reconciled with God." (Banko sent A.U. a copy of Robertson's letter.) The next chapter looks at how Robertson views faiths other than fundamentalist Christianity.

As the controversy over *The New World Order* and anti-

Semitism swirled around him, Robertson broke out one of his tried-and-true tactics: attacks and name-calling against the people who raised the issue. Calling the complaints about the book "specious objections," he insisted they come from "the radical left in America desperately looking for an opportunity to discredit the role of religious conservatives in politics."[21] Unfortunately for Robertson, that simply was not the case. Both Lind and Heilbrunn, who first circulated the charges against Robertson in the mass media, have conservative pedigrees. Lind served in the Bush administration, and Heilbrunn headed a branch of the College Republicans while a student at Oberlin College. (These days both men call themselves "former conservatives," but that hardly makes them members of the "radical left.") The two put the information before the public in the hope that the *conservative* community would be shamed into confronting Robertson and demand that he rescind the statements or be disowned. Not only did that not happen, but the far-right quickly began circling the wagons.

Ironically, the right wing's failure to condemn—or even criticize—Robertson for the excesses of *The New World Order* actually increased his power. Robertson demonstrated that his political movement is so influential in the GOP that he has in effect become untouchable. Emerging from the controversy with his reputation unscathed, he was given license to more or less say anything with impunity, safe in the knowledge that should anyone dare to criticize him, a flock of well choreographed advocates would soon rise up in indignation. The silence of the conservatives had the effect of saying, "Robertson may be a crackpot, but he's our crackpot."

New York Times columnist Frank Rich had it exactly right. Had the bizarre ravings found in *The New World Order* been uttered by another, they would have been speedily and repeatedly denounced. When a well known anti-Semite such as Louis Farrakhan makes similar statements, he is roundly condemned by liberals, moderates, and conservatives alike—and rightly so. But because Robertson controls a large bloc of right-

wing votes, conservatives refuse to join the chorus of denun-
ciation, and he gets an exception from the normal rules of
human decency. Even some Jews, it seems, who ought to be
sensitive to the dangers of anti-Semitism, are willing to put
politics above principle when it comes to Robertson.

As Rich pointed out, Robertson's theories are more than
just harmless eccentricity. As the 1990s progressed, many Americans awakened to the fact that extremist movements were
gaining in power in the United States. Members of the shadowy
militia movement, who call for armed resistance to the federal
government, became the subject of heightened media scrutiny
following the tragic bombing of a federal building in Oklahoma City in April of 1995. Rich pointed out that the rhetoric of
many militia backers sounded familiar to Robertson's rants.
Consider, for example, the views of militia leader Mark Koernke, alias "Mark of Michigan," who broadcasts over short-
wave radio. Koernke believes that a one-world government
will soon be established under the auspices of the United Nations and that the right to bear arms will be abolished, along
with other constitutional freedoms. Koernke signs off his broadcasts with, "Death to the new world order!"

In his book, Robertson also wonders if someday the "government of the United States [might] defer to the United Nations" and warns that if this happens "our constitutional right
to keep and bear arms would be one of the very first casualties."

Notes Rich, "Koernke transcripts on the Internet . . . reveal
that his ideas are not only incendiary but mimic the published
credos of Pat Robertson, president of the Christian Coalition and
a major force within the Republican party."[22] Rich acknowledged
differences in what Kornke and Robertson chose to emphasize,
but concluded that both "have thrown gasoline on the psychotic
fires of the untethered militias running around this country."

Not surprisingly, militia rhetoric has popped up in the
Christian Coalition. In September of 1994, the Rev. James W.
Watkins, pastor of a United Church of Christ congregation in
Kirtland, Ohio, attended a meeting of the Lake County, Ohio,

chapter of the Christian Coalition and found some members babbling ominously about "black helicopters." In militia lore, black helicopters are used by the federal government (or the United Nations) to harass freedom-loving Americans who dare to stand up to the New World Order. One man at the Ohio gathering claimed to have seen them "right here in Lake County!" Another couple at the meeting asserted that some U.S. military bases slated for shutdown were being secretly converted into detention centers to house President Clinton's political enemies. Another person asserted that UN troops were already stationed on U.S. soil, poised and ready to strike. Participants watched an anti-Clinton video that accused the president of numerous crimes, from drug running to murder, with no substantiation. (Clinton was blamed for just about everything at this particular meeting. One attendee lamented the fact that the new owners of a local radio station had seen fit to hire a repulsive "shock jock" and asserted, "The new owner is from Florida and obviously tied in with [Attorney General Janet] Reno and Clinton.") Concluded Watkins, "I spent the evening listening to unexamined paranoid speculations, swallowed whole and validated by bobbing heads and frequent amens. The entire thing reminded me or my pastoral visits to a psychiatric unit. Between the video and the general rumor sharing, Bill Clinton was blamed for everything from the decline of moral fiber to bad breath."[23]

In Rensselaer County, New York, the local Christian Coalition unit went totally around the bend. In its publication, *Capital Christian News*, one writer warned that a United Nations seizure of the U.S. government was imminent, saying the country would be occupied by international troops, including Russians. According to the Coalition newsletter, once the UN took power, New York state and local jurisdictions would lose their power to govern. Dissenters would be packed off to converted military bases, and all Americans would be forced to carry a national identity card. Asserted the newsletter, "Forms are already at the post office in boxes marked, 'For Emergency

Use Only.'" (Oddly enough, not one of the Postal Service's thousands of employees thought to blow the lid off the nefarious scheme by sneaking one of these forms out and slipping it to the media. But then, that just proves that the media is in on the whole thing.)

Perhaps most shocking of all was the revelation that the conspiracy theory espoused by the Rensselaer County Christian Coalition was apparently lifted from the *Spotlight,* a publication of the far-right Liberty Lobby, a group that frequently criticizes the Trilateral Commission and is considered by many observers to be anti-Semitic.

One would think Robertson and Reed would have enough common sense to put a lid on such excesses before they got out. Not only did they not do that, but Robertson himself fed the paranoia in July of 1995 with a series of "700 Club" broadcasts attacking the FBI and the Bureau of Alcohol, Tobacco, and Firearms (BATF). Across the nation, militia adherents fear and loathe the BATF because the agency has some authority to regulate weapons and enforce what few firearms laws there are. To militia members, any law—even one banning the sale of assault weapons or "cop killer" ammunition designed to rip through bullet-proof vests—is tantamount to putting the Bill of Rights through a paper shredder. Robertson's broadcasts played right into these fears. Relying on "dramatizations" of storm-trooper-like thugs breaking into the homes of innocent citizens, Robertson portrayed a government agency gone amok.

There was a time when a law-and-order conservative like Robertson would have never criticized federal police agencies. In the 1960s, for example, when the FBI was engaging in illegal domestic spying on left-wing groups, and the National Guard was beating up student war protesters on college campuses, many conservatives rushed to the defense of the federal government. But in 1995, Robertson saw an opportunity to attack a Democratic president, and of course he took it. The FBI and the BATF, he asserted, used to be good agencies, until they fell into the clutches of Clinton and Attorney General

Janet Reno. "You know, here on this program and at CBN we have been strong supporters of law enforcement," Robertson said on "The "700 Club," July 11, 1995. "We feel that the law enforcement officers, the police, and up to a time the FBI were outstanding agencies, doing a superb job. But since the advent of the head of the Justice Department, Janet Reno, things have gotten out of control. Something is just going on that is just very unwholesome in this nation, and you look for an explanation of this craziness in Oklahoma City and a lot of it goes right back to what happened with the Branch Davidians, Randy Weaver, and these other people. . . . It's reminiscent of the Nazis, and something has got to be done."

In his eagerness to smear Reno, Robertson failed to point out that the incident involving Randy Weaver, a white separatist whose wife and son were killed by the FBI during a siege in 1992, occurred while George Bush was president, prior to Reno's tenure as attorney general. (Weaver, who was accused of shooting a federal agent, was later acquitted by a sympathetic local jury.)

One of the "experts" on the FBI and the BATF that Robertson featured on the show turned out to be Bob Fletcher of the Militia of Montana. Other "experts" interviewed were advocates of the National Rifle Association—hardly objective sources. Although Robertson insisted that CBN does not "approve of some of these militias," his choice of interviewees led him to air a biased piece that trumpeted the charges of extremist groups as if they were accepted fact.

Law enforcement agencies do overstep their bounds from time and time, and Janet Reno's handling of the Branch Davidian standoff outside Waco, Texas, has been justifiably questioned. But to compare federal agents to Nazis goes beyond the pale. In his rush to discredit Clinton, Robertson was willing to crawl into bed with anyone, even, it seems, a band of heavily armed Rambo-wannabees and go so far as to compare portions of the government to the Third Reich.

With all of the controversy over *The New World Order*'s anti-

Semitism, all of the book's other extreme features were sometimes overlooked. For example, in the tome Robertson asserts that "the Establishment" has rigged the 1996 election and that Senator Jay Rockefeller, a West Virginia Democrat, will be elected president. As of this writing, President Bill Clinton had no challengers in the Democratic party for 1996, and Rockefeller had given absolutely no indication that he would run for president.

For someone who claims a direct pipeline to God, it's amazing how often Robertson's prophecies are simply wrong. In 1981 he noted in his newsletter *Pat Robertson's Perspectives*, "The odds are very high that there will be a major worldwide economic debacle of unprecedented magnitude. It could come at any time, but an informed guess would say that there will be some type of recovery in 1982, then rapid inflation, followed by a major worldwide crash sometime between 1983 and 1985. The wise man prepares himself." Robertson has been predicting economic doomsday for years. While there certainly have been economic downturns and even recessions, nothing like a "debacle of unprecedented magnitude" has occurred yet.

Robertson's claims about international warfare have also been breathtakingly off base. Religion journalist Russell Chandler reports that Robertson once "guaranteed" there would be a 1982 Tribulation, "sparked by a Russian invasion of Israel."[24] Chandler also reports that in 1990 Robertson told "700 Club" viewers that the "Middle East is going to explode. It's exactly what the Bible said." Predictions that there will be tensions in the Middle East are generally a safe bet, given that region's troubled history, but one must wonder how Robertson balances all of this with the current trend toward peace in the Middle East. Also, one must speculate why Robertson misses so many big developments. He never predicted the circumstances under which the Soviet Union would fall or the collapse of Europe's Eastern Bloc, for example—until it had already begun to happen. Then Robertson conveniently altered his scenario to fit new developments. One would think God would want to keep him apprised of the big developments.

On January 1, 1980, Robertson decided to ring in the new year by calling together the CBN staff for a prayer meeting. During this event, which was tape recorded, he outlined a nightmarish scenario for world war and international collapse that, he asserted, came to him directly from God. Recounting his dialogue with God, Robertson told the crowd, "At least for the last decade, I have said to the Lord, 'What kind of a year is it going to be?' And each year the Lord has said to me, 'It's going to be a good year for the world.' I'd come back the next year and think, 'It's going to be terrible,' and the Lord said, 'It's going to be a good year for the world. . . .' Year after year, that's what He said. I asked the Lord, 'What about this year?' and I didn't get that same answer. I got a different answer. He said, 'It will be a year of sorrow and bloodshed that will have no end soon, for the world is being torn apart, and my kingdom shall rise from the ruins of it.' " Continued Robertson, "The Lord has showed some things to me. I believe it's of God."

What God supposedly showed Robertson was an Armageddon-style scenario for the end of the world. Under the plan, the Soviet Union would invade several Middle Eastern nations, seize access to the world's oil reserves and plunge Western Europe and the United States into economic chaos. "You'll see Chrysler Corporation in a tailspin, you'll see hundreds of thousands of people out of work, you'll see all kinds of problems with the gold market and the oil and people in long lines, and you're not going to be able to do this and do the other thing," he predicted. "If I'm hearing Him right, things are starting to happen," said Robertson. "What has started over in the Middle East is not going to stop short of a war. I believe that in the next two years—I would put it at '82, but dates are risky—there's going to be a major war in the Middle East. I don't see how it can stop."

Once the Soviets cut off the oil supply, "the game's over," Robertson asserted. "Europe would fall in ninety days, and the United States would be all by itself. Now, they're going to make this move. And that's what God is saying. We've got a couple of years. They're not going to let up from now on. I mean, from now on it's going to be bloodshed, war, revolution, and trouble because the prize is too big. It's just too big."

With Europe in economic ruins, the United States would soon crash. "People are out of work. There's an awful lot of dislocation. There's going to be starving, there's going to be bread lines. There are going to be riots. People are going to go crazy," he said.

This setting, Robertson asserted, would be the perfect breeding ground for the Antichrist, who would rise up out of the chaos of Europe. "Now, what happens when economies get in critical condition? Well, they look for a strong leader to get them out of it. And they'll give their power to anyone, be he devil, be he God, anyone who can give the answers. . . . That sounds to me like the perfect setting for the guy who may be called the Antichrist."

Although Robertson hedged his bets a few times throughout the speech by saying "dates are risky," he seemed confident that the prophecy would come true. "I do not see how there's any possibility this is going to be delayed," he said at one point. "The maximum peril is in the next two years."[25]

Robertson did get one prediction correct—that the Soviet Union would fall, but even here he had the circumstances wrong. According to Robertson, the USSR was to collapse after a seven-year "tribulation" period played out within the context of worldwide war. Needless to say, that's not the way it happened.

Despite his dismal track record of prophesy, Robertson continues making predictions about dire economic upheavals and worldwide conflict. He still claims the Bible calls for this, but in light of recent history he has simply changed some of the characters in the cast.

Robertson's 1990 book, *The New Millennium*, explores ten trends that will affect Americans by the year 2000. In the tome Robertson still warns of worldwide conflict, but the villains have shifted away from the now defunct Soviet Union and toward tin-horn dictators like Saddam Hussein of Iraq. The last chapter of the book contains vintage Robertson musing about the end of time. It may be coming sooner than we think, Robertson says. When Israel gained military control over Jerusalem during the Six Day Way in June of 1967 it fulfilled a biblical prophecy and started the end-times clocking ticking. "When that event took place a clock began to tick that signaled the downfall of the great Gentile powers, the last and greatest of which is the United States of America," writes Robertson. "It also began the rise of Israel. What we would like to learn now is, very simply, how long will the clock be ticking."[26]

To answer that question, Robertson engages in some creative biblical numerology. He asserts that a biblical generation is forty years, and says that if June 1967 began a "generation" marking the end of the time of the Gentiles, then the magic date for the end of it all is 2007. Furthermore, Robertson asserts that the year 2007 has special significance for the United States since it is four hundred years from the date of the first permanent settlement in America, in what is now Virginia. The landing occurred April 29, 1607. "Four hundred years from the beginning of America—ten full biblical generations—takes place on April 29, 2007," he writes. "By some amazing coincidence— or might we not say foresight of God—the 400th anniversary of the greatest Gentile power that the world has ever known coincides precisely with the 40th year conclusion of the generation of the 'end of Gentile power.' . . . Could this be a time of collapse of the Gentile powers? None of us knows the times and seasons which God has reserved for Himself, but this scenario is fascinating to contemplate. If correct, it reinforces some of the other conclusions of this book that indicate the long cycle of Western European ascendancy has come to an end."

The following year, at the first meeting of the Christian Coalition, Robertson was casting around for new villains. With the Soviet Union gone, the United Nations became the big bogeyman. He told conference attendees that the collapse of the Soviet Union would have financial repercussions all over the world and said, "The United Nations is going to rule the world. . . . We're to cede the sovereignty of America to this organization. One world currency. One world army. One world court system, very possible. And it can happen overnight."[27]

Fears of one-world government have been stock-in-trade among the paranoid right for years. In the mid-1990s they flared up again as a new round of UN-bashing broke out, courtesy of the militia movement. As we have already seen, some local Christian Coalition chapters were eager to feed this paranoia about UN troops hiding in the national parks and ominous "black helicopters."

One-world government may exist in episodes of the television show "Star Trek," but it is unlikely to make much headway in the real world. At the very time Robertson was floating these speculations about the UN, countries like the Soviet Union and the former Yugoslavia were breaking down, creating more governments all over the globe. Despite organizations like the European Union and discussions of a "Eurodollar," the trend hardly favors consolidation.

In the mid-1980s Robertson was so confident of his abilities as a prophet that he announced plans to film the Second Coming of Christ. According to *The Freedom Writer*, a newsletter that monitors the Religious Right, Robertson made the statement while speaking on a Satellite Network Seminar held December 9 through 12, 1984, at the Word of Faith World Outreach Center, a complex in Dallas owned by fellow television evangelist Robert Tilton.

Robertson referred to a prophecy he received in May of 1986 during which God told him, "I have chosen you to usher in the coming of My Son." According to Robertson, God said, "I'm going to let you usher him in. Now, where do you usher in the Coming? You usher in the Coming where He's going to come." Robertson announced that CBN would provide worldwide coverage of the event from the Mount of Olives in Jerusalem but did not say exactly when it will occur.[28]

Incredibly, prophecies like these and end-time rantings have not damaged Robertson's reputation in the political sphere one bit. He even survived *The New World Order* debacle and went on to produce two more books—*The Turning Tide,* a routine attack on liberalism that failed to attract much attention, and his first novel, *The End of the Age,* a clumsily written hodgepodge of science fiction mixed with Robertson's end-times theology. (In the novel, a meteor hits California, killing millions and setting the stage for the rise of the Antichrist and one-world government.)

Once again the amazing teflon televangelist had dodged the bullet. Oblivious to the controversy, Republican presidential hopefuls or their emissaries were soon lining up to meet with Pat Robertson or Ralph Reed. In the "new world order" of the 1990s conservative political scene, it seems, being a paranoid exponent of conspiracy theories who relies on known anti-Semites for "research" is not enough to get one exiled from the movement.

Although the controversy over *The New World Order* briefly brought some of Robertson's more extreme views to the forefront, even that incident didn't begin to scratch the surface of his highly unusual worldview. Over the years he has been responsible for an amazing variety of statements that, looked at it in their totality, should make him a pariah in decent society. The next chapter examines some of these.

Notes

1. Pat Robertson, *The New World Order* (Dallas: Word Publishing, 1991), p. 37.

2. Joe Queenan, "New World Order Nut," *Wall Street Journal* (December 31, 1991).

3. Joseph L. Conn, "Apocalypse Now: Pat Robertson's New World Order—And Your Place In It," *Church & State* (June 1992).

4. Michael Lind, "Rev. Robertson's Grand International Conspiracy Theory," *New York Review of Books* (February 2, 1995).

5. Jacob Heilbrunn, "On Pat Robertson: His Anti-Semitic Sources," *New York Review of Books* (April 20, 1995).

6. Lind, "Rev. Robertson's Grand International Conspiracy Theory."

7. Heilbrunn, "On Pat Robertson: His Anti-Semitic Sources."

8. Heilbrunn, "On Pat Robertson: His Anti-Semitic Sources," quoting Nesta Webster, *World Revolution* (New York: Gordon Press, 1973), pp. 91–92.

9. Heilbrunn, "On Pat Robertson: His Anti-Semitic Sources," quoting Nesta Webster, *Secret Societies and Subversive Movements* (Hollywood, Calif.: Angriff Press, 1972), p. 383.

10. Heilbrunn, "On Pat Robertson: His Anti-Semitic Sources," quoting Webster, *World Revolution*, p. 169.

11. Heilbrunn, "On Pat Robertson: His Anti-Semitic Sources," quoting Webster, *Secret Societies*, p. 368.

12. Heilbrunn, "On Pat Robertson: His Anti-Semitic Sources," quoting Webster, *World Revolution*, p. 309.

13 Gustav Niebuhr, "Pat Robertson Says He Intended No Anti-Semitism in Book He Wrote Four Years Ago," *New York Times*, March 4, 1995.

14. Ephraim Radner, "New World Order, Old World Anti-Semitism," *Christian Century* (September 13–20, 1995).

15. Michael Lind, "On Pat Robertson: His Defenders," *The New York Review of Books*, April 20, 1995.

16. Robertson, *The New World Order*, p. 72.

17. Norman Podhoretz, "In the Matter of Pat Robertson," *Commentary*, August 1995, pp. 27–32.

18. Jeffrey Goldberg, "Are You a Completed Jew?" *New York* (October 2, 1995).

19. Frank Rich, "The Jew World Order," *New York Times* (March 9, 1995).

20. Pat Robertson, *The New Millennium* (Dallas: Word Publishing, 1990), pp. 290–91.

21. Quoted in Joseph L. Conn, "Power Play," *Church & State* (April 1995).

22. Frank Rich, "New World Terror," *New York Times* (April 27, 1995).

23. James W. Watkins, "The Christian Coalition's Gonzo Gospel: Politics and Paranoia in the Heartland," *Church & State* (November 1994).

24. Russell Chandler, *Doomsday: The End of the World—A View Through Time* (Ann Arbor, Mich.: Servant Publications, 1993), p. 257.

25. "Pat Robertson's Prophecy," CBN Staff Prayer Meeting, January 1, 1980, audio recording distributed by Institute for First Amendment Studies, Great Barrington, Mass.

26. Robertson, *The New Millennium*, p. 312.

27. Frederick Clarkson, "The Christian Coalition: On the Road to Victory?" *Church & State* (January 1992).

28. "Robertson to Televise Second Coming," *Freedom Writer* (September 1986, reprinted November 1995).

6

The World According to
Pat Robertson

"You say you're supposed to be nice to the Episcopalians and the Presbyterians and the Methodists and this, that, and the other thing. Nonsense! I don't have to be nice to the spirit of the Antichrist. I can love the people who hold false opinions, but I don't have to be nice to them."
—Pat Robertson, "The 700 Club," January 14, 1991

One can tune into "The 700 Club" on virtually any day and see and hear remarkable things. On one July 1995 broadcast, for example, Robertson held forth about the coming return of Jesus and the end times, always a favorite theme. A segment was aired featuring "700 Club" viewers giving their thoughts on the matter. One man said with a straight face that he was disturbed by the fact that people can now pay for gas at the pump with a credit card. Many Americans see something like this as a simple convenience, but to this Robertson devotee it was something much more ominous. The devil, it seemed, just might be lurking in that gas tank.

Weeks later, on July 31, 1995, Robertson explained how the heat wave that was gripping the nation was more than just

149

a summertime inconvenience. Robertson explained that God had personally given him word that the hot weather was yet another sign that the end of the world was not far off. To most people, the fact that it gets uncomfortably hot and humid in parts of the United States in late July is somewhat unremarkable, but then, most people are not blessed with Robertson's unique theological insights, which enable him to transform even the most mundane event into an ominous warning that we're all doomed.

Groups like Americans United for Separation of Church and State, People for the American Way, and the Institute for First Amendment Studies monitor Robertson regularly. They have collected many of his statements, especially his utterances on "The 700 Club," which airs five days a week. Robertson appears most days. Without his speech writers and other staff members to screen everything he says, it is inevitable that the "true Robertson" comes to the fore on a regular basis. Thus, the show has been a gold mine for collectors of "Pat-speak."

A complete listing of all of the unsettling, extreme, and downright peculiar things Robertson has uttered on "The 700 Club" over the years would fill another book, a tome that could be supplemented annually. While I lack the space for such a project, it is worth looking at some highlights. Topics frequently covered on "The 700 Club" and which will be examined in this chapter include religious freedom, feminism, race relations, and homosexual rights, among others.

As a religious broadcaster, it's not surprising that Robertson would have a special interest in religious freedom, a subject that comes up regularly on "The 700 Club." Robertson, however, has an odd definition of religious liberty. To him, it seems to mean primarily the freedom to be a fundamentalist Christian, as he regularly bashes other religions. He reserves special contempt for Eastern faiths, which, since he apparently does not understand their doctrines, are equivalent, in his mind, to devil worship.

Robertson has unleashed especially vile invective against

Hinduism, which he believes is somehow tied in with the "New Age" philosophies that he so much detests. Speaking of the "New Age," on the January 7, 1991, edition of "The 700 Club," he asserted, "What you've got to recognize is it is Hinduism in another guise, and what is Hinduism but devil worship, ultimately?"

More recently, Robertson attacked Hinduism again on the July 4, 1995, "700 Club." In a special taped segment on what various religious denominations believe, Robertson purported to explain the doctrines of Hinduism while expounding on the beliefs of Hare Krishna, an American Hindu offshoot. Pointing out that India is plagued with poverty and overpopulation, Robertson asserted, "It seems strange that religions which have brought such trouble to India would be imported to the West, where we have flourished and prospered under Christianity for many centuries."

Later in the same segment, Robertson lumped Hinduism in with spiritualism, psychic groups, and other offbeat modern movements. He called them all "cults" and insisted, "These groups . . . are actually not in touch with some great God consciousness or even psychic power, but they're in touch with Satan and demon spirits. . . . Demons work behind the Hindu and other Oriental religions, and as well as behind the teaching of mind control."

Like many Americans, Robertson is obviously not acquainted with the doctrines of this "exotic" faith. Thus he has no problem lumping Hinduism in the same category with New Age fads or the spiritualist movement of Edgar Cayce. In fact, Hinduism is an ancient religion, predating Christianity by several centuries. Its theology is complex. Across the world, it claims an estimated seven hundred million adherents. It most assuredly does not advocate worship of Satan.

As one scholar has observed, "For most Americans the Orient remains a land of mystery. American schools teach children about their European heritage, regardless of where their parents were born. American concepts of Hinduism and Buddhism are both in error and negative. These ancient religions are usually treated as only pagan superstitions, barely worth study or respect."[1]

Coming from a poorly informed person, such an attitude might be understandable, but Robertson has studied theology; one would think that he learned at least a little about non-Christian faiths. While Hinduism obviously isn't Robertson's favored faith, for him to label it as devil worship unveils either ignorance or simple mean-spiritedness.

Robertson is also quick to label Hinduism or other religions he doesn't understand or like as "cults," and he uses this term widely. To Robertson, the definition of "cult" would appear to be "Any religion I don't like."

A CBN pamphlet titled "Cults" dated 1992 defines the term as "any group that has a form of godliness, but does not recognize Jesus Christ as the unique son of God." Elsewhere it states, "One test of a cult is that it often does not strictly teach that Jesus is the only begotten Son of God who Himself is God manifested in the flesh." Under a definition this broad, Judaism, Islam, Buddhism, Taoism, Shintoism, and virtually any non-Christian religion would qualify. Even groups that acknowledge Christ can't escape being labeled cults by Robertson. The pamphlet defines the following groups as "Christian-oriented cults": the Church of Jesus Christ of Latter-day Saints or Reorganized Church of Latter Day Saints (Mormons), the Worldwide Church of God, Christian Science, Unity, Unitarianism, The Way International, Rosicrucian Society of America, Bahai, Hare Krishna, Scientology, the Unification Church, and the Jehovah's Witnesses.

Some of the groups on this list are accustomed to being labeled cults. The Unification Church and the Church of Scientology, for instance, have been trying to avoid the label and its negative connotations for years. But the inclusion of mainstream groups such as the Unitarians, Mormons, and Christian Scientists seems a bit extreme. It's to be expected that Robertson would take issue with the theological beliefs of these denominations, but for him to label them as "cults" is unjust. It would appear that Robertson uses the term "cult" merely to defame religions he does not like or with whom he does not agree.

Robertson's attack on Mormons is especially impertinent. Most Mormons are politically conservative and share common goals with the Christian Coalition. In the U.S. Senate, for example, Utah's Orrin Hatch is a conservative whose votes have pleased the Christian Coalition. One has to wonder how Hatch, who by all reports is a genuinely devout man who takes his religion seriously, feels about his faith being described as a "cult" by Robertson? However, Hatch and other Mormons in Congress are apparently willing to let these insults go unanswered for the greater good of advancing their right-wing political agenda. After the GOP takeover of Congress in 1994, the Christian Coalition announced its support for a "Religious Equality Amendment" to the U.S. Constitution to allow official prayers in public schools and government funding of religious organizations and schools. The issue was farmed out to Representative Ernest Istook of Oklahoma, a Mormon. Istook was more than happy to work with the Christian Coalition, apparently not bothered by the fact that Robertson believes he is a cult member.

Discussing the Mormons during a pretaped segment that aired on the July 4, 1995, broadcast of "The 700 Club," Robertson praised them as "exemplary human beings in regard to their behavior pattern and the adherence to the fundamental values of society." But he was quick to add, "But their religious beliefs are, to put it simply, wrong. . . . Mormonism teaches that God is not the only deity and that we all have the potential of becoming gods. You can remember that Satan's fall came about because he wanted to be like God." Mormons, Robertson concluded, "are far from biblical truth." According to Robertson, Mormons may be nice people, but they're still going to burn in hell.

Robertson has made derisive comments about mainstream

Protestant religions over the years, too, although he hasn't labeled them "cults." Robertson once asserted that more than half of all Protestants who attend services every Sunday are not really Christians and that they are going to hell because they are not "born again."

During a June 5, 1995, "700 Club" interview with evangelical pollster George Barna, Robertson asserted that "sitting in church Sunday after Sunday and not being a Christian is not unusual at all. According to recent statistics, half of all adults who attend Protestant churches on a typical Sunday morning are not born-again Christians." When Barna asserted that the non-born again go to church because it is a "comfortable place" for them, Robertson quickly interjected, "It couldn't be comfortable if they had a minister who told them they were going to hell if they don't get born again!" Robertson went on to say that Barna's findings would "tear the so-called mainstream churches up. I think they're peripheral these days. The Episcopal church, the Presbyterian church, the Lutheran church, the Methodist church, etc. are the ones that you're speaking about primarily, and if the people begin to confront their membership with the fact that they need to be born again, they'd lose half of their memberships."

Robertson insisted that ministers in the Presbyterian, Lutheran, United Methodist, and Episcopalian churches must preach that their congregants become born again. It apparently never occurred to Robertson or Barna that such activity would in fact be highly unusual in these denominations. The need for a "born again" experience, while required in Robertson's brand of theology, is not shared by all Christian denominations. While doctrinal matters obviously differ from group to group, most mainline Christian groups believe one can be a good Christian and get into heaven without being "born again." Robertson assumes that every Christian will naturally want to believe as he does. This incident is a good example of how Robertson creates his own definition of the word "Christian." When he speaks about wanting America to be a "Christian" nation or spouts off about the country returning to its "Christian" roots, it is important to understand that he means "Christian" in a very narrow sense.

Many Americans have not been threatened by Robertson's pronouncements about the need for a "Christian" America because people view Christianity favorably and interpret it in light of the Christian churches with which they are familiar. Liberal and moderate Christians who define Christianity in light of social justice, equality, and helping the poor should understand that this type of activity is not what Robertson means when he speaks of a "Christian nation." Instead, he links the theological term "Christian" to a whole host of ultraconservative political issues, some of which may be far-removed from theology.

According to Robertson, those who fail to accept such right-wing pontifications and don't adopt his narrow definition of what it means to be a Christian—primarily the born-again experience—are not really Christians.

The quote that opens this chapter reinforces this assertion. Robertson was explaining to viewers of the January 14, 1991, "700 Club" that they ought to flee any church that fails to preach that the only path to salvation is to become "born again" through Jesus Christ. Churches that don't do this, he said, are not just wrong, they are reflecting the spirit of the Antichrist! Because of the severity of this quote, allow me to repeat it here, as transcribed exactly from a videotape of the broadcast: "You say you're supposed to be nice to the Episcopalians and the Presbyterians and the Methodists and this, that, and the other thing. Nonsense! I don't have to be nice to the spirit of the Antichrist. I can love the people who hold false opinions, but I don't have to be nice to them."

Robertson has a history of criticizing other religions and even labeling other branches of Christianity as "false religions." In a 1987 interview with the *Washington Post* Robertson even criticized the notion of religious pluralism, saying, "Pluralism is the name given to the transition period from one orthodoxy to another. . . . Every other great nation has unified around some ethical standard. Lack of unity is a sign of ultimate destruction."[2]

Robertson's relationship with Roman Catholics has also been rocky over the years. While he has refrained from overt anti-Catholicism, Catholics who have worked in Robertson's organizations have reported incidents of bias. Some were pressured to change their religious views and convert to fundamentalist, Protestant Christianity.

In 1986, the Catholic League for Religious and Civil Rights, an organization of ultraconservative Catholics, complained to Robertson after one of its members protested anti-Catholic bias at a Houston office of "The 700 Club." The Catholic League member was a volunteer at CBN and alleged that telephone counselors were making anti-Catholic comments to callers. Reportedly, Catholic callers were told that their church is the "Whore of Babylon" and were urged to "come out of her" to be saved. When the Catholic League volunteer complained about the matter, he was told his services were no longer needed at CBN. In response to the complaint, CBN official Thomas Victor said that despite "careful instruction," some counselors had expressed "personal bias" to callers. Such incidents, Victor insisted, were "isolated."[3]

An earlier incident of anti-Catholicism at CBN, much more serious in nature, was reported in the Catholic newspaper *Our Sunday Visitor* in 1981. According to the report, a Catholic CBN member named Val Doering of Fort Madison, Iowa, wrote to CBN in 1979 requesting a story be aired on reported appearances of the Virgin Mary around the world. In response, Robertson co-host Ben Kinchlow sent Doering a letter accompanied by two comic books—*Angel of Light* and *Sabotage.* Both comics were produced by Jack T. Chick, a fundamentalist publisher who has been cranking out anti-Catholic literature for years. *Sabotage* asserted that the Catholic Church has elevated the Virgin Mary to the status of a goddess and likened veneration of Mary to devil worship. In the letter, Kinchlow wrote, "Both are easily readable, and both deal with a subject that I think you will find interesting. My only hope is that you will not simply consider them as 'vicious attacks on your faith' and throw them out without reading them."

Deeply offended, Doering wrote complaint letters to both Kinchlow and Robertson. Robertson's response, dated February 27, 1980, and printed in full in *Our Sunday Visitor*, read in part, "While we certainly are not in the process of 'running down the Catholic Church' we do want to challenge people to know exactly what they believe. While we certainly do not agree with every book that is written, we do believe that there are certain books that challenge people to examine their theological position. I believe *Sabotage* is one of those kinds of books, that if taken as a probe will cause people to examine what they really believe and why and the end result will be a stronger faith."[4]

Pressed by *Our Sunday Visitor*, Kinchlow later called the mailing to Doering "a mistake" and apologized. He admitted that CBN had been purchasing material from Chick for some time, saying that previous shipments had not contained anti-Catholic tracts. Kinchlow also acknowledged that he knows Chick personally, saying, "I still have the highest regard for him as a man, even though I don't agree with the tactics he uses in these books." In a separate statement, Robertson said the Chick comics had been sent "without my knowledge."

Robertson tried to dissuade *Our Sunday Visitor* from running the story. In a column, Editor Richard McMunn noted that the paper had requested a short interview with Robertson but was denied. After that, McMunn said, "We got a phone call from a well-known Catholic figure who told us he had been asked if we might not be willing to reconsider the story."[5] Although the paper ran the story, it later accepted Robertson's invitation to visit CBN and observe the operation first hand.

Today Robertson actively courts right-wing Catholics to join the Christian Coalition, and has made it a point to put a few Catholics in high profile positions in his various organizations. Keith Fournier, executive director of the American Center for

Law and Justice, is an example. In May of 1988, Robertson traveled to New York to meet face-to-face with Cardinal John J. O'Connor. The two discussed social issues for thirty minutes, and when they emerged Robertson proclaimed, "We are one. . . . I believe frankly that the evangelicals and the Catholics in America, if they work together, can see many pro-family initiatives in our society, and we can also be an effective counterbalance to some of the radical, leftist initiatives, the gay rights and the prochoice, and many of the radical groups that are seeking to disrupt and destroy the family values of America."[6]

In 1993, O'Connor joined forces with the Christian Coalition to influence local school board races in New York City. The Archdiocese of New York distributed Christian Coalition voter guides in all 213 of its parishes. O'Connor and Robertson were both opposed to plans to distribute condoms in high schools to combat AIDS and over a multicultural curriculum called "Children of the Rainbow" that urged tolerance of homosexuals. Results were mixed and could not be linked to the guides. Conservative candidates were successful in working-class neighborhoods where they had held seats for years. In more liberal boroughs, the right-wing fared poorly. Nevertheless, Reed and Robertson proclaimed a great victory.

At Christian Coalition conferences, great pains are taken to show that the organization has Catholic support. Every year the group honors a "Catholic Layman of the Year." (U.S. Representative Henry Hyde, R-Ill., was one recipient.) Catholics are placed on the conference program and featured as speakers. During Pope John Paul II's visit to the United States in October of 1995, Robertson scored an even bigger coup: a personal meeting with the pope. After the meeting, Robertson told the Associated Press, "We're laying the foundation for some very significant harmony, socially and spiritually." He also reported that he had told John Paul, "The American people love you."

Despite the posturing, the Christian Coalition's own figures show that Catholics make up a small percentage of the group's membership. A survey of members published in the *Christian American* in 1994 showed that only 5 percent of the group's membership comes from the Catholic church. The survey indicated that most members come from fundamentalist Protestant denominations. However, a Coalition survey released the following year claimed a higher percentage of Catholic members—16 percent. Nevertheless, it is clear that many American Catholics—quite a few of whom break with the church's conservative hierarchy on questions of abortion, birth control, and married clergy—harbor reservations about Robertson.

In late 1995 Robertson apparently believed he could drum up enough Catholic support to start a Catholic auxiliary of the Christian Coalition. Called the Catholic Alliance, the group remains subservient to Reed and the Coalition. Hoping to find members for the new unit, Robertson mailed one million solicitation letters to right-wing Catholics across the country. About four hundred people turned out for the Catholic Alliance's first meeting in Boston on December 9, 1995. But the *Boston Globe* reported that only 30 to 50 percent of those attending were actually Roman Catholics. Noted Republican Party activist Frank Flynn, "These are not exactly the faces that you see at mass on Sunday, if you know what I mean."[7]

Why is Robertson so eager for Catholic support? Aside from giving his Coalition the appearance of ecumenism, Catholic membership also boosts the Coalition's power in states where it is weak—primarily the northeast and the Midwest "Rust Belt" along the Great Lakes.

It's not surprising that the Coalition is strong in states like South Carolina, Texas, and Florida—places where many people are fundamentalist Protestants. In the northeast and in New England, where states have high Catholic populations, the Christian Coalition has had a tougher time making headway. Tapping into established Catholic power in those states could give Robertson's political arm a much-needed boost.

It is ironic that even as Robertson labors to bring Catholics into his religious-political empire, he has the audacity to continue attacking their theology. On a taped segment that ran on "The 700 Club" June 8, 1995, Robertson was asked, "What part does the Virgin Mary play in my salvation?" He responded, "There are some who teach that the Virgin Mary is a co-redemptress, that she assists people in attaining salvation because she has special access to her son. Now, these are very well-meaning people, sincere people, but the Bible does not support their point of view. The Bible teaches, in the writings of the apostle Paul particularly, that there is one mediator between God and man: the man—Christ Jesus." Those "some" Robertson refers to are the world's estimated one billion Roman Catholics, including twenty-five million in the United States. Robertson, it seems, is eager to have them be a part of his political crusade, even if their theology is faulty. The amazing thing is that there are Catholics who not only tolerate this, but actively work with Robertson to further his goals.

While Robertson's Coalition has enjoyed some success in wooing Roman Catholics, its efforts to court Jews have met with much less success. A smattering of Orthodox Jews have endorsed Robertson's crusade, but the majority of American Jews remain wary of his goals. The most prominent rabbi to work with Robertson is Daniel Lapin of California, who heads a group of right-wing Jews called Toward Tradition and leads a right-leaning synagogue. According to the Anti-Defamation League, Lapin once endorsed the activities of retired Washington Supreme Court Judge William C. Goodloe. Goodloe, the league reports, has been active in the extremist Lyndon LaRouche political movement and once addressed a rally of the Populist party, a racist and anti-Semitic, far-right unit that is espoused by many militia activists.

At the Christian Coalition's 1995 "Road to Victory" gathering in Washington, Lapin defended Robertson against charges of anti-Semitism lodged in the wake of the fiasco surrounding *The New World Order*. Lapin's argument was novel, if not convincing: Robertson, he said, can't be an anti-Semite because once Lapin attended a weekend meeting at the

Robertson-owned Founders Inn in Virginia Beach and the hotel arranged for Lapin to have a ground floor room, knowing that the Orthodox rabbi could not use electrically powered elevators on Saturday. Lapin then launched into a barely coherent, poorly reasoned speech against evolution, implying that the scientific principle can't be true because if it were, baboons would still be turning into people.

Many Jews find Robertson's rhetoric distasteful. Robertson, for example, has never hesitated to compare the alleged "persecution" of Americans Christians by "the liberals" to what the Jews experienced in Nazi Germany. On September 14, 1993, syndicated columnist Molly Ivins reported the following Robertson quote: "Just like what Nazi Germany did to the Jews, so liberal America is now doing to the evangelical Christians. It's no different. It is the same thing. It is happening all over again. It is the Democratic Congress, the liberal-biased news media, and the homosexuals who want to destroy all Christians. Wholesale abuse and discrimination and the worst bigotry directed toward any group in America today. More terrible than anything suffered by any minority in our history."[9]

As I pointed out in my previous book *Why the Religious Right Is Wrong About Separation of Church & State*, there is no systematic, widescale persecution of Christians in the United States today. (In fact, the United States enjoys the highest degree of religious freedom found in the world today.) What the Religious Right calls "persecution" is, in actuality, opposition to its theocratic goals or a refusal by the government to actively subsidize and promote fundamentalist Christian dogma at every turn. In public schools, for example, the courts have ruled that fundamentalist Christians have no right to force children to say prayers in class. This is persecution to the Religious Right. Religious conservatives, like any segment of the American religious community, have the right to preach and spread their message. They don't have the right to ask for government help in achieving this goal, nor should they expect the state to endorse their religious choice. When the government refuses to extend that endorsement, this is viewed as "persecution" to the Religious Right.

Robertson attempts to make a case for persecution by dredging up Nazi imagery. Is it any wonder Jews are offended by this? Many Jews quite forcefully point out that the Holocaust was a unique historical event. No other people have faced such a systematic, well-executed plan to wipe them off the face of the planet. At least six million people died; families were torn apart, people were forced into exile; and countless other millions suffered imprisonment, psychological damage, and other injuries. Even if we were to assume that there have been some instances of discrimination against Christians in America, such as a misguided teacher taking away a student's Bible or an employer ordering a worker to remove a religious sign from his desk, would these things possibly compare to what the Jews endured during the Holocaust? Any violation of an American's constitutional rights is unfortunate and ought to be corrected, but Christian Americans have never undergone anything that even remotely resembles what the Jews experienced in Nazi Germany. For Robertson to say the two are "the same thing" is simply fallacious.

During the July 11, 1995, "700 Club" broadcast on the BATF mentioned in chapter 5, Robertson struck this note again. He called some recent actions of the FBI and BATF "reminiscent of the Nazis, and something has got to be done." As I've already said, yes, police agencies do abuse their power from time to time, but nothing the FBI or the BATF has ever done can be compared to the horrors of the Nazi government. The BATF's handling of the Branch Davidian affair in Waco has been justly criticized, but it in no way compares with a premeditated, systematic plan to exterminate millions of people. When Robertson compares the two, he doesn't intensify the Waco tragedy or other FBI/BATF failures to the level of the Holocaust as he had hoped. Instead, he trivializes the experiences of the millions who suffered and died under the Nazis and detracts from the historical uniqueness of the Holocaust.

By the way, it would not be difficult to find Americans who would disagree with Robertson's insistence that the alleged persecution of Christians in the United States is "more terrible than anything suffered by any minority in our history." Ask some African Americans, whose ancestors lived in slavery, about that. Or, take up the issue with Native Americans, who saw their lands seized as they were chased across an entire continent, their traditional way of living destroyed.

Aside from his views on other religious groups, Robertson has unusual opinions on a number of other topics. The rights of women are an example. In Robertson's view, the husband is the head of the household. Many of the problems experienced by the American family today would vanish, he says, if women would simply learn to submit. "I know that this is painful for you ladies to hear," remarked Robertson on "The 700 Club" on January 8, 1982, "but if you get married, you accept the headship of a man, your husband. Christ is the head of the household, and the husband is the head of the wife. And that's just the way it is. This is the way the Bible set it up."

Robertson has returned to the theme many times. "Why are so many marriages falling apart?" Robertson asked on the May 22, 1986, episode of his program. "Why is the divorce rate so high? Why is there such tragedy in marriage? Now, the basic answer to the basic problem of today is a question of surrender. We don't like to surrender, and we don't like to serve. . . . There is a question of headship. The wife actually makes the husband the head of the household, and she looks to him and says, 'Now you pray, and I'm going to pray for you that the Lord will speak to you.' "

On "The 700 Club" aired November 28, 1989, Robertson was expounding on the differences between men and women and uttered this gem: "[T]here's a difference from birth. Now, the male mind thinks in certain attitudes. . . . But the key in terms of mental—it has nothing to do with physical [ability]—is chess. There's never been a woman Grand Master chess player. And if, you know, once you get one, then I'll buy some of the feminism, but until that point. . . ." At the time Robertson made the comment there were already two women chess Grand Masters. Since then, three more have joined them. One of them, Judit Polgar of Hungary, defeated Boris Spassky, a man widely regarded as one of the best chess players in the world, in an exhibition match when she was fifteen. However, Robertson has yet to explain what facets of feminism he now accepts.

On the July 6, 1995, "700 Club," Robertson quoted the apostle Paul to buttress his case for female subordination:

> [The husband] should love his wife as Christ loves the church and gave himself for her [the Church]. . . . And the woman should be in submission to the man as under the Lord. . . . People who speak the biblical truth are reviled and ridiculed. I personally have been ridiculed on television and other places because of speaking the Christian truth. The man is to love the wife as Christ loved the church. What woman wouldn't want a man who was willing to die for her? What woman wouldn't want a man who puts her interests ahead of his? What woman wouldn't want a man who was willing to do anything possible to bless her and cherish her and nurture her and look after her? In those circumstances, wouldn't the woman be delighted to say, "I acknowledge your headship because God is head of you and together we are one flesh?"

What may be Robertson's most foolish statement concerning the issue of women's rights was made in 1992. Denouncing an Equal Rights Amendment that was on the ballot in Iowa, he wrote in a fundraising letter, "The feminist agenda is not about equal rights for women. It is about a socialist, anti-family political movement that encourages women to leave their husbands, kill their children, practice witchcraft, destroy capitalism, and become lesbians." (A Robertson ally, Marlene Elwell, headed up a successful campaign to defeat the amendment).

At first, Ralph Reed tried to brush off the complaints, claiming he had received "nothing but accolades" about the letter, but he and Robertson shifted gears as the controversy increased. The letter in question bore Robertson's signature, but when he was asked about its outlandish charges, he tried to disclaim responsibility. Robertson said he does not personally write his own fundraising mail and that every day he signs many things he hasn't personally written.

No one expects that Robertson would actually sit down and write his own fundraising mail. Such letters are routinely prepared by outside firms. Due to the vehemence of this particular letter, however, one would be hard pressed to believe that an independent organization actually authored it. Regardless, it doesn't seem to be too much to ask for Robertson to actually look at the letters before hundreds of thousands of copies are produced for distribution. If his name is going to go on it, one would think Robertson would at least spare a few minutes to make certain the letter writer didn't get carried away. Because he did not, it's easy to get the impression that Robertson does agree with the sentiments in the letter and only tried to distance himself from them later when so much criticism came rolling in. The dodge is sloppy at best.

On race relations, Robertson has been more circumspect. Although he supported the apartheid government in South Africa until the very end, he has generally been careful to avoid racially charged rhetoric in his publications.

He did slip up once, however. In *The New World Order* Robertson raises the specter of black troops running amok under the United Nations flag. Citing civil unrest in the Belgian Congo (now Zaire) in 1960, Robertson writes, "I cannot forget the bloody picture in *Life* magazine of the young Belgian settler in Katanga whose wife and children lay dead behind him in a little Volkswagen, brutally killed by black African soldiers serving in a United Nations contingent. If it happened there, it can happen here."[10]

Concerning South Africa, Robertson was never one to criticize the apartheid regime. Appearing on government-run television in Johannesburg on February 12, 1988, he asserted that black Americans in the United States have made this whole matter into an extension of the United States civil rights movement, and I think they don't understand what they're dealing with really in this South African thing. And so it becomes an American political issue to say if you want support among American blacks for American political office you have to bash South Africa. I think that's bad. . . . The media has just done an absolute hatchet job on South Africa, and I think the reason, very frankly, is because the left wants to see South Africa fall. They don't want a free government.[11]

On the March 18, 1992, "700 Club" Robertson went even further, saying about South Africa, "I think 'one man, one vote,' just unrestricted democracy, would not be wise. There needs to be some kind of protection for the minority which the white people represent now, a minority, and they need and have a right to demand a protection of their rights."

Aside from race relations and women's rights, Robertson also holds unusual views on America's system of public education. He reserves special venom for public schools. According to Robertson, the public schools actively seek to recruit young people into an anti-God philosophy he calls "secular humanism." In a fall 1981 issue of a newsletter entitled *Pat Robertson's Perspective*, he charged, "Humanist educators are forcing sex education without any moral standards upon little children. Courses in sex education are being offered which advocate masturbation, premarital sex, and homosexuality." No evidence was offered to support this claim, and Robertson did not give the names of the public schools that are allegedly encouraging young children to masturbate.

Always eager to promote conspiracy theories, Robertson asserts in his 1993 book, *The Turning Tide*, that public education was the brainchild of a secret society founded by the followers of Robert Owen, a nineteenth-century Welsh social reformer whom Robertson identifies as "the founder of modern socialism." Concludes Robertson, "Thus, one of the fathers of modern compulsory state education was also the first modern socialist, and education in his eyes was the means to accomplish his program."[12]

Robertson asserts that Owen set forth "essentially the program for progressive education that John Dewey promulgated a century later." In this passage we see Robertson once again employing his own version of literary sleight of hand. Reading it, an uninformed reader might assume a connection between Owen and Dewey. There is no evidence indicating Dewey was influenced by, or even knew of, Owen. In fact, the concept of public education predates both men, having its genesis with a Massachusetts law of 1647. The idea of public education really began to grow in the United States in the middle of the nineteenth century and spread rapidly in the post-Civil War period. Furthermore, Owen is hardly the "father of modern socialism." He advocated communal living and headed up an experimental community in Indiana called New Harmony, which failed. Robertson's source for his claim is Samuel Blumenfeld, author of various texts which denounce public education. Blumenfeld is active in the Christian Reconstructionist movement, a collection of far-right types who believe that democracy in the United States should be replaced with a theocracy consistent with their interpretation of the Old Testament's harsh legal code. Robertson, not surprisingly, doesn't bother to point this out.

In Robertson's view, the schools were doomed that day in 1962 when the U.S. Supreme Court ruled in *Engel* v. *Vitale* that mandatory programs of government-sponsored classroom prayer violate the First Amendment. In *The New World Order* he writes, "The Supreme Court of the supposedly Christian United States guaranteed the moral collapse of this nation when it forbade children in the public schools to pray to the God of Jacob, to learn of His moral law or even view in their classrooms the heart of the law, the Ten Commandments, which children must obey for their own good or disobey at their peril."[13] In his follow-up book, *The Turning Tide*, Robertson asserts that numerous societal trends, such as increasing teen pregnancy rates, the escalating divorce rate, and a rise in the number of single-parent families, are due to the Court's school prayer rulings. "One or two isolated trends could be dismissed as arising from other causes, but there is no way to explain all of these extraordinary happenings originating in a single year except as a sign of the lifting of God's blessing from our land," he writes.[14]

Speaking on "The 700 Club" on October 5, 1981, Robertson outlined the problems in the schools as part of a broader conspiracy. "There are two major elites who are working in conjunction to take away the religious heritage from our nation," he said. "The first is the educational elite. . . . In league with them are many people in the judicial system, the legal system."

On the May 13, 1984, edition of "The 700 Club" Robertson again dragged Nazis into the picture, asserting, "The state steadily is attempting to do something that a few states other than the Nazis and the Soviets have attempted to do, namely, to take the children away from the parents and to educate them in a philosophy that is amoral, anti-Christian, and humanistic and to show them a collectivistic philosophy that will ultimately lead toward Marxism, socialism, and a communistic type of ideology."

In *Answers* (1994) Robertson asserted that the federal government once published a curriculum designed to "indoctrinate young children into the teachings of humanism." He goes on to write, "Humanist values are being taught in the schools through such methods as 'values clarification.' All of these things constitute an attempt to wean children away from biblical Christianity."[15]

According to Robertson, Supreme Court decisions designed to uphold separation of church and state in public education are equivalent to a vicious sexual assault. In one of his ugliest speeches ever, Robertson, in February of 1995, likened the Court's school prayer rulings to gang rape. Speaking at William and Mary College in Virginia, Robertson began by describing, in lurid detail, a widely publicized pool hall rape that had occurred in a New England community. "Rape is a horrible crime, but my message is not about the brutal rape of a young woman," he said. "I want to tell you about a much more insidious rape that has been repeated over and over— one that was not directed against the virtue and self worth of a few individuals but our entire society. A rape of our nation's religious heritage, our national morality, of time-honored customs and institutions. Especially, a rape of our governing document, the United States Constitution."

Robertson listed the following as "suspects" in this awful crime: the Supreme Court, legal scholars, the American Civil Liberties Union, and atheist Madalyn Murray O'Hair, the woman who brought one of the first school prayer cases to the Supreme Court. The school prayer decision of 1962, Robertson said, raped America and sparked a rash of social problems, such as teenage pregnancies, abortion, drug use, alcoholism, suicide, declining academic performance, and violent crime. Robertson might have thought he was being clever by using this metaphor, but in fact he was merely being grotesque. To compare the fallout from a Supreme Court ruling with the trauma undergone by rape victims is appalling. Yet he was so proud of this speech that he had it published in full in the April 1995 edition of the *Christian American*.

Robertson's rantings about the public schools are too numerous to list in full. It will suffice to say that attacks on the hard-working people who make up the public education community are a staple of his broadcasts. To hear Robertson tell it, teachers are either communists, atheists, devil worshippers, or dupes for any and all of these things. The following is a sampling of Robertson's rhetoric about public schools:

- "It's time to say we must take back the schools. We've got to do something in America and take away the school system from the left-wing labor union and their left-wing cohorts that are destroying the moral fiber of the youth of America." ("The 700 Club," January 22, 1995)
- In his 1993 book *The Turning Tide*, Robertson praises vouchers and writes, "They say vouchers would spell

the end of public schools in America. To which we say, So what? For all we've been getting for our tax dollars out of the public schools, they should have disappeared years ago. So long as we have standards that ensure that our goals of quality education are achieved, then the very idea of maintaining an antiquated and ineffective public education system is absurd."[16]

- "The public schools are actually agencies for the promotion of another religion, which is the humanist religion." ("The 700 Club," October 2, 1981)
- "No nation has the right, according to the freedom we enjoy, to take tax money to inculcate the people with a repugnant philosophy. They're going to take your tax money and insist on forcing your children to learn a philosophy that is contrary to what you believe very deeply. That goes to the very heart of freedom. And if the public schools are going to do that, then the public schools are illegal nationwide, and we're going to start lawsuits, saying the whole public school system, if that's the way they're going to have it, is illegal." ("The 700 Club," November 23, 1982)
- In his book *Answers to 200 of Life's Most Probing Questions*, Robertson writes, "The humanism that is being taught in our schools, media, and intellectual circles will ultimately lead people to the Antichrist, because he will be the consummate figure of humanism."[17]
- "The teachers who are teaching your children . . . are not necessarily nice, wonderful servants of the community. They are activists supporting one party and one set of values and a number of the values which they espouse are affirmative action, ERA, gun control legislation, sex education, illegal teachers' strikes, nuclear freeze, federal funding for abortions, decriminalization of marijuana, etc." ("The 700 Club," November 20, 1984)
- Even Head Start, one of the most successful government programs for disadvantaged children, gets a blast

from Robertson. Such programs are wasteful, he told "The 700 Club" audience on March 28, 1984, because "if you're smart you'll catch up anyway."[18]

Robertson has long advocated "returning" education to local control. (In fact, public schools in the United States are already under local control. They answer to democratically elected school boards, and local officials have wide latitude over curriculum; there is no national curriculum.) As the 1980s progressed, he began to express increasing interest in voucher plans, which would divert money away from public education by allowing parents to enroll their children in private religious and other nonpublic schools at state expense. Critics say such plans would bankrupt public education, segregate children along religious lines, and violate separation of church and state, but Robertson doesn't seem to care.

Robertson's comments on a host of other social issues have been just as extreme. He has attacked civil rights laws, blasted as "wasteful" the Great Society programs of the 1960s that lifted many out of poverty, and ridiculed environmental protection laws.

Even the relatively innocuous children's festivity Halloween has been a Robertson target. He sees it as a Satanic plot. "I think we ought to close Halloween down," he said on "The 700 Club" on October 29, 1982. "Do you want your children to dress up like witches? The Druids used to dress up like this when they were doing human sacrifice. . . . [Your children] are acting out Satanic rituals and participating in it, and don't even realize it." The same thing could be said for Christmas, a holiday whose secular aspects, including yule logs, mistletoe, wassail bowls, Christmas trees, and gift giving all have pagan origins, having grown out of the ancient Roman festival of Saturnalia. Robertson is surprisingly silent about this.

Halloween bothers Robertson so much that CBN has issued a critical pamphlet titled *Hallowed or Harmful: Christian Perspective on Halloween.* "During Halloween little children in particular are the weak ones," asserts the pamphlet. "On TV, in movies, in school, and with their playmates, many children today are exposed to occult influences. We may be opening our children to these influences if we approve of these things in Halloween fun. We adults may be fully aware that we are only spoofing witches and ghosts, but the young may not be so sure."

When attacking Halloween or other aspects of life that he does not like, Robertson frequently cites the Bible, insisting that it should be read literally and that every word is true. However, on at least one occasion Robertson felt free to edit the Bible because one of its stories failed to comport with his political views. On February 9, 1995, Robertson was discussing capital punishment on "The 700 Club" with co-hosts Terry Meeuwsen and Ben Kinchlow. Robertson, who despite his "pro-life" views on abortion defends the death penalty, said, "I don't know that Jesus ever got involved in the judicial system or judicial punishment. The Bible says, 'Thou shalt not murder,' but judicial executions went along. And even His own death was an illegitimate execution, but He was executed and He never criticized the state of Rome for doing it. . . . I don't know if I've ever read anything in the New Testament saying the Roman system of execution was to be abolished."

Meeuwsen brought up the story of the woman arrested for adultery, which appears in the chapter 8 of the Gospel of John. In the story, Jesus is asked what should be done with a woman accused of adultery. The Pharisees plan to execute the woman by stoning, but Jesus tells the mob, "He that is without sin among you, let him cast a stone at her."

This is one of the Bible's best-known stories, but Robertson did not hesitate to exclaim, "But this wasn't judicial, this was a mob. . . . Besides, I might point out that the better manuscripts of the New Testament don't have that passage. It is really considered a later amendment. As much as I like the story, it is not a good part of the New Testament." Although many Bible scholars agree that the story is not found in early texts of the New Testament, one must wonder how fundamentalist Christians, who believe the Bible as a whole is inerrant, feel about Robertson's attempt to edit the Scriptures.

Not surprisingly, the very notion of homosexual rights is abhorrent to Robertson. He seems to have an obsession with the idea of female homosexuality, and often attempts to link it to feminism and women's rights in general. According to Robertson, lesbians have created a plot to stop heterosexual women from having children by promoting abortion. Robertson raised the theme on the June 26, 1990, edition of "The 700 Club," saying, "If the lesbians who don't have babies, if they can get their sisters to be less than the fulfilled women they could be—willing to forfeit that—then of course they've brought them down to their level. There's such an incredible militancy on the part of lesbian women to get heterosexual women to abort their babies."

Less than a month later, Robertson was harping on the alleged lesbian plot again. Discussing abortion on "The 700 Club" on July 15, 1990, Robertson remarked, "You know who's pushing it. You saw some of those women out there. I mean, those women aren't ever going to have a baby by anybody. I mean, these are primarily lesbians, and lesbians don't have babies. And it's the one thing a mother has that a lesbian can never have is this femininity, and they can never achieve that. And so, in order to level the field, they say, 'Hey, let us abort your baby so you'll be like us, because we don't have them.' . . . They don't like families."

Robertson's attacks on gay people should surprise no one. In his worldview, homosexuality is not only unbiblical, it's an illness, and he feeds existing homophobia. Discussing the matter on "The 700 Club" on March 7, 1990, he called homosexual activity "antisocial" and said, "It is a pathology. It is a sickness, and it needs to be treated." On the same program he also claimed that, "Many of those people involved with Adolf Hitler were Satanists, many of them were homosexuals. The two things seem to go together." In a 1981 newsletter he fulminated that because homosexual acts cannot result in procreation, they are therefore "not sexual" and wrote, "Homosexuality and lesbianism always remain a form of autoeroticism. Yet those who practice these abominations desire not only legal but even scriptural assent to their actions." A CBN pamphlet titled *Freedom from Demon Bondage* goes so far as to assert that homosexuality may be caused by demon possession.

In late 1995 the group Parents, Families, and Friends of Lesbians and Gays (PFLAG) launched a nationwide advertising campaign condemning violence against gay people. One TV spot interspersed clips of Robertson ranting against homosexuality with a dramatization of a young man being assaulted by a gang, a scene designed to depict an incidence of "gay bashing."

Robertson was furious. Lawyers for CBN drew up an open letter to "all General Managers" threatening legal action if the ads were aired. "The spots contain defamatory material and cast Pat Robertson and CBN in a false light by implying that Pat advocates/promotes heinous crimes against gays. . . . This is outrageously false and severely damaging to the reputation of Dr. Robertson and this ministry," warned Bruce D. Hausknecht, CBN associate general counsel. Any station that aired the ads, Hausknecht said, would force CBN to "immediately seek judicial redress against your station."[19] The threat had results. CNN considered running the ad during "Larry King Live," but backed down. PFLAG reported that eight stations in Houston and Atlanta also rejected the ad campaign. It is a sad day when Robertson's attorneys can successfully intimidate television stations because *his own words* might be defamatory.

Robertson's rants against homosexuality reveal an ignorance of the subject. This is not surprising, as he never hesitates to speak on issues he knows little or nothing about. On the August 17, 1995, edition of "The 700 Club," for example, he commented on an extremely biased CBN report on the environment that clearly sought to portray environmentalists as extremists who place the well-being of owls before people. According to Robertson, it's no big deal if an endangered species such as the spotted owl loses its home to logging. "This is the idiocy of bureaucracy," he ranted. "You know, seriously, you're an owl, you're sitting on a limb. That's where you live. Okay, somebody cuts the tree down. What are you going to do as a smart owl? You're going to go to the next tree and set up house, right? I mean, they're not going to die on you; they're just going to move to another tree. That's what owls do. Can you imagine the inconvenience and the trauma of having to move to another tree? Just think, an owl becomes an alcoholic—alcoholic owls! I mean, you know, that's terrible. Psychotic owl, roaming the woods. I mean, it's nuts."

An understanding of how the natural world operates has never been Robertson's strong suit. On his television show he frequently rails against the teaching of evolution in public schools and insists that creationism—the biblical account of world origins—is a valid scientific alternative.

Robertson's musing about science may be ridiculous, but most of his rhetoric on other topics isn't funny, it's ugly. Robertson reserves his strongest invective for his numerous enemies; in his world, "the left," who are always out to get him. "The left" consists of anybody who takes issue with Robertson's ultraconservative theological views. Sometimes they are more than just "the left" they can also be "the radical left," the irreligious, or the anti-Christian forces.

"The left's" plan is usually to sneak communism into the United States, and then smash Christianity. As Robertson explained in *The New World Order*: "Irreligious liberal groups like the American Civil Liberties Union, People for the American Way, the American Jewish Congress, Americans United for Separation of Church and State, the National Organization for Women, and the liberal media are doing everything in their power to drive the United States into the same moral abyss that the Eastern Bloc countries are clawing their way out of."[20]

In the April/May 1992 edition of the newsletter *Pat Robertson's Perspective*, Robertson really lost his temper. "The ACLU, NOW, People for the American Way, Americans United for

Separation of Church and State, the Gay-Lesbian Caucus, the National Education Association, the Communist Party U.S.A., the National Council of Churches, and all of their left wing allies have lost," he wrote. "The strategy against the American radical left should be the same as General Douglas MacArthur employed against the Japanese in the Pacific. . . . Bypass their strongholds, then surround them, isolate them, bombard them, then blast the individuals out of their power bunkers with hand-to-hand combat. The battle for Iwo Jima was not pleasant, but our troops won it. The battle to regain the soul of America won't be pleasant either, but we will win it!"

Reading this passage, one is struck by a few things. First, note how Robertson couldn't resist the effort to throw in some more red-baiting by raising the specter of the Communist Party U.S.A. The American Communist party has never had more than a handful of members and has never been taken seriously by the liberal community. Nevertheless, Robertson couldn't resist including them and implying by association that all the organizations listed were guilty of communist sympathies. Robertson has raised the cheap smear to an art form.

Second, and perhaps even more strikingly, one is struck by the mean-spiritedness of this passage. It simply drips with hate. Fundamentalist Christians who follow Robertson often spout lines like, "We love the sinner but hate the sin" when talking about their enemies in the public policy arena. Such pop theology is mere verbiage, especially in this instance. Robertson hates his enemies, or else he would not speak of blowing them up and annihilating them. Such a violent, ugly, and blood-soaked metaphor is miles removed from the biblical Christianity Robertson claims to champion.

After the ACLU, the organization that Robertson despises the most is Planned Parenthood. Speaking on the April 9, 1991, "700 Club" program, he had this to say about the group: "What Planned Parenthood is doing is absolutely contrary to everything Christian. It is teaching kids to fornicate, teaching people to have adultery, teaching people to get involved in every kind of bestiality, homosexuality, lesbianism—everything that the Bible condemns. And teaching without absolutely any moral restraint."

Americans, of course, differ on the question of birth control and sex education. Some Americans contend that teenagers should not be taught about birth control or sex in public schools because it might encourage them to experiment. Others say young people must be fully informed about how the human reproductive system works and learn the best methods for preventing pregnancy and disease. Planned Parenthood clearly favors the latter view, but that does not make the organization an advocate of humans having sex with animals. Nor does the group advocate adultery. Planned Parenthood's main goal is to make certain that people make rational choices about family size. They want men and women to understand the full range of birth control options open to them. Many of the group's services are available at a reduced cost to the poor.

Planned Parenthood is Robertson's mortal enemy because the group provides abortion services at some facilities. Robertson ignores the fact that Planned Parenthood also provides breast cancer screening for women, AIDS tests, and information about how to prevent or treat venereal diseases. In any case, the charges against Planned Parenthood that Robertson makes are typical of his hyperbole. One would think that these types of reckless assertions would have discredited him long ago. For Robertson, though, it's never enough to say that he disagrees with his foes, or to even call them misguided. They have to be enemies of God, under the spell of Satan, members of the "radical left," or proponents of revolting ideas such as bestiality and child sexuality.

Consider this Robertson statement from *New York* magazine, published in August 1986: "It is interesting that termites don't build things, and the great builders of our nation almost to a man have been Christian, because Christians have the desire to build something. He is motivated by love of man and God, so he builds. The people who have come into institutions [today] are primarily termites. They are destroying institutions that have been built by Christians, whether it is universities, governments, our own traditions that we have. The termites are in charge now, and that is not the way it ought to be, and the time has come for a godly fumigation." Thus we see that those who disagree with Robertson aren't just wrong, they are active agents of destruction, out to bring society's foundations crashing down. It's proper, indeed *useful*, to annihilate them. This manner of accusation, that entire groups of people have become demonized, has served to drag the political discourse in the United States down to new depths.

According to Robertson, entire regions of the country can be under demon control. In *Answers to 200 of Life's Most Probing Questions* he writes, "Just as the angels have archangels and higher powers, the demons have what are called 'principalities and powers.' It is possible that a demon prince is in charge of New York, Detroit, St. Louis, or any other city. Particular sins are prevalent in certain cities. One city might have rampant homosexuality, while another might be troubled by excessive lust. In another, it may be witchcraft or spiritism. Nations, as well as cities, can be gripped by demon power."[21]

In fall of 1981 Robertson wrote in his newsletter, *Pat Robertson's Perspective*, "There is in the air today the unmistakable scent of the Antichrist spirit." He goes on to assert that the people have given into a malign force "which will both permit and personify their basest desires . . . in the United States it is the central government under the religion of secular humanism." Observes Robertson, "No society under the grip of the Antichrist spirit has ever survived. With it comes a period of lawlessness and virtual anarchy. Then an economic collapse followed by a reign of terror. Then a strong-man dictator who plunders the society for his own personal aggrandizement. Then wars to fulfill the leader's insane dream of empire. Then defeat and collapse." In *Answers* he goes so far as to assert, "There is always the possibility that the Antichrist is already in the world."

Many fundamentalist Christians who follow Robertson complain that they are the ones being demonized. When asked to back up this assertion, they often complain that they are stereotyped in popular culture. There is probably some of that going on, but it comes nowhere near to matching the offensiveness level of what Robertson says about those who oppose him. Nearly every day of "The 700 Club" program, one can hear Robertson rant, rave, ridicule and demean "liberals," "the left," or anyone who dares to object to his political agenda. This type of vituperation makes his television show more of a political program than a religious one. Robertson's enemies aren't just wrong or misguided; they are responsible for ushering in the "Antichrist spirit."

Robertson has been a master of this type of hate-mongering for more than fifteen years. Some time ago, he chose to become a public figure by stepping into the political arena. His views are controversial; some would say dangerous. Not surprisingly, they have generated much criticism. According to Robertson, this criticism is religious bigotry. But is it really? Just about all of the criticism Robertson engenders springs from this ultraright-wing *political* agenda. Few people attack Robertson for his theological beliefs, even if many people consider them unusual. Just about every day "The 700 Club" pictures Robertson claiming that God is healing people of life-threatening diseases and afflictions through prayer. This type of faith healing, common in Pentecostal circles, is surely not everyone's cup of tea, but if it were all Robertson were doing, he would not be a controversial figure, and few would pay attention to him. The First Amendment protects Robertson's right to believe whatever he wants concerning God and Christianity, and advocates of separation of church and state would go to bat for him any day of the week were that right ever genuinely threatened.

What has so many people concerned about Robertson is that in between healings and stories about religion, he attacks church-state separation, labels his enemies as "anti-Christian," develops strategies to have his pet theological notions written into the secular law, and builds a grassroots army working day and night to transform the United States into a theocracy. When Robertson attacks the First Amendment, he is attacking something that is a cornerstone of the American way of life. It is proper that such attacks should generate forceful responses.

In short, Robertson wants a free ride. He wants to expound his own political agenda, attack all of those who disagree with him, and label anyone who responds negatively a bigot. American politics doesn't work that way. Anyone who holds extreme views, as Robertson does, should be willing to accept the criticism they engender.

As chapter 2 pointed out, Robertson complained that he was being manhandled by the mainstream media during the 1988 presidential campaign when in fact all of the candidates were undergoing tough scrutiny. (Just ask Gary Hart about scrutiny.) Robertson continues to complain that the media abuse him. Given his ambitions and the growing power of the Christian Coalition, it is only natural that he would be the subject of increased media attention, some of it probing and perhaps even critical.

Robertson has little room to complain. Every weekday he enjoys a ninety-minute block of time on "The 700 Club" during which he can preach his political views. CBN, the Christian Coalition, and other Robertson projects produce numerous publications, tapes, and books that reach millions of Americans and people overseas. The bulk of his activities enjoy non-profit status, even if they are overtly political. His personal fortune runs in the hundreds of millions. These projects give Robertson more than enough outlets to respond to his critics.

It's hard to say who started the shouting match, Robertson or those who oppose him. But Robertson can't claim that his critics are getting the best of him and expect to be taken seriously. In fact, Robertson has weathered a number of revelations that would have penetrated the armor of just about any other public figure. Many of his most vocal critics are small organizations with modest budgets who don't reach the vast audience Robertson does. The mainstream media pay only intermittent attention to his activities. The key role he has played in orchestrating the Christian Coalition's enormous influence within the Republican party, for example, is one of the great, underreported stories of the 1990s.

One would think Robertson would have little about which to complain. His empire, fortune, and power continue to grow, and the American people seem unconcerned or unaware that an extremist TV preacher is on the verge of seizing control of the country's dominant political party, rapidly putting himself in the position of having enough political power to make or break presidents.

What more could a simple man of God want?

Notes

1. Charles R. Monroe, *World Religions: An Introduction* (Amherst, N.Y.: Prometheus Books, 1995), p. 88.

2. T. R. Reid, "Robertson's Ever-Changing Approach," *Washington Post* (February 11, 1988).

3. "Anti-Catholic Bias 'Isolated,' TV Evangelist Responds," *Catholic League Newsletter* (December 1986).

4. Frank Franzonia, "TV Evangelist's Ties to Anti-Catholicism a 'Mistake,' " *Our Sunday Visitor* (May 17, 1981).

5. "Pressure Aside, the Story Must Be Told," *Our Sunday Visitor* (May 17, 1981).

6. " 'We Are One,' Says Robertson After Meeting With Cardinal O'Connor," *Church & State* (July/August 1988).

7. Charles M. Sennott, "Christian Right Woos Catholics," *Boston Globe*, December 10, 1995.

8. David Cantor, *The Religious Right: The Assault On Tolerance & Pluralism In America*, 2d ed. (New York: Anti-Defamation League, 1994), p. 39.

9. Quoted in Cantor, *The Religious Right*, p. 4.

10. Pat Robertson, *The New World Order* (Dallas: Word Publishing, 1991), p. 208.

11. "Robertson Asserts Blacks in U.S. Fail to Understand South Africa," Associated Press dispatch, *New York Times*, February 14, 1988.

12. Pat Robertson, *The Turning Tide: The End of Liberalism and the Rise of Common Sense* (Dallas: Word Publishing, 1993), p. 229.

13. Robertson, *The New World Order*, p. 233.

14. Robertson, *The Turning Tide*, p. 233.

15. Pat Robertson, *Answers to 200 of Life's Most Probing Questions* (Nashville: Thomas Nelson Publishers, 1984), p. 192.

16. Robertson, *The Turning Tide*, p. 239.

17. Robertson, *Answers*, p. 155.

18. Jim Castelli, "Pat Robertson—Extremist with a Baby Face," People for the American Way report (August 1986).

19. David D. Dunlap, "Gay Advertising Campaign on TV Draws Wrath of Conservatives," *New York Times* (November 12, 1995).

20. Robertson, *The New World Order*, p. 233.

21. Robertson, *Answers*, pp. 116–17.

7

Big Business

"Yes, unbridled capitalism must be restrained, or people will get too
much money and too much power and will use it to oppress others."
—Pat Robertson, *Answers to 200 of Life's Most Probing Questions*

The Christian Broadcasting Network is more than just a television ministry. It is also a hugely profitable enterprise for Pat
Robertson. From the humble beginnings explored in chapter
1, Robertson built CBN into a vast complex in Virginia Beach.
Today CBN—which during a successful year can pull in $75
million to $97 million in clear, tax-free profit[1]—is the money
generator that finances or provides the seed money for so
many other Robertson projects, including those of a political
nature. In time, CBN became so successful that it was necessary for Robertson to convert some of it into a purely secular
operation, the Family Channel. Now the nation's seventh
most popular cable channel, the Family Channel airs mostly
reruns of westerns and sitcoms. The only religious program it
carries on a regular basis is "The 700 Club," a program that is
as much about politics as it is religion.

But CBN and the Family Channel only scratch the surface of Robertson's business empire. A millionaire many times over, Robertson heads a complex and growing financial domain that over the years has experimented with numerous money-making ventures. While not all have been successful, on the whole Robertson's business sense is excellent. That does not mean his business ventures have been without controversy. To the contrary, some of Robertson's projects have been quite controversial, sparking lawsuits and charges that he has abused the nonprofit status of CBN. The Family Channel is a case in point. Founded in 1977 as a division of CBN, the Family Channel was a vehicle to give "The 700 Club" a national outlet. At first the old westerns, movies, and sitcoms were seen as filler, but Robertson underestimated the American public's appetite for nostalgia. Viewers wanted to see these old programs, such as "The Adventures of Dobie Gillis" and "Father Knows Best," as well as squeaky clean dramas like "The Waltons." Reporter John Taylor of *Esquire* magazine, who has investigated Robertson's finances in depth, tells what came next: by 1989 the Family Channel was making so much money that it could not legally remain a part of CBN, a nonprofit enterprise. Robertson insists he tried to find an outside buyer for the channel, but everyone to whom he talked wanted to axe "The 700 Club." This was anathema to Robertson.

Robertson and his son Tim joined forces with John Malone, founder of Tele-Communications, Inc., the largest cable operator in the United States, to keep control of the Family Channel. Malone contributed $45 million, and Robertson and his son invested $183,000. To pay CBN for the Family Channel, a new corporation, International Family Entertainment, issued $250 million in cash and notes that could eventually be converted into IFE stock.[2]

Business transactions can seem complex and intricate to the average person unschooled in the ways of the stock market. The bottom line of this deal, a form of leveraged buyout, is that it eventually brought both Robertsons quite a windfall of profits. The two had purchased 1.5 million shares of the company's common stock at 2.2 cents per share. In 1992, the stock was offered to the public for fifteen dollars a share. Robertson and his son had converted their modest investment of under $200,000 into a deal worth $90 million. Even the most aggressive venture capitalist would be hard pressed to find an investment that could reap such huge profits so quickly.

Robertson aggressively defends the transaction. After the *Philadelphia Inquirer* ran a series of articles on nonprofit groups that mentioned the CBN deal, Robertson sent the paper a lengthy letter, which was subsequently printed, insisting that the Family Channel buyout had been entirely above board. The purpose of the transaction, he insisted, was not to enrich himself but to place CBN on sound financial footing. Nevertheless, in 1991 Robertson received $371,000 in compensation from IFE; Tim Robertson received $446,000.[3] Pat Robertson later donated $117 million in CBN cash and stock options to Regent University—formerly CBN University—the graduate school he founded in Virginia Beach. "The actions that Tim and I have taken to enhance CBN's value and its religious mission do not sound like the actions of insiders who are attempting to benefit personally from their positions with a tax-exempt organization," wrote Robertson. "I have dedicated my life to CBN and to its religious mission. I expect to continue to do so as long as God is willing. At this point, I am proud of what we have been able to accomplish in His service."[4]

Although apparently legal, Robertson's CBN–Family Channel deal garnered plenty of criticism. Many critics expressed the view that it was unethical of Robertson to raise money for CBN, devoted to spreading the gospel, and use those funds to build a massive and hugely profitable secular media enterprise.

One critic, the owner of a group of Christian radio stations, who wishes to remain anonymous, told syndicated columnist Michael McManus, "There is a trend of soliciting donations from the public to build television facilities to spread the Gospel. Then at some later date, those facilities are converted to private, for-profit, commercial, secular business investments. It smacks of some kind of ethical fraud on the public. You can't take money freely given for one purpose and then convert it to an entirely different purpose without somehow being held accountable to the public that gave the money in the first place. It may be legal, but it is not right."[5] Another critic, Jeffrey K. Hadden, a sociology professor at the University of Virginia and author of books on televangelism, told the *New York Times*, "Pat built the company from the faithful who contributed money to his ministry, and what is happening now is scandalous."[6]

Robertson never denied that CBN money had been used to launch the Family Channel. He told *Christianity Today* that it was "a very limited amount in the beginning, a few hundred thousand dollars at most."[7] Robertson never let the criticism slow him down. In fact, IFE continued to grow. In 1993 the company purchased MTM Entertainment, whose catalog includes such popular television shows as "The Mary Tyler Moore Show," "Lou Grant," and "Hill Street Blues." It later purchased the Ice Capades and three South Carolina-based businesses that put on shows at Myrtle Beach. In 1993 IFE's profits reached $208 million.

The Family Channel also has a global presence. It now works with broadcast operations in the United Kingdom, South Korea, Canada, Australia, and the Czech Republic. In addition, CBN operates out of about fifty international ministries, including Middle East Television in Lebanon. In recent years, Robertson has even targeted communist countries such as North Korea and Vietnam for broadcast opportunities.

I will discuss Robertson's international wheeling and dealing later. Back at home, Robertson couldn't resist using IFE for political purposes. During Virginia's statewide elections in 1991, IFE gave a total of $11,000 to five Virginia Beach Republicans running for Senate and House of Delegate seats. Given the popularity of the Family Channel—it reaches an estimated sixty million households—one has to wonder how many people realize the political agenda behind all of those old reruns. Viewers who dislike Robertson's political views may tune in for a little nostalgia and end up indirectly helping Robertson unseat politicians who fail to toe his political line.

Not satisfied with acquiring millions of dollars through IFE, Robertson has worked repeatedly to become a true media mogul. Over the years he has expressed an interest in purchasing secular news operations and once tried to start a radio network from the ground up. Robertson clearly has a great interest in the media. At Regent University, one of five graduate degrees offered is in communications. In 1992 he told *Christianity Today,* "I believe that [Jesus Christ] is lord of the government, and the church and business and education, and, hopefully, one day, lord of the press. I see him involved in everything. And that's why I don't want to stay just in the church, as such. I want the church to move into the world."[8]

CBN operates a news division that offers regular reports on "The 700 Club." Some reports are objective, but evidence of bias does creep into many others. (For an example, see the discussion of CBN's report on abuses by the FBI and other federal police agencies in chapter 6.) Also, the ministry's news division tends to give more coverage to the moral and social issues that are so dear to Robertson.

Robertson frequently analyzes the stories that appear on CBN News. Flanked by his co-hosts, he doesn't hesitate to tell the viewer how to interpret what was just aired. Undoubtedly this type of activity affects the way the viewer perceives the news he gets from CBN. Also, "The 700 Club" tends to give a lot more air time to the moral issues with which Robertson is chiefly concerned. Stories that might get scant attention on the network news are sometimes given big play on the program. This is especially true with "nonrulings" by the Supreme Court.

The Supreme Court refuses more than 98 percent of all the cases it is asked to hear during each term. When the Court refuses a case, the lower court opinion stands. It does not mean that the Supreme Court affirms or approves the lower court ruling. In many cases, the Court has refused a particular legal question one year only to accept a similar case raising an identical question the next. These "nondecisions" become big news to Robertson's CBN, especially when they concern hot-button issues such as religion in public schools. Robertson gives them much more play than they deserve, which can confuse the viewer. Many CBN devotees know little about the law and how the Supreme Court operates. They may be led to believe that these "nonrulings" are equivalent to Court opinions. (I will discuss this phenomenon in more detail in the next chapter, which concerns Robertson's legal activities.)

While "The 700 Club" does have a large audience, it tends to be limited to those who already accept Robertson's message. In a sense, he is preaching to the converted. Robertson has a great interest in breaking out of this mold and gaining control of a news operation that is not tied explicitly to his ministry. To further this aim, in May of 1992, Robertson made a bid to buy United Press International. The Robertson-founded U.S. Media Corporation offered $6 million for the financially troubled news agency, contingent upon an examination of UPI's books. Less than a month later, he announced that the deal was off. Robertson said his accountants had looked over UPI's finances and decided the deal was too risky. "My auditors told me that we would have to invest $31 million over the next eighteen months, and that didn't guarantee a turnaround," he said during a Washington, D.C., press conference. Robertson proceeded to offer $500,000 for the rights to UPI's name and some of its archival photos, but the news agency rejected the offer.

Robertson may have been scared away from the UPI deal because in his financial world, debt is discouraged. In *Answers to 200 of Life's Most Probing Questions* he denounces debt twice. He believes that a financial crash is imminent and warns that debt will financially ruin many Americans. "Of course, the happiest people in this regard are those who have no debt on anything, who have paid cash for their cars, their furniture, and their houses, and who have funded their businesses out of either equity or cash flow," writes Robertson. "These people are better off in times of recession or even in times of rampant inflation."[9]

Indeed they are. Unfortunately, very few Americans are wealthy enough to pay cash up front for every purchase, including big-ticket items such as cars and houses. Thankfully, Robertson asserts that some debt is okay, and that many people view a home mortgage as a "monthly budgeted expense" and not really debt.

Robertson's desire to buy the UPI name is interesting, in light of what happened next. The following February Robertson announced the formation of Standard News, a nationwide radio news service based in Washington. It's possible that Robertson wanted to call this new service UPI, thus getting all the prestige of the older service without any of the debt. Despite the big splash, Standard News did not remain a Robertson enterprise for long. In 1995 Robertson sold the company to a Chicago-based media concern called Major Networks. Terms were not disclosed.

Around the same time he sold Standard News, Robertson also dumped another struggling business, this one unrelated to the media. In 1990, under the name American Benefits Plus (ABP), Robertson launched Kalo Vita, a vitamin and cosmetics company. In its original incarnation, the firm sold home-study Bible courses. Two years later, however, Robertson recreated the company to pitch a secular product line: coupon books containing discounts for a variety of goods and services. One year after that, the company metamorphosed again and changed its name to Kalo Vita, this time selling vitamins and nutritional supplements. Among the products it sold were nutritional supplements called "The American Whey" and "Sea of Galilee" skin care and cosmetics.

ABP and Kalo Vita were based on "multilevel" or network

marketing, whereby distributors recruit family, friends, and coworkers to help them sell the product. The main distributor then takes a cut of each sale. (The Amway company is probably the most familiar proponent of this sales arrangement.) More than twenty thousand people signed up for Robertson's program. According to Robertson, multilevel marketing has a biblical basis. In a 1991 promotional video hawking American Benefits Plus, he called it "one of the greatest expressions of the biblical principles of prosperity that I know of."[10] What Robertson didn't tell people was that multilevel marketing companies experience an exceedingly high rate of failure. According to Les Garringer, Florida's deputy attorney general, at least 95 percent of all multilevel marketing companies fail within two years.

In 1992, Florida officials began investigating American Benefits Plus. Lead investigator Jim Lyons told ABC, "We found all sorts of rife income claims that were entirely inappropriate." Two Florida distributors were subsequently fired.

On October 27, 1994, ABC News' "PrimeTime Live" newsmagazine ran a major exposé on American Benefits Plus/Kalo Vita. During the broadcast, Garringer said, "I believe those at the top can gain a lot of income. I believe the average 'Joe citizen' who participates will never make a significant amount of money."

"PrimeTime Live" had interviewed a group of disgruntled ABP distributors in Pittsburgh. Two distributors claimed Robertson told a crowd they could make upwards of $20,000 per month, though they admitted they had no tapes to prove the assertion. Said one man, "You weren't allowed [to tape]. Every video was confiscated. His bodyguards would confiscate . . . videos." Kerry Young, who helped Robertson set up the ABP meeting told ABC, "The instruction from his security people was no videos, no audios." Young, who eventually broke with Robertson, told the newsmagazine that he regretted his involvement with the company. "I'm the guy that sat down at their kitchen table and got them involved—Aunt

Mildreds and Uncles Joes and retired pastors," he said. "They're the innocents and they're totally operating on a dream with no substance behind it."

The shift from American Benefits Plus to Kalo Vita and the accompanying new product line created hardships for some distributors. Suddenly the coupon books were out, replaced by a line of high-potency vitamins, nutritional supplements, and skin care products. According to *Newsweek* magazine, Robertson made the change after listening to a pitch from Jim Heflin, a body builder. Kalo Vita adopted Heflin's line of products, leaving earlier investors stuck with coupon books they could not sell. Many investors were left high and dry. "It was a catastrophe," Lois Flockhart, a seventy-six-year-old retiree from Indianapolis told *Newsweek*. Flockhart says she lost more than $7,000 and was forced to refinance her home. Another investor, Ron Santom of Pittsburgh, tried to send back $750 in coupons for a refund, only to be told that the company had changed its policy and was no longer buying back the books. Said Santom, "I didn't think a company backed by Pat Robertson would do that."

Robertson used his personal stature and charisma to push Kalo Vita aggressively to his followers. Ads for the firm frequently ran in the *Christian American*, the Christian Coalition's newspaper, and attendees at Christian Coalition conferences were exhorted to sign up. Robertson also made personal appearances in hotels around the country to plug Kalo Vita's precursor, American Benefits Plus. He did not hesitate to stress the religious themes he knew would resonate well with the audience. Robertson told the potential sales force that unlimited profits could be earned. "With God there is no cap," he said. "In the multilevel business, the sky is the limit."

Robertson's vitamins were sold to the public at a huge mark-up. Former Kalo Vita president Mark Peterson told Newsweek, "We were buying it for $7 to $8 a bottle and selling it for $49.95. What I didn't understand is a man of [Robertson's] stature putting his name on products like that." (Peterson was fired by Robertson in 1992, and Robertson later changed vitamin suppliers.) Peterson also told ABC, "We were getting letters every day saying, 'What kind of operation is this?' "[11]

Florida officials were not impressed by Robertson's shift from ABP to Kalo Vita. Garringer noted that a Kalo Vita recruiting letter included a sample $15,000 monthly commission check accompanied by the words, "Can you imagine what you could be earning?" "If you are advertising that people who join your plan could make $15,000 a month, and there is no disclaimer, you have committed an unfair and deceptive trade practice in the state of Florida," Garringer said. "You just can't make those kinds of claims and if you can, if you do makes those kinds of claims, you've got to be prepared to substantiate them." (The letter did include a disclaimer, but Florida officials said it was insufficient and continued their investigation.) Robertson refused to grant "PrimeTime Live" an interview to discuss the allegations. But, aware that the story was coming up, he began doing damage control, telling "700 Club" viewers that it was all part of a plot by the media to discredit him for his political activity. "Well, the truth is, in two weeks, a little bit less than two weeks, there's going to be a major election and, of course, I get to be a target."

In his interview with ABC, Kerry Young concluded, "The normal, average, American Christian person out there, they won't point the finger and blame, because that's not the Christian thing to do. But I've prayed about this. There needs to be an apology made to everybody who ever got involved in American Benefits Plus, or Kalo Vita, as it's called now."

Perhaps most shockingly, it was revealed during the Kalo Vita debacle that CBN money had been used to prop up American Benefits Plus during its early years. When *Newsweek* and ABC News inquired about the CBN-Kalo Vita financial link, Robertson staffers insisted that the money used was from CBN's reserves, not donations, and said all the loans were paid back.[12] A year before the ABC "PrimeTime Live" report, the Norfolk *Virginian-Pilot* reported that CBN pumped $2.8

million into American Benefits Plus to keep the fledgling company alive. The arrangement raised the eyebrows of some in the nonprofit world. "It violates acceptable standards," said Gerald Kaufman, co-chairman of the National Council of Nonprofit Associations. "It's charity dollars. You don't risk a charity's money. You risk your own money." Dan Langan of the National Charities Information Bureau, another watchdog group, also criticized the deal. "The idea that nonprofit money is being used to fund a for-profit enterprise in which he's a partner—it sounds like a conflict."

Robertson was livid over any suggestion that he had engaged in unethical practices. In a statement issued to the *Virginian-Pilot,* Robertson said the deal was "entirely ethical, in the best interest of CBN and its donors, and in no way constitutes any conflict of interest or impropriety under Virginia corporate law or under the moral code that I live my life by."[13] Robertson's son Gordon explained to the newspaper that his father was trying to establish for-profit groups to provide CBN with a regular income after his death. A statement issued by CBN insisted that Robertson received no salary from Kalo Vita, although the statement acknowledged that the firm did pay Robertson $38,600 for various "services" to the company.

Eventually, Kalo Vita's financial troubles became too much for Robertson to bear. In 1995 he sold the firm to an unnamed Dallas company for one dollar, just one month after the critical reports about Kalo Vita in *Newsweek* and on "PrimeTime Live."

The American Benefits Plus/Kalo Vita enterprise led to some interesting fallout. In May of 1995 former American Benefits Plus president Mark Peterson filed suit against Robertson in a North Carolina court. The suit contends that Robertson unjustly fired Peterson and then blamed him for the company's problems. Peterson also charges that Robertson threatened him in September of 1994 after he refused to stop speaking publicly about his experiences at American Benefits Plus. Court papers filed by Peterson in the lawsuit assert that Peterson's wife taped a phone call from Robertson in September of 1994 during which he allegedly said, "If a stallion bites and kicks, he might break his leg. I've had horses break their legs. When a horse breaks his leg, they put him to sleep."[14] Saying he never made the statements, an angry Robertson counter-sued Peterson for $1.35 million. He contended that his ex-employee had defamed him with his critical comments about Robertson's business dealings, citing the "PrimeTime Live" story and *Newsweek* article. The remarks, Robertson's suit says, "impugn [Robertson's] reputation in his business and profession, impute a lack of integrity . . . and allege criminal and unlawful conduct."

Yet another Robertson business venture, Founders Inn, has come under fire, but for a different reason. The inn, a luxury hotel in Virginia Beach, hires only born-again Christians. Prospective employees are asked to "briefly state your Christian testimony" on the job application. They are also expected to describe "My life before receiving Christ," "How I became aware of my need for Christ," "How I came to Christ" and "My life since receiving Christ." Robertson claims that because Founders Inn is a division of CBN, it is permitted to discriminate on the basis of religion. And discriminate it does. Says CBN spokesperson Frankie Abourjilie, Jews and Muslims "at this point would not be eligible. We would exercise our right to discriminate on religion."[15]

Once the policy came to light, community groups began pressuring local organizations to refrain from holding events there. In 1991, both the Virginia Opera and the Virginia Symphony cancelled fundraising events they had planned for Founders Inn, citing the "Christians only" policy. While Founders Inn may not want non-Christians on the staff, it absolutely wants them as customers. One advertisement that ran in Norfolk's *Portfolio* magazine in August of 1991 called Founders Inn a "magnificent four-diamond hotel" suitable for "weddings, receptions, reunions, *barmitzvas*, corporate dinners and meetings, and parties for any occasion." (Emphasis mine.) To the Jewish community of Virginia, Founders Inn appears to be saying, "Yes, we'll take your business, but don't expect to work here."

There is one group, however, that Founders Inn does not want at the hotel even as paying guests: homosexuals. This policy led to an amusing incident in May of 1992 after a gay group in Virginia rented space at the hotel under the name "Gala Fundamentalist Christians" for a Sunday brunch. Hotel staffers got wind of the true nature of the group, a local branch of Queer Nation, after someone sent them a notice about the event that appeared in a gay newspaper. The inn then cancelled the reservation and went so far as to close the facility for the day. J. Patrick Evans of Queer Nation called closing the inn "the ultimate in homophobia" and added, "They don't want queers to eat in their restaurant and get cooties on the china."[16]

Some of these business ventures are apparently designed to keep CBN financially strong after Robertson dies. But Robertson's concern over keeping CBN afloat after he is gone may be a bit overblown. The ministry has a huge endowment. It was reported in the *Virginian-Pilot* to stand at $1 billion in May of 1992, with Robertson planning to double it by the year 2000. The paper also reported that CBN has a well-organized campaign to encourage supporters to give through wills or trusts. The organization retains a full-time staff of thirty-four financial planners who work with potential donors all over the country.[17] In addition, CBN holds financial planning seminars in large cities around the country every year. Observed Stephen D. Halliday, a Norfolk estate-planning expert who has worked with CBN, "CBN has certainly been at the forefront in terms of their [fundraising] techniques. They have been very sophisticated. They have a networking system with national contacts."

Despite the size of the endowment, Robertson keeps asking his supporters for more money. CBN sponsors regular telethons during which viewers are exhorted to send donations. Viewers are asked to become CBN "partners"—at twenty dollars a month. Robertson has even implored financially strapped people to give, implying God will reward them later many times over. Robertson also cranks out fund-raising mail at regular intervals. The *Virginian-Pilot* reported that just before Easter of 1994, Robertson mailed supporters an "urgent-gram" imploring them to send "$100 or more over and above your regular giving" so CBN could air an animated special called "The Easter Story" in media markets around the country. At the bottom of the appeal, in small print, appeared this cryptic notice: "All funds are used for designated projects and for the worldwide ministry of CBN in accordance with Ezra 7:17-18." The biblical passage cited reads, "With this money, therefore, you shall diligently buy bulls, rams, and lambs with their grain offerings and their libations and offer them on the altar of the house of your God which is in Jerusalem. And whatever seems good to you and to your brothers to do with the rest of the silver and gold, you may do according to the will of your God." CBN officials would not elaborate on the meaning of this verse, but the gist seems clear enough for donors: you may give money thinking that it will be used for airing an Easter special, but in reality CBN will use it for whatever project Robertson sees fit.

Arthur C. Frantzreb, a consultant to hospitals, universities, and other nonprofits, told the newspaper, "Poor little John Q. Public who is sending them $100 or $1,000 a year isn't able to digest the consolidated financial reports they send out. I think there will be a real problem coming up."[18] A former CBN financial planner echoed those comments. Remarking on Robertson's plan to create a $2 billion endowment, he said, "They really don't want people to know how much they have raised this way. Who is going to want to send in their $20 a month to 'The 700 Club' when they see that CBN has $1 billion in trust money?"[19]

Questions of accountability have been raised concerning CBN. In October of 1992 the ministry pulled out of the Better Business Bureau, calling the BBB's requirements "unreasonable and unacceptable." The bureau later reported that CBN had failed to provide a list of its governing board and a complete breakdown of its financial picture. CBN officials claimed it would have cost the ministry too much money to comply, but a BBB official noted that groups like the American Cancer Society, the American Heart Association, and other large organizations have no problems meeting the requirements.[20] For a time, the ministry had no membership in any oversight agency. However, to remain a member of the National Religious Broadcasters, Robertson had to bring CBN into compliance with the standards established by the Evangelical Council for Financial Accountability. Despite its innocuous sounding name, the NRB is a front group for the ultraright wing and toes the Religious Right's line on separation of church and state and various social issues. Robertson, who often speaks at NRB conventions, would not want to give up his ties to this organization.

Despite the $1 billion endowment, despite (until recently) the lack of accountability, the money keeps pouring in to CBN and related Robertson organizations. How does Robertson square all of this cash with the Bible's frequent warnings about acquiring too much wealth? In *Answers to 200 of Life's Most Probing Questions* he laid it all out. He pointed out that the Bible is often misquoted on this subject. The first book of Timothy (6:10) states that the "love of money is the root of all kinds of evil," not merely money itself. This leads Robertson to state, "The question is, what is money being used for? It is being used for God's glory, or is it being used only for pleasure? Is it being used for pride, to support dictators, and for the purchase of arms with which to kill people, or is it being used for a higher purpose?"[21] The passage is interesting in light of some of Robertson's activities overseas. Robertson says it is wrong to use money to "support dictators," yet that is exactly what he has done in at least two cases—Zaire and Guatemala.

In the central African nation of Zaire, Robertson has been a consistent ally of President/Dictator Mobutu Sese Seko, in the face of near universal condemnation of Mobutu's brutal one-party rule. Under Mobutu, Zaire has an abominable human rights record. For thirty years he has ruled Zaire, propped up by a variety of Western governments that found him useful during the Cold War. In 1993, with the Cold War a memory, those nations grew so disgusted with him that they finally withdrew support. Since then, Zaire has rapidly descended into anarchy.

The average resident of Zaire lives on an income of less than $500 a year. But Mobutu is a millionaire many times over, having plundered the nation's lucrative diamond trade. (He is, by some accounts, one of the richest men in the world.) Mobutu is considered persona non grata as far as the United States is concerned. In 1993 the State Department, under orders from the Clinton administration, issued a ban forbidding Mobutu and members of his family from visiting the United States. In 1995 Robertson began lobbying intensely to have the ban lifted. According to the *Washington Post*, Robertson threatened to enlist the aid of Senator Jesse Helms (R-N.C.) to have the ban removed, but Helms, normally a Robertson ally, balked at the request. Robertson, meanwhile, has blasted the State Department's policy as "outrageous." State Department officials insisted that Mobutu wanted to travel to the United States to polish up his image before holding mock elections that would enable him to further his stranglehold on Zaire. U.S. officials said they had no desire to play any part in this sham. Mobutu is so desperate for the visa that he paid a conservative U.S. lobbying firm $30,000 to spruce up his image and apply pressure in Washington. A Clinton administration source noted in the *Washington Post* that "Robertson's hand is all over" the effort to win a visa for Mobutu. "Mobutu hasn't changed," a source in the State Department told the *Post*. "What he wants is a transition from the second Mobutu republic to the third Mobutu republic." Mobutu, the source said, pretends he wants democracy in the country but "has blocked the process of transition every step of the way."[22]

Aware of Robertson's dealings, some members of Congress

wrote to the State Department urging that Mobutu be kept out of the United States. Assistant Secretary of State Wendy Sherman responded, "We assure you that President Mobutu will not be coming to Washington." Sherman noted Mobutu's "obstruction of Zaire's transition to democracy" and wrote, "The visa sanction has been, and remains, one of our most effective measures to influence Mobutu and his entourage, and we have seen no change on the part of the Zairian president which would warrant a reversal of this policy."[23]

The State Department maintains a long list of grievances against Mobutu. According to the *Washington Post*, it includes "massive corruption, personal enrichment on a spectacular scale at his country's expense, indifference to the physical deterioration of what should be a prosperous country, connivance at rearming the murderous Hutu militias of neighboring Rwanda, and repeated maneuvers to frustrate the process of transition to democracy that he has promised to support."[24]

Mobutu has dealt harshly with his political enemies. In February of 1992 groups of Protestants and Catholics protesting in the streets of Kinshasa, the capital, were gunned down when government troops opened fire without provocation. Perhaps as many as sixty were killed, and Mobutu promptly outlawed public demonstrations of dissent. Robertson visited Mobutu in Zaire less than a month after the incident, ignoring pleas from Christian missionaries who had fled the country that he stay away. The missionaries said Robertson's hobnobbing with Mobutu would fuel anti-American sentiment and jeopardize future missionary activity there. Even the State Department, then under conservative Republican President George Bush, urged Robertson to stay home. Noted State Department official Makila James, "Honestly, we had concerns about the public relations impression that would be conveyed."[25] Robertson went anyway.

Ken Giacoletto, a businessman and former missionary to Zaire, said Mobutu used Robertson during a previous visit in

July of 1991 to enhance his own prestige. "Pat Robertson's going over there just makes it demoralizing for people who are working as Christians and being killed," he said. Giacoletto recalled seeing Mobutu on television bragging about Robertson as "being a friend of the country and as a supporter of the president." Then, the ex-missionary said, Mobutu went on to talk about how "he [Mobutu] fights to rebuild the country and all this kind of stuff." Concluded Giacoletto, "I don't know if Pat believes all that stuff, but nobody else does in Zaire." Another missionary, Evelyn Millman of the American Baptist Churches, said many people in Zaire interpreted the earlier Robertson visit "as an endorsement and another instance of the U.S. supporting a terrible dictator."[26]

Mobutu will not stand for criticism. According to a 1995 report issued by the Committee to Protect Journalists, Mobutu's regime has a dismal record when it comes to tolerating a free press. The organization charged that Mobutu's security forces have murdered some journalists.[27] The Zairian strong man also has a poor understanding of religious freedom. In 1989, the government announced a crackdown on what were termed "unrecognized" religious groups. More than four hundred organizations were banned and ordered to cease all activities. When it was all over, six religious groups were deemed recognized: the Roman Catholic Church, the Eglise du Christ au Zaire (an umbrella group for most Protestant denominations), Islam, Judaism, the Greek Orthodox Church, and the Kimbanguist Church (a regional faith founded in 1921).

Mobutu's poor understanding of religious freedom hasn't scared off Robertson. According to *Time*, the two get along famously. The magazine reported that "some years ago" Robertson and his wife were flown to Zaire on board Mobutu's personal jet and, once in the country, they were entertained on his presidential yacht. They cruised up the Congo together to Mobutu's presidential estate. An American executive who went along on the trip remarked, "The atmosphere was very congenial. Pat Robertson and Mobutu get along extremely well. Mobutu was interested in bringing in people to get the mining and agricultural operations going again."[28]

Why would Robertson consort with such an individual? The anonymous business executive quoted in *Time* put his finger right on it: the bottom line is money. Robertson has formed a company called African Development Company to head up diamond mining and harvesting of the nation's forests. As the State Department noted, Zaire should be a prosperous nation, and might be today were it not for Mobutu. The country has rich reserves of copper, cobalt, zinc, diamonds, gold, silver, bauxite, iron, and coal. Many of these industries have been idle or nearly idle for years. Robertson apparently sees the potential to make huge profits in Zaire, although he insists that any money made will be plowed into humanitarian work being conducted in Zaire under the Robertson-run Operation Blessing, a relief agency.*

Zaire is not the only country where Robertson has meddled and backed cruel dictators. He also has long-standing ties to Jorge Serrano, former president of Guatemala. Robertson's ties to Serrano are harder to figure out, because there apparently is no economic motive behind them. Instead, Robertson says he supports the Guatemalan president because he is a fellow Pentecostal Christian.

Serrano is a protégé of General Efrain Rios Montt, a cruel dictator who seized power in March of 1982 in a coup. Shortly after taking control, Rios Montt unleashed a program of terror upon Guatemala's citizens, insisting that he was acting to wipe out a leftist insurgency led by guerrilla fighters. In fact, as the human rights watch-dog group Amnesty International has documented, thousands of people who had no connection

---

*Critics have asserted that even in his humanitarian work, however, Robertson has a second agenda. During relief operations in Rwanda in 1994, Operation Blessing staffers were criticized for proselytizing too much and helping too little. One American aide worker told *Time*, "They were laying on hands, speaking in tongues and holding services while people were dying all around."

to the guerrillas were killed in the most horrible ways. As Carlos Salinas, government program officer for Amnesty International noted in a letter to the *Washington Post*, "In just the first four months of Gen. Rios Montt's rule, Amnesty International had documented more than 2,000 extrajudicial killings attributed to the Guatemalan army. Furthermore, these killings were done in horrible ways: people of all ages were not only shot to death, they were burned alive, hacked to death, disemboweled, drowned, beheaded. Small children were smashed against rocks or bayoneted to death." Salinas reported that Guatemala under Rios Montt was so bloody that just two months after he assumed power, the nation's Roman Catholic bishops issued a report stating in part: "Numerous families have perished, vilely murdered. Not even the lives of old people, pregnant women or innocent children were respected. Never in our national history has it come to such extremes."[29]

Yet, in *The New World Order*, Robertson writes, "Serrano continues the enlightened leadership of his patron, former President Rios Montt, who insisted on honesty in government and then had every key official sign a pledge that read, 'I will not steal; I will not lie; I will not abuse.' I was in Guatemala City three days after Rios Montt overthrew the corrupt Lopez Garcia government. The people had been dancing in the street for joy, literally fulfilling the words of Solomon who said, 'When the righteous are in authority, the people rejoice.'"[30] The people of Guatemala may indeed have danced for joy when Rios Montt overthrew General Romeo Lucas Garcia—whose name Robertson got wrong in the above passage—because he, too, was a cruel dictator responsible for many deaths. But they did not dance for long; Rios Montt merely continued the killings.

If Rios Montt's reign of terror is an example of "enlightened leadership," then perhaps it is best to remain in the dark. One wonders if Robertson was really taken in by Rios Montt's pledge for government officials (which, perhaps, should have been modified to say "I will not engage in mass murder") or simply refuses to acknowledge that the man's hands are forever bloodstained. In any case, at this writing Rios Montt had announced his intention to lead Guatemala again, undoubtedly to continue that nation's fine tradition of "Godly government." Guatemalan courts, however, declared Rios Montt ineligible to run the country again.

Back in Africa, Robertson has a special interest in Zambia. Zambian President Frederick Chiluba is a Robertson associate who in 1991 officially declared the country a "Christian nation," and followed this up by changing some of the nation's laws to reflect the new Christian status. Robertson hailed this action while interviewing Chiluba during a taped segment that aired during the April 25, 1995, edition of "The 700 Club" and lamented the fact that no such declaration can occur in the United States. "Your country is a standard for not only Africa but the rest of the world," gushed Robertson. Following the interview he asked the audience, "Wouldn't you love to have someone like that as president of the United States of America? . . . The term 'Christian nation' seems to scare a lot of people in this nation of ours, but what Chiluba said is that it gives us a yardstick to measure the performance of the government. Otherwise we have no yardstick."

Anyone wondering what Robertson's "Christian nation" would look like in the United States need only examine Zambia. Since Chiluba took office, the country has been gripped with a wave of religious fanaticism. One of Chiluba's first acts was to announce that henceforth all public schools in the country would be saturated with fundamentalist Christianity. Members of the country's Islamic, Hindu, and animist minorities, who together comprise an estimated 25 to 50 percent of the population, were told they would have to build their own schools. Chiluba also announced that state-run television and radio would broadcast only fundamentalist Christian religious programming, again telling members of minority religions that they would have to build their own facilities. Soon all abortions were outlawed. Police raided and shut down every clinic, and many doctors and staffers were attacked and beaten. Next, an "antipornography" crusade was launched, and fundamentalist ministers and missionaries were given license to work with the police to publicly burn any material deemed obscene.

The country is now swarming with fundamentalist Christian missionaries, many of them affiliated with the radical Christian Reconstructionist movement, a collection of reactionary extremists who want to impose a fundamentalist Christian version of Iran on the United States. Under their plan, the harsh legal code outlined in the Old Testament would be the basis for U.S. law. Adultery, speaking in disrespect to parents, "witchcraft," and a whole host of other offenses would be punishable by death through stoning. Reconstructionists apparently see Zambia as a laboratory in which they may conduct experiments designed to fuse church and state into one inseparable mass. In the Reconstructionist magazine *Chalcedon Report*, one writer gave a glowing summary of the events in this "Christian nation" and urged activists to support Zambia. "A reconstructed Zambia could be the beginning of a worldwide revival," wrote the Rev. Brian M. Abshire. "As central Africa is depopulated by AIDS, a strong Christian nation, blessed by God, could spread throughout the continent. Who knows, in a few decades, we may need their missionaries to put our nation back together again!"[31]

Robertson often says Americans who disagree with his theological views have nothing to fear from his efforts in the political arena. The experience in Zambia proves otherwise. If Zambia is a model for a "Christian nation," many Americans will say no thanks. The type of intolerance that is rife there has no place in the United States, a diverse country where people of many faiths and philosophies seek to live together in peace. We cannot meet this goal by, for instance, following Chiluba's example of declaring the public education system the exclusive property of the ultraconservative, fundamentalist Christian community that encompasses only a narrow segment of the population, and in effect telling everyone else, "Too bad for you. Your tax dollars built and support this institution, but don't expect to be able to send your children here. Go off and build your own school."

Some right-wingers have actually praised Chiluba, asserting that he is tolerant for allowing other religions to exist in his "Christian nation." But it is fair to ask if the type of religious fanaticism and intolerance Chiluba has fostered continues, how long will it be before bulldozers come bearing down on Zambia's mosques and temples? Christian Reconstructionists, after all, believe that no one has the right to worship a false god, and in *The New World Order* Robertson warns that "false religious worship" is forbidden.[32] Under Reconstructionist thought and Robertson's view, the government may not execute any laws that conflict with "God's law." Logically, under their system, the government would be justified in taking all steps to stamp out "false religious worship." Who knows how many faiths—including many Christian ones— would be declared off limits if the decision were left to Robertson. Robertson has always denied being a Reconstructionist. Some of his religious-political rhetoric, however, sounds uncomfortably similar to what those groups proclaim. However, Robertson clearly does disagree with the Reconstructionists on some matters, such as end-times theology.*

But Zambia is hardly the paradise that Robertson and the Reconstructionists would have people believe. The country remains bitterly poor. The average worker makes less than $400 per year, and 70 percent of the country's residents live in poverty. The adult life expectancy is only forty-eight years for men, forty-nine and a half for women, and the infant mortality rate is actually rising. Chiluba has also been criticized for failing to move the country closer toward democracy.

---

*For more information about Reconstructionism, see my previous book *Why the Religious Right Is Wrong About Separation of Church & State.*

Robertson's overseas adventures may do more than give him good copy for "700 Club" stories. Robertson has a keen eye for the bottom line, and he has demonstrated an interest in developing nations, where he can mix business with theology and achieve two purposes: spread the gospel according to Pat among populations that haven't heard it, and make a few dollars while doing it.

Notes

1. Joseph Coccaro, "CBN Sowing Seeds for Day Leader Goes," *Virginian-Pilot* (May 24, 1992) and Mark O'Keefe, "Robertson Built Empire on Theology of Capitalism," Religious News Service (July 8, 1994).

2. John Taylor, "Pat Robertson's God, Inc." *Esquire* (November 1994).

3. Michael McManus, "Televangelist Pat Robertson Grows Ever Bolder," *Pueblo Chieftain* (October 24, 1992).

4. Pat Robertson, *Philadelphia Inquirer* (May 2, 1993). Reprinted in *The Exempt Organization Tax Review* (July 1993).

5. Michael McManus, "Pat Robertson & Son: Greed vs. Gospel," *Muncie Star* (October 17, 1992).

6. Anthony Ramirez, "From Evangelical TV Roots to a Stock Offering's Riches," *New York Times* (April 18, 1992).

7. "Robertson Bullish on Family Channel, UPI," *Christianity Today* (June 22, 1992).

8. Ibid.

9. Pat Robertson, *Answers to 200 of Life's Most Probing Questions* (Nashville: Thomas Nelson Publishers, 1984), p. 242.

10. Michael Isikoff and Mark Hosenball, "With God There's No Cap," *Newsweek* (October 3, 1994).

11. Ibid.

12. Ibid.

13. Mark O'Keefe, "Watchdogs Wary of CBN-Robertson Deal," *Virginian-Pilot* (August 20, 1993).

14. Marc Davis, "Pat Robertson Sues Executive He Fired," *Virginian-Pilot* (October 11, 1995).

15. Louis Jacobson, "Christians Only: Hiring Bias a Fact at Founders Inn," *Virginian-Pilot* (July 29, 1991).

16. Bill Geroux, "Group Dances, But Inn Is Closed," *Richmond Times-Dispatch* (June 1, 1992).

17. Coccaro, "CBN Sowing Seeds."

18. Mark O'Keefe, "Robertson: Faithful Servant or Shrewd Investor?" reprinted from the *Virginian-Pilot* by Religious News Service (July 8, 1994).

19. Coccaro, "CBN Sowing Seeds."

20. Mark O'Keefe, "CBN Withdraws from Better Business Bureau," *Virginian-Pilot* (October 30, 1992).

21. Robertson, *Answers*, p. 205.

22. Thomas W. Lippman, "Conservative Activists Seek U.S. Visa for Mobutu," *Washington Post* (August 5, 1995).

23. Ibid.

24. Ibid.

25. Gustav Spohn, "Ire Is Response to Pat Robertson's Trip to Zaire," Religious News Service (March 16, 1992).

26. Ibid.

27. "Enemies of the Press," *Parade* (September 17, 1995).

28. Andrew Purvis, "Jewels for Jesus," *Time* (February 27, 1995).

29. Carlos Salinas, "Shattered Lives in Guatemala," *Washington Post* (August 15, 1995).

30. Pat Robertson, *The New World Order* (Dallas: Word Publishing, 1991), p. 228.

31. The Rev. Brian M. Abshire, "Those Who Live in a Dark Land, Will Have a Great Light: The Christian Reconstruction of Zambia," *Chalcedon Report* (August 1995).

32. Robertson, *The New World Order*, p. 234.

8

The American Center for
Law and Justice:
Pat Robertson's Legal "SWAT Team"

"The Apostle Paul said there is a door wide open and effective and
the gospel has been opened unto me. You and me together have
opened a wide and effective door for the Christian people in this
nation to proclaim their faith. . . . This thing, the American Center
for Law and Justice, is God's answer at the right time."
                                    —Pat Robertson, "The 700 Club"[1]

There is probably no organization in the country that Pat
Robertson despises more than the American Civil Liberties
Union. Though Robertson takes frequent potshots at the National Organization for Women (NOW), Planned Parenthood,
Americans United for Separation of Church and State, teachers' unions, homosexual rights groups, and others, no organization can raise his ire like the ACLU.

Although he can't stand the ACLU, Robertson has tried on
two occasions to imitate the group by creating Religious Right
versions of the organization. The first effort, the National
Legal Foundation, was abandoned by Robertson in the 1980s
after he had some kind of falling out with its director, Robert

Skolrood. The second attempt, the American Center for Law and Justice (ACLJ), has been much more successful.

Robertson first began soliciting support for the ACLJ in the summer of 1990. He announced that the ACLJ would be a joint project of the Christian Coalition and Regent University. That soon changed, however, and today the ACLJ has no official connection to the Coalition. Soon Robertson recruited Jay Sekulow, a Jew who had converted to evangelical Christianity, to head up the ACLJ. Sekulow had been running Christian Advocates Serving Evangelism, his own small Religious Right legal group, in Atlanta.

The ACLJ got off to a slow start. But a year after it was founded, Robertson began an aggressive direct-mail fundraising campaign from his supporters. Raising the standard right-wing bogeymen, he promised that contributions would be used to build a state-by-state network of attorneys, springing from Regent University. "To enter lawsuits, prepare briefs, travel to places of injustice costs money," observed one Robertson ACLJ fundraising letter. "But with the present conservative majority on the Supreme Court we can begin to win. We can drive the ACLU back into the fringes of society from where they came and guarantee to our children a society that once more is 'One nation under God.' . . . This is America, founded as one nation under God. A Christian country. Yet we have permitted the courts and the schools at taxpayers' expense to launch an unbelievable vendetta against every expression of religion in our society. . . . This is our country and you can no longer take it away from us."[2]

It wasn't until April 1992 that the ACLJ really began to take off. Addressing his "700 Club" audience, Robertson announced plans to dramatically expand the ACLJ, including opening an office in every federal appellate court district. Today the organization boasts an annual budget of $8 million and thirteen full-time attorneys on staff. It claims nearly half a million contributors and says it has five hundred volunteer attorneys around the country willing to donate time to its cases.

Robertson was exuberant in announcing the hiring of Sekulow. "It's going to be good," Robertson crowed. "It's an important thing we've been hoping for." Later in the same broadcast he and Sekulow railed against public education, with Robertson asserting, "Children are being beat up by humanist teachers and misguided educators all over America. It's happening every day, isn't it?"[3]

Sekulow was a good choice for Robertson. Loud, aggressive, and occasionally rude, Sekulow is the type of person who can match Robertson word for word in rhetorical exchanges. Even his critics admit that Sekulow's legal skills are top notch, and, despite his frequent rhetorical excesses when appearing on "The 700 Club" with Robertson, he can appear quite reasonable. Sekulow, like many Robertson employees, seems to have two different personae. When on camera with Robertson he doesn't hesitate to rage militantly against the courts and public education and denounce the plot to keep Christians from exercising their rights. In other forums, he appears to be a moderate who simply wants to guarantee that evangelical Christians and other religious people enjoy their free speech rights.

Sekulow made his name in evangelical circles early on by defending antiabortion protesters, especially Randall Terry of Operation Rescue. During the summer of 1991, when Terry's followers besieged abortion clinics in Wichita, Kansas, Sekulow worked doggedly to keep Terry out of jail. Later Terry remarked, "Jay's courtroom savvy and constitutional knowledge have been absolutely critical in the growth and survival of Operation Rescue. Without his intervention, I believe several judges would have tried to crush the life out of our movement."[4]

The ACLJ has continued to defend radical antiabortion activists in a series of cases around the country. Its attorneys have argued in court that judges have no right to establish "zones" around abortion clinics where protesters may not enter. The goal of the "zones" to is to keep the clinics open while still permitting antiabortion protesters to demonstrate. The group also filed suit against the Freedom of Access to

Clinic Entrances Act, a federal law designed to keep anti-abortion extremists from denying women the right to physically enter abortion clinics. The group's track record in defending antiabortion protesters has been spotty. On June 29, 1994, the Supreme Court ruled 6 to 3 that these "zones" do not violate the First Amendment's free speech clause. Sekulow was devastated. "By endorsing a zone of exclusion, the Court crushes both the pro-life message and its messengers," he said with characteristic hyperbole. "This decision has devastating consequences for the pro-life movement."

In the decision, written by conservative Chief Justice William H. Rehnquist, the Court's majority upheld the creation of a thirty-six-foot "zone" around an abortion clinic in Melbourne, Florida. Rehnquist said creation of the "zone" was necessary to "accomplish the government interest at stake": protecting access to the clinic. Nothing in the *Madsen* v. *Women's Health Center* decision curtails abortion opponents' rights to physically visit the clinic and demonstrate. From a distance of thirty-six feet, they can still wave signs, yell slogans, and attempt to persuade clients to change their minds. What Operation Rescue and similar extremist groups had sought was constitutional protection for their efforts to physically bar women from entering the clinics; in essence, they wanted legal protection of their efforts to stop others from exercising their legal rights. The Court didn't buy their argument.

Samuel Rabinove, legal director for the American Jewish Committee, summed up well the flaw in the ACLJ's argument. "The tactics of the antiabortion zealots go far beyond protected speech," he said. "Their unlawful conduct aims to force the closing of every abortion clinic in the country, notwithstanding the constitutional right of a woman to choose abortion." Mark Freedman, a regional director for the American Jewish Congress, similarly noted, "The majority of the Supreme Court has recognized that free speech rights do not include harassment, intimidation, and physical violence."

Even before the ruling, antiabortion extremists vowed to continue their activities regardless of what the Court said. "We must continue to do as our Lord commands us, and work at 'abortuaries' to save mothers and babies from the horror of the abortion holocaust," said Don Treshman, national director of Rescue America, in a statement. By constantly looking for loopholes in cases with which it disagrees and recommending evading the clear meaning of the Supreme Court in religion-in-public-schools cases, the ACLJ may fail to make it clear to its clients that they are not free to ignore court rulings that don't go their way.

The abortion clinic "zone" case was a rare loss for Sekulow. Generally speaking, his legal track record is impressive. He argued his first case before the Supreme Court in 1986. Sekulow's first big crack at a religious liberty case occurred when he was asked to defend Jews for Jesus, an evangelical Christian group that targets Jews for conversion. The organization had filed suit challenging a Los Angeles ordinance curbing the distribution of religious literature at Los Angeles International Airport. The case went all the way to the Supreme Court, where it was an easy win for Sekulow. The ordinance, passed in 1984 in preparation for the Olympic Games, was clearly unconstitutional. Nevertheless, Sekulow's first visit to the Court was not without flaws. *American Lawyer* magazine reported he was "rude and aggressive" as well as "so nervous that at times he appeared to be out of control."[5] Sekulow has since argued five cases before the Supreme Court, and he is no longer rude before the justices (though he is still aggressive) and certainly he is not visibly nervous.

Before turning to First Amendment law, Sekulow was a prosecutor with the tax litigation division of the IRS. He later entered private practice, establishing a firm with Stuart J. Roth, a friend who is also a converted Jew. The law practice grew rapidly. By the mid-1980s, reported the *Los Angeles Times*, Sekulow "was earning $250,000 a year and had bought a large house in the suburbs, entertaining frequently and lavishly."[6] But in 1987 the firm abruptly crashed, and Sekulow filed for bankruptcy. The practice had been plagued by financial problems, and some former employees had sued Sekulow. One woman, Joyce F. Glucksman, left a job she had held for eight years to go to work for Sekulow, only to be subsequently fired in what was called a cost-cutting move. Glucksman, who suffers from spina bifida, lost her health coverage and sued, winning a judgment of $1.8 million.[7] The bankruptcy filings showed just how dire Sekulow's financial situation had become. According to the papers filed in bankruptcy court, Sekulow's law firm had debts of $13,071,748 against assets of $638,000 when it went under.[8]

Shifting gears, Sekulow began working to make a name for himself in religious liberty cases. He soon came to the attention of Paul Crouch, Sr., of the Trinity Broadcasting Network. Shortly after he won the Jews for Jesus case, Sekulow appeared on Crouch's "Praise the Lord" talk show, in what was to become the first of many visits to TBN. At the time, Sekulow was just getting his group, Christian Advocates Serving Evangelism, off the ground. He was amazed at how much contributions to the organization escalated after his appearances on Crouch's show. In one year alone, donations to the group quadrupled, a phenomenon Sekulow attributes solely to his appearances on Trinity. "I was personally shocked at the reach of television, and I still am," Sekulow said. "I saw that this could be a very important part of what I do in the education process. . . . I really believe the Lord used TBN to open a complete array of ministries that I work with."[9]

Crouch gave Sekulow his own show, "Call to Action: Legal Issues Facing Christians Today." Staged in a set designed to look like a courtroom, the show features Sekulow interviewing law professors, attorneys, and clients of Religious Right legal groups. Crouch also featured Sekulow prominently in TBN publications and hosted more appearances by him during annual fundraising appeals.

Crouch also sponsored Sekulow's own foray into the business side of broadcasting. In 1989 Sekulow and Crouch's son, Paul Crouch, Jr., established Sonlight Broadcasting System by purchasing three television stations in the South for $2 million. The elder Crouch propped up Sonlight by pouring $3 million of Trinity money into the venture. Sonlight, which is tax exempt, now owns full-power stations in six cities—Mobile, Alabama; Holly Springs, Mississippi; Montgomery, Alabama; Chattanooga, Tennessee; Dalton, Georgia; and Hendersonville, Tennessee. The firm also owns ten low-power stations. Stuart Roth, Sekulow's old law firm partner, runs the company. "For this lawyer, to be able to communicate the message that I feel I'm supposed to communicate, it's important to be on as many television stations as you can be on," Sekulow told the *Los Angeles Times*. "And being director of Sonlight gives you a little bit different flexibility."[10]

Crouch, Sr., was so pleased with Sekulow that he wrote to Robertson urging the Virginia evangelist to invite him to be a guest on "The 700 Club." Robertson agreed, leading to the close association between the two men and eventually Sekulow's ascension to chief counsel for the ACLJ.

Although Sekulow is undoubtedly the ACLJ's star, technically he is not the top man at the organization. The group's executive director is Keith Fournier, a "charismatic" Roman Catholic who practices a Pentecostal theology and strident opponent of legal abortion. Fournier has been at the forefront of one of the ACLJ's more distasteful activities: the coining of the phrase "religious cleansing" to describe the alleged "persecution" of right-wing Christians in the United States. The ACLJ began pushing this phrase shortly after civil war erupted in Yugoslavia. Every day the newspapers were full of horrific tales of "ethnic cleansing"—entire categories of people being systematically killed, abused, or forcibly relocated simply because of their ethnic background.

For some reason, ACLJ staffers thought it would be appropriate to pick up on this theme for advertising. One ACLJ ad that ran in newspapers in the fall of 1993 deplored the tragedy in the Balkans but then went on to make the following assertion: "Tragically, this pattern of intolerance is being

applied to a very large number of our fellow Americans today
. . . God-fearing Americans. Advocates of 'religious cleansing'
will not rest until every vestige of religion is erased from the
public arena. Our public interest law firm is all too familiar
with the zeal of their attack." The ad goes on to warn: "The
censors and bigots must be stopped. Or one day, the world
will witness Balkan-style persecution and destruction in a
place it never expected. The United States of America."

Fournier penned a booklet, *Religious Cleansing in the American Republic,* which was offered to people during the ad campaign. In the booklet Fournier asserts, "Just as ethnic cleansing attempts to rid certain ethnic groups and their influence
from public life, so religious cleansing attempts to do the same
with religious groups, their beliefs, and their values. How?
Not by physical extermination—at least not in the United
States—but by political and legal containment."[11] Discussing
a Supreme Court action over graduation prayer a June 9, 1993,
on "The 700 Club," Robertson said, "This is like Bosnia. The
ACLU becomes the Serbs of America." Added Sekulow, "They
are the new censors."

Robertson occasionally compares the alleged persecution
of Christians in America to what the Jews endured during
Nazi Germany. In a previous chapter, I discussed how offensive this tactic is. Fournier's "religious cleansing" claims are
just as repugnant and in equally poor taste. In the former Yugoslavia, people have been murdered, men have been im-
prisoned and starved, women have been raped, and families
have been divided and driven from their homes. Can this type
of abuse possibly compare with a court ruling striking down
the display of a religious symbol on government property? Is
a valedictorian who is told to refrain from turning her speech
into a sermon because of the captive nature of the public
school audience on the same level with a Bosnian woman
whose husband has been murdered and whose children are
missing? *Nothing* that is going on the United States today can
compare to the horrors of the Balkan civil war, and Fournier

and Robertson should both be ashamed of themselves for making such a suggestion so casually.

Not content with linking advocacy of separation of church and state to Nazis and Balkan hoodlums, the ACLJ has also labored to tie the concept to communism. It is incredible that years after the collapse of the Communist Bloc that any organization would still be engaging in red baiting, yet the ACLJ does so without shame. In 1994 the organization ran ads in right-wing publications under the headline, "HAVE WE WON THE COLD WAR . . . ONLY TO LOSE OUR OWN FREEDOM?" The ads compared the wall of separation between church and state to the Berlin Wall. The organization actually had the unmitigated gall to refer to that protective barrier as "America's Wall" and said its effects have been "devastating."

In many Soviet-controlled East Bloc countries, religion was either co-opted by the government or suppressed. In Albania, for example, all religious expression was outlawed under communism. In the United States, we enjoy complete religious freedom for everyone. The two situations are absolutely not comparable, and again, nothing that has occurred in the United States in recent years comes even remotely close to the oppression of freedom those who lived behind the Berlin Wall experienced.

The ad's imagery was misleading. Two photos were used: one showing the collapse of the Berlin Wall and another depicting police dragging away an Operation Rescue (OR) antiabortion protester. Can these two images be reconciled? Of course not. The ACLJ's implication is that in arresting OR members, police are denying Americans their free speech rights. What the group does not point out is that most overzealous antiabortion protesters are arrested for acts that go way beyond simple marches or pickets. As has been mentioned, OR members seek to shut down abortion clinics, and to that end they frequently block access to the facilities, chain themselves to cars that block driveways, padlock doors, squirt glue in locks, or slip foul-smelling substances or acid into clinics through mail slots. These types of activities are not examples of constitutionally protected free speech, and the police are right to arrest those who engage in them.

Operation Rescue members have the right to protest abortion, but they have no right to physically block buildings and deny women their right to enter the clinics. Whether the ACLJ likes it or not, abortion is currently a legal practice, and no OR supporter has the right to use intimidation to stop women from availing themselves of the procedure. When the police use a modicum of force to remove OR members, which they often must do because the protesters "go limp" and refuse to cooperate, they are protecting the rights of women and others to enter the clinics, not denying OR members' rights to free speech or assembly.

A final offensive metaphor that the ACLJ uses frequently is "religious apartheid." Actually, this phrase isn't even original, having been coined some years ago by John Whitehead of the Rutherford Institute, another extreme Religious Right legal group. The ACLJ has adopted it, and it often pops up in the group's ads and writings.

The apartheid regime of South Africa was a moral outrage that earned the country international ostracism and condemnation. Under an official policy of racial discrimination, whites enjoyed privileges and a standard of living that blacks and those of mixed race could not achieve because of legally imposed barriers. Today, South Africa has finally dismantled apartheid. No Christian in modern-day America experiences anything like what blacks went through in South Africa under apartheid. Despite the incessant whining from the Religious Right, Christians in America enjoy an unparalleled measure of religious freedom. They may attend any church they like, print and distribute religious publications, engage in door-to-door evangelism, own and operate television and radio ministries, run schools and universities, take part in social service ministries, and address moral and political issues. And they can do all of these things without paying one dime in federal, state, or local taxes. It is a great irony that separation of church and state—the very mechanism that ensures Robertson's right to spread his propaganda—is so often attacked by him.

Can religious individuals or religious groups expect the government's help in spreading these sectarian messages? Absolutely not. The government, in fact, is forbidden from assisting in evangelism. To do so would be an establishment of religion in violation of the First Amendment. Can religious groups and people demand financial aid from the government to run wholly sectarian programs? They can demand it, but the state can't give it.

Nevertheless, the ACLJ continues to send out fundraising mail that is typically extreme. One ACLJ letter, signed by Robertson, warned that "[T]oday we see a deliberate, all-out effort to eradicate religious belief from every vestige of public life." Another letter, signed by Keith Fournier, insisted, "Our culture is under fire. The beliefs we cherish are being attacked at every point. It is time to take a stand." In another letter Robertson declared, "It is time to stop the ACLU, secular humanists, and anti-family organizations that are destroying our freedoms."

In the ACLJ's universe, anyone who dares to disagree with the group's oppressive agenda is labeled "anti-family," "anti-God," or a "secular humanist." Advocates of separation of church and state are trying to "destroy Christianity." The organization seems to have learned all it knows about rhetorical excess from its sibling, the Christian Coalition.

And, like the Christian Coalition, ACLJ staff members frequently tell the American public one thing and the true believers quite another. Like Robertson, Fournier and Sekulow have been all over the map on the matter of separation of church and state. As indicated previously, the ACLJ has attacked the wall of separation in its publications and even likened it to the Berlin Wall. But on other occasions, Fournier has claimed to support church-state separation. Addressing a conference sponsored by Americans United for Separation of

Church and State in October of 1995, the ACLJ director said, "Properly understood, separation of church and state is a principle that is important and that we must not abandon."

Note the qualifier "properly understood." This type of hedging language is the same device Robertson employs to have it both ways on church-state separation. He can ridicule the constitutional principle on "The 700 Club" and later tell Larry King he supports it 100 percent. Fournier's "properly understood" church-state separation means essentially no established church. He made it quite clear to Americans United that he disagrees with the modern body of church-state law, which includes the rulings striking down school-sponsored prayer in public schools and unrestricted government aid to religious institutions. Like Robertson, Fournier's notion of separation of church and state is so limited as to be virtually meaningless.

The ACLJ's hyperbole is matched only by its erroneous interpretations of the law. Although the organization hires skilled attorneys, it insists on distorting the law and the opinions of the U.S. Supreme Court. What's worse, it spreads these distortions throughout the country in letters to public school officials and municipal leaders. These missives are generally thinly veiled threats to sue unless the public officials start doing what the ACLJ wants. A prime example of this type of ACLJ-sponsored intimidation occurred after the Supreme Court struck down clergy-led graduation prayer at public schools in 1992. The decision in the *Lee* v. *Weisman* case was close, 5 to 4, but nevertheless the Religious Right lost. Robertson, Sekulow, and the ACLJ immediately began looking for ways to circumvent the ruling.

Some months after the decision, a federal appeals court upheld a graduation prayer scheme from a public school in Texas that permitted prayer as long as it was student-led as well as "nondenominational" and "nonproselytizing." As an added feature, a majority of the students had to first vote on the prayer, with the majority vote carrying the day. Why this scheme was upheld by a federal court remains a mystery, but nevertheless it became law in three states—Texas, Louisiana, and Mississippi. The Supreme Court later refused to hear an appeal of the ruling, which is not surprising, since the Court on average hears less than 2 percent of the cases appealed to it. Also, the Supreme Court usually does not take on cases until split decisions have occurred in the lower courts.

As graduation season 1993 approached, the ACLJ sent mailings to every public school district in the country informing the officials that "student-initiated" prayer at commencement was a constitutionally protected right and threatening to sue any school that did not buckle under. An ACLJ press release promised that the group would dispatch "SWAT TEAMS to communities around the country to meet with school and government officials to inform them that student-initiated prayer is a constitutionally protected right."

The organization ignored a few salient points, however. First, the Fifth Circuit Court of Appeals never ruled in the Texas case that public schools were *required* to permit student prayer. It simply declared that the mechanism used by one school district in the state to allow it was constitutional. Second, and more importantly, the scope of that ruling (*Jones* v. *Clear Creek Independent School District*) was limited to the three states already mentioned. Public schools in other parts of the country were not affected by it in the least.

Critics pointed out that the Robertson legal unit was trying to mislead school officials and trying to evade the clear intent of the Supreme Court. In Michigan, state education officials knew what the group was trying to do. Frank Kelley, the state's attorney general, advised local schools to ignore the ACLJ missive. "It's just a plaintive wish on Pat Robertson's part," Kelley told the Associated Press. "I've yet to read any place that he's a constitutional scholar. They've got a dissident ruling from a lower court in some other part of the country, and they're jumping upon it and trying to give it precedent value and that's a legal argument that can't be followed. That has no effect." Linda Bruin, general counsel for the Michigan

Association of School Boards, was equally blunt. "They can say what they want," she said, "but they've not done a very good job of presenting what the law is. I just don't think they've done a very good legal analysis."[12]

In pushing the "student-initiated" graduation prayer scheme, the ACLJ was trying to make history repeat itself. After the 1962 and 1963 Supreme Court rulings striking down government-sponsored religious exercises in public schools, a few states tried to get around the ban by passing laws reinstating daily, vocal, classroom prayers as long as they were led by student "volunteers." The federal courts quickly struck down these obvious attempts to circumvent the Court's decisions.

When the Supreme Court refused to hear an appeal of the *Jones* case, Robertson and Sekulow celebrated as if the school prayer decisions of the early 1960s had been overturned. A beaming Robertson appeared on "The 700 Club" with Sekulow, insisting that the Court's inaction was in fact an affirmative decision in favor of "student-initiated" graduation prayer. Speaking of *Jones*, Sekulow asserted, "In one sentence, the Supreme Court affirms the decision below." This was totally incorrect. The Supreme Court did not affirm the ruling in *Jones*; the justices simply decided not to hear an appeal of it. When the Court refuses a case, the lower decision stands, but this is not the same as an affirmance. Sekulow surely knows this. It is the type of information that law students learn during their first year of study. Why then did he choose to mislead the "700 Club" viewing audience, most of whom, not being lawyers and not understanding the intricacies of how the Supreme Court operates, must have concluded that something significant had occurred?

The same day that the Court refused to hear an appeal of *Jones*, the justices issued an opinion in a separate case, *Lamb's Chapel* v. *Center Moriches Union Free School District*. In this case the Court ruled unanimously that a public high school in New York must allow a Christian group to rent its facilities after hours because nonreligious groups had been given the same right. The Court's ruling was no surprise. In fact, the decision merely restated previously settled law. Use of a public school or other government-owned facilities after hours by religious groups normally does not present church-state problems. After all, if it's a weekend or 7 P.M., the students aren't present and no one is required to go. As long as the events are not school-sponsored, there should be no problems. The Court's action in *Lamb's Chapel* gave religious groups no rights they didn't already have, but according to Sekulow, it was as if the Court had knocked down the wall of separation between church and state. He insisted that the ruling would give groups the right to sponsor baccalaureate services in public schools and ensure that students could give "Christian testimony" in schools. All of this was wishful thinking. As Steven K. Green, a lawyer with Americans United for Separation of Church and State, pointed out, "Nothing in the *Lamb's Chapel* ruling changes the law concerning school prayer. Sekulow's analysis reflects wishful thinking on the part of the ACLJ. It's either that or a deliberate distortion designed to convince viewers of 'The 700 Club' that Robertson's attorneys have won a great victory so they will send money."

During the broadcast, both Sekulow and Robertson gleefully attacked advocates of church-state separation and ridiculed their views. An uninformed viewer might have assumed that groups like the ACLU and Americans United had sided with the New York school district. In fact, both organizations, citing freedom of religion and the right of all groups to use public facilities, filed court briefs on the side of the church.

Keith Fournier, the executive director of the ACLJ, has apparently learned nothing from Sekulow's missteps. In June of 1995, the Supreme Court dismissed another graduation prayer case, this one from Idaho, declaring the case moot since the student who brought the challenge had graduated. Fournier appeared on Robertson's program and distorted the Supreme Court's action in *Joint School District 241* v. *Harris,* saying the court had declared student-led prayer "constitutionally protected." Like Sekulow, Fournier gave the misleading impression that the Court's action made graduation prayer legal in the western states. Fournier went so far as to assert, "The issue is settled." He also asserted that the Court's action set aside the Ninth Circuit Court of Appeals ruling but left the District Court ruling (which upheld student-led prayers) intact. That is simply wrong; when the Court vacates a judgment for reasons of mootness, all lower court opinions are dismissed.

Other members of the evangelical legal community interpreted the Court's action honestly. Steve MacFarland of the Christian Legal Society pointed out in a press statement that the Court's action had not resolved the question of graduation prayer and, like separationist groups, criticized the Court for dodging the issue. Why couldn't the ACLJ do the same? One is tempted to believe that these gross distortions of Supreme Court actions by ACLJ staffers are done deliberately. After all, distortions do serve an important purpose: they lead the ACLJ's donors to conclude that great victories have been won. Many of the ACLJ's donors are probably concerned over the issue of prayer in public schools. Many might like to see the Supreme Court's school prayer rulings overturned. But the truth is, there simply hasn't been much progress in this area for the Religious Right. The Supreme Court has shown no inclination to strike down the 1962 and 1963 decisions. The type of religious activity in public schools the Court has upheld, such as the Equal Access Act, deals with truly voluntary activity by students. Even groups that advocate church-state separation don't take issue with this. Lacking any meaningful victories over the issue of prayer in schools, the ACLJ is forced to invent them. But the reality remains: *nothing has changed.* School-sponsored or mandatory prayer or religious exercises are still illegal in public schools.

The ACLJ has distorted other religion-in-public-school issues as well. In February of 1994, the ACLJ sent a letter to U.S. Attorney General Janet Reno, urging the Justice Department to investigate alleged widespread abuses of the Equal Access Act. The act permits students in public secondary schools to form voluntary religious clubs during noninstructional time. The clubs must be student run; teachers may be present at the meetings to keep order, but they may not participate in religious activities with the students. In 1990, the Supreme Court upheld the constitutionality of the law by an 8 to 1 vote, in a case argued by Sekulow.

Even though he defended the Equal Access Act before the high court, Sekulow did not hesitate to distort its provisions for the purpose of aiding the ACLJ's publicity stunt. In a press release about the letter to Reno, Sekulow is quoted as saying, "If a school permits a French club or a science club to meet, they must permit the formation of a Bible group or a prayer group. It's that simple."[13] In fact, the Equal Access Act says exactly the opposite. Public secondary schools are required to permit Bible groups on campus only if other "noncurriculum" related groups are permitted to meet. Obviously, French and science clubs would be curriculum related; their presence would not trigger the act. Separationist groups wrote to Sekulow and asked him to correct the record. He never did.

Shortly after the Equal Access Act was upheld in 1990, Sekulow proclaimed that born-again Christians must use the act to evangelize in public schools. "Our purpose must be to spread the gospel on the new mission field that the Lord has opened— public high schools," he wrote in the July newsletter of Christian Advocates Serving Evangelism. "This victory that the Lord has provided affirms that it is okay to have Christian beliefs and to share them with others. Yes, the so-called 'wall of separation' between church and state has begun to crumble."[14]

This was a clear distortion of the act's provisions. It allows only for *student-initiated, purely voluntary* religious clubs on the campuses of public secondary schools under certain conditions. These clubs cannot be sponsored by the school and cannot be engineered by outside religious groups. Nothing in the act gives outside religious groups the right to proselytize on public school grounds.

A more recent ACLJ legal effort underscores how much of what the group does just happens to benefit Robertson. In

April of 1995, a phalanx of ACLJ attorneys came to Washington to announce that the organization was suing the Internal Revenue Service on behalf of a fundamentalist church in New York that lost its tax-exempt status for partisan politicking. Under the IRS code, churches and other tax-exempt organizations are not permitted to engage in partisan politicking. The prohibition is designed to keep organizations that supposedly operate in the public interest from becoming front groups for political campaigns. Office-seekers must run their campaigns through political action committees (PACs). Were nonprofit groups like churches permitted to go political, there would be no more need for PACs, and Americans would lose control of a large portion of the political process. PACs, for example, must meet stringent reporting requirements and maintain lists of donors for public inspection.

During the closing days of the 1992 presidential campaign, the Church at Pierce Creek in Vestal, New York, placed full-page newspaper ads in *USA Today* and other publications warning people not to vote for Bill Clinton. Headlined "CHRISTIAN BEWARE," the ad charged that Clinton "supports abortion on demand . . . the homosexual lifestyle . . . and giving condoms to teenagers in public schools." Concluded the ad, "Do not put the economy ahead of the Ten Commandments. The Bible warns us not to follow another man in his sin, nor help him promote sin—lest God chasten *us*. How then can we vote for Bill Clinton?" Americans United for Separation of Church and State promptly filed a formal complaint with the IRS, including a copy of the ad. The IRS investigated and pulled the church's tax exemption.

IRS rules forbid churches and other nonprofits from endorsing candidates for public office or giving a "negative endorsement" by attacking one candidate to the extent that his or her opponent is effectively endorsed. Nonprofit groups accept this stipulation as a condition of receiving tax exemption. Churches and other nonprofits are not required to accept the deal. They remain free to endorse candidates all they want, but if they do, they have to pay taxes just like a PAC. The Church at Pierce Creek and its pastor, Daniel Little, decided they wanted all of the benefits of tax exemption and none of the responsibilities. Hence the lawsuit.

Why the ACLJ's involvement? Sekulow appeared on "The 700 Club" and tried to frame the issue as one of religious freedom. The church, he said, was being muzzled by the IRS for its conservative political views. Sekulow also called the *Church at Pierce Creek* v. *Richardson* suit "our most important religious freedom case." "The IRS has set a very dangerous precedent that now reaches into the four walls of the church . . . ," Sekulow insisted. "We're not going to allow this church or any church to be told what they can or cannot say because the IRS doesn't think the position of the church is in some way politically correct."

Political correctness, of course, had nothing to do with the case. The Church at Pierce Creek did not lose its tax-exempt status for being right-wing. It lost it for engaging in partisan politics in violation of the IRS code. Had the church wanted to get political, all it had to do was give up its tax exemption and jump right into partisan politics. No liberal or mainstream church had been so brazen to place such blatantly political ads. If one had, it's a safe bet the IRS would have cracked down on it as well.

Consider, for a minute, what will occur if the ACLJ wins this case (which, at this writing, is still in court). Every church in the country will be able to get as heavily involved in politics as it chooses and still not pay anything in taxes. Politicians could virtually run their campaigns out of churches. Why establish a PAC, which must pay taxes and meet government reporting requirements, when a nonprofit group or church can do the work free from regulations?

Now consider this: through the Christian Coalition, Pat Robertson has been trying to enlist evangelical and fundamentalist churches in his political machine. Some church leaders have resisted, believing that partisan political work might violate their tax-exempt status. Now imagine that the IRS is ordered by the court to stop enforcing the ban on political activity by churches. Who benefits? Robertson, for one. Every on-the-fence or wavering church now has no excuse for not backing his highly partisan crusade. All over the country, churches could become little more than cogs in Robertson's giant right-wing political machine.

The ACLJ denies that's what the Church at Pierce Creek case is about, but one can be forgiven for doubting them. Anti-abortion activist Randall Terry sits on the church's board of directors. Terry has known Pastor Little for many years and looks to him as a mentor. Given Sekulow and Terry's prior relationship, one can see the interest Robertson must have in this case. Shortly after the case was filed, I debated an ACLJ lawyer on a talk radio program and brought up the Robertson connection and his motives for being interested in this case. The man began issuing frantic denials. However, ACLJ attorneys generally dislike being reminded that they work for Pat Robertson. Those of us in the separationist camp always make it a point during debates and talk radio and television appearances to mention that Robertson founded the group. If left to them, ACLJ attorneys would never mention this salient point. One wonders of what they are ashamed.

Finally, I should point out that the ACLJ, like other Robertson projects, has been guilty of associating with extremists. On April 19, 1995, Benjamin Bull, senior trial counsel for the ACLJ, addressed the Phoenix Business and Professional Chapter of the John Birch Society, a far-right organization that has been lurking on the fringes of American politics for decades. According to the *Phoenix Gazette,* Bull's topic was "Government's War on Religious Expression."

The ACLJ also has ties to Paul Hill, an antiabortion extremist and defrocked preacher who admitted shooting Dr. John Britton to death outside of a Pensacola, Florida, abortion clinic in July 1994.* Three ACLJ attorneys had been defending Hill in

---

*Hill has been convicted and sentenced to die in Florida's electric chair, but the case is being appealed.

a separate case against charges that his loud protests at the clinic violated the city's antinoise ordinance. After the shooting, the ACLJ tried to drop Hill as a client, but a county judge in Florida ordered attorneys Michael Hirsh, John Stepanovich, and Charles Hoskins to stay on the case. The Norfolk *Virginian-Pilot* later reported that Hirsh had authored an article for the law review at Regent University Law School arguing that killing abortion doctors is justifiable homicide. Citing the murder of Dr. David Gunn at a Florida abortion clinic in 1993, Hirsh noted that state law permits the use of deadly force if it will prevent "imminent death or great bodily harm."

Regent officials ordered the article pulled from all copies of the journal, but the *Virginian-Pilot* obtained one in August of 1994. Some students complained about censorship, but Terrence R. Lindvall, Regent president, insisted that Hirsh had requested the article be pulled. The ACLJ subsequently fired Hirsh.[15] Shortly thereafter the ACLJ hired Paul Schenck, a radical antiabortion activist, to edit a publication called *Liberty, Life and Family*. Schenck's employment was delayed while he finished a thirty-day prison sentence for lying under oath during a federal trial in 1991. Fournier blithely dismissed Schenck's conviction, saying, "Although we do not condone the incident which gave rise to [the sentence], Mr. Schenck has acknowledged his culpability and is accepting the punishment."

In 1992 Schenck and his twin brother, Robert, who are both ministers in the Assemblies of God, a rigidly fundamentalist denomination, led Operation Rescue protests in Buffalo, New York, designed to close down the city's abortion clinics. They also participated in an incident in which what was claimed to be a dead fetus was presented to then-presidential candidate Bill Clinton.

The existence of the ACLJ gives law students at Robertson's Regent University a place to get experience outside the classroom. Regent is a graduate-level university that offers majors in just five subject areas: law, communications, education, business, and theology. Robertson, who founded the school in 1977, serves as Regent's chancellor. The law school was added to Regent in 1986 after Oral Roberts closed a law school he had been running at Oral Roberts University and donated its library to Robertson.

The secular far right has shown some interest in Regent. Holly Coors, wife of Joe Coors, head of the ultraconservative Coors beer empire, sits on Regent's board of directors. In 1988, the Adolph Coors Foundation gave Regent $50,000. The foundation had made previous grants to the school totaling in the hundreds of thousands.[16] In *Answers to 200 of Life's Most Probing Questions,* Robertson warns against drinking alcohol, but he seems to have no problems accepting money from a foundation that makes its millions selling beer. (Coors money also helped start the Heritage Foundation and the Free Congress Foundation, two largely secular right-wing groups.*)

Coors money has not been enough to shore up Regent, however. In 1992, Robertson's Christian Broadcast Network donated $117 million to Regent to put the school on sound financial footing. At the time he said he hoped to boost enrollment to three thousand students and add several buildings to the campus. Those plans have since been scaled back, and the university currently enrolls fewer than 1,500 students.

As of this writing, Regent's law school had only provisional accreditation from the American Bar Association (ABA) but is seeking full accreditation. The path Robertson chose to meet this goal has not been without controversy. In 1993,

---

*The Heritage Foundation was founded in 1973 by New Right strategist Paul Weyrich, who said he formed the group as a right-wing alternative to the Brookings Institute, a well-known liberal think tank in Washington. He served as president for only a year, however, before using more Coors money to form a political action committee called the Committee for the Survival of a Free Congress. Relying primarily on direct mail solicitations, Weyrich raised millions for the Free Congress PAC, and four years later, in 1977, created another far-right think tank as an adjunct to it called the Free Congress Foundation. Weyrich remains head of the Free Congress Foundation today. The Heritage Foundation and the Free Congress Foundation share similar political goals, although Free Congress has much more interest in the types of social issues championed by the Religious Right.

Robertson and the Regent Board of Trustees fired Law School Dean Herbert W. Titus. The dismissal of Titus, a Religious Right hardliner with unusual views about religion and the law, was widely interpreted as an attempt to move Regent into the legal mainstream. No fan of church-state separation, Titus attempts to fully integrate his interpretation of the Bible into the law. According to the *Virginian-Pilot* newspaper in Norfolk, he has argued that birth control, public education, and affirmative action all violate biblical principles.[17]

Robertson tried to portray Titus's firing as a promotion. He offered to make him an endowed scholar and give him time off to conduct research, travel, and write articles. An angry Titus accepted dismissal instead and later charged to local reporters that Robertson was trying to moderate his image in preparation for another presidential run. Robertson, through spokespeople, denied the charge.

Although Robertson insisted that Titus was not let go for philosophical reasons, the ex-dean argued otherwise. Titus produced memos from former Regent President David Gyertson that criticized his opinions. One noted that the school's board of trustees was concerned about "teaching that did not make a clear distinction between personal points of view and institutional positions." An October 1992 report to the board by the school's provost referred to Titus as "a brilliant and compelling individual," but noted, "while the dean holds some views that are quite diverse, those that seem to receive the greatest amount of attention are considered by some to be overtly rigid and to reflect a narrow view of Scripture."

Titus pointed out that an ABA site team that visited the school lauded him in a report, calling him "an able and dedicated founding dean who, by virtue of his teaching prowess and scholarly productivity, serves as a powerful role model for the faculty."[18]

Following Titus's dismissal, eight Regent faculty members signed a statement protesting the move, which they filed with the ABA. Robertson became livid. He accused the professors of acting like cultists "after the order of Jim Jones or the Branch Davidians" and wrote in a letter to them, "I have never encountered a group of supposedly educated people who were so myopic, so lacking in common sense, or so inept as lawyers." In a letter to the dissenting professors Robertson wrote, "No rational person burns down the house he occupies. No rational professional person seeks to destroy the source of his own employment and career advancement." Robertson asserted that the professors' letter "merely served to reinforce the view held by leaders at the ABA that the Regent Law School was in the grip of extremist fanatics."

Robertson subsequently fired three of the dissenting law professors. J. Nelson Happy, Titus's replacement, denied that the firing had anything to do with the trio's views about the ex-dean and said they were let go for "a lack of scholarship" and having poor attitudes. Some student leaders, however, disputed Happy's contention. "I would say it's definitely in retaliation," said Dean Broyles, 1994 class president. "No question about it. There is no legitimate academic reason to terminate these three people. All were good professors. Academic freedom at Regent is a joke. There is none."[19]

The situation deteriorated during the summer of 1994, when three other Regent professors filed suit against the school challenging its tenure policy. They were joined by two of the law professors who were fired for signing the pro-Titus statement. The five sought reinstatement under Regent's original tenure policy, which granted three-year contracts that were automatically renewed. School officials responded that Regent could not offer lifetime job security and said there was no tenure policy.

The issue of ABA accreditation is a continual thorn in Regent's side. Without accreditation, Regent graduates will not be able to take the bar exam in most states, making their degrees next to worthless. In 1989 a group of university law school graduates filed suit against the ABA, seeking to force the organization to accredit the school. A federal court quickly quashed the lawsuit.

Regent, then CBN University, was initially denied accreditation in 1987. The ABA cited several areas of concern, including fears that the school's requirement that all faculty members sign a statement of faith may jeopardize academic freedom. The state of Virginia later agreed to allow law school graduates to take the bar exam in that state while the question of the institution's accreditation status played out. Now, with provisional accreditation, Regent grads may take the bar.

Regent students may take the bar exam, but can they pass it? The university's law school graduates rank last in passing the Virginia bar. Regent officials say that fact in itself is not significant and argue that students come from all over the nation and return to take bar exams in their own states. Few, they say, take bar exams in Virginia. However, we know that during the period Regent's accreditation was denied, students could take the bar only in Virginia and a few other states, which indicates that higher numbers of Regents grads may have tried to pass the test there.

Despite the attempt to clean house, Regent continues to have credibility problems. In March of 1994 university officials were criticized when it was revealed that the school subscribes to an anti-Semitic magazine that supports the view that the Holocaust never occurred. Regent President Lindvall defended the subscription to the *Journal of Historical Review,* saying, "The university is the best place to confront lies."

The Regent University Law School and the ACLJ enjoy a close relationship. In Virginia Beach, the ACLJ has its offices at the law school. Regent students do work for the Robertson-founded legal organization, and some have been hired by the group after graduation.

Robertson still has a long way to go before the ACLJ can match its archenemy the American Civil Liberties Union. The ACLU has an affiliate in every state. Robertson's ACLJ has a main office in Virginia Beach with branches in Atlanta; Washington, D.C.; Phoenix; and New Hope, Kentucky. The budget of the ACLU dwarfs that of the ACLJ. But the ACLJ has been growing rapidly, and like any Robertson project, it bears watching. Especially if the composition of the Supreme Court changes and a majority of justices turn away from separation of church and state, the group may find its narrow vision of the constitutional rights of Americans transforming into actual law.

Notes

1. Quoted in Mark O'Keefe, "Holy Warriors," *Student Lawyer* (December 1993).

2. Quoted in "Discriminatory Hiring at Robertson Hotel Stirs Virginia Debate," *Church & State* (October 1991).

3. Quoted in Joseph L. Conn, "Courtroom Contender," *Church & State* (June 1992).

4. Mark L. Pinsky, "Legal Weapon," *Los Angeles Times* (September 2, 1993).

5. Ibid.

6. Ibid.

7. Ibid.

8. Ibid.

9. Mark I. Pinsky, "Attorney Convert Wins Again," *Los Angeles Times* (June 8, 1993).

10. Ibid.

11. Keith A. Fournier, *Religious Cleansing in the American Republic* (Washington, D.C.: Liberty, Life, and Family Publications, 1993).

12. Jeff Holyfield, "Attorney General Disputes 'Loopholes' in Ban on School Prayer," Associated Press dispatch, *Ann Arbor News* (March 14, 1993).

13. Quoted in Americans United for Separation of Church and State, letter to Attorney General Janet Reno, February 25, 1994. Also People for the American Way letter to Jay Sekulow, February 25, 1994.

14. "Equal Access Ruling Opens 'Mission Field' in Public Schools, Says Bible Club Attorney," *Church & State* (September 1990).

15. Joe Taylor, "Norfolk Clinic Has History of Violence," Associated Press, printed in the *Washington Times* (January 2, 1995).

16. Russ Bellant, *The Coors Connection* (Boston: South End Press, 1988), p. 50.

17. Mark O'Keefe, "Ex-Regent Dean: His Views Got Him Fired," *Virginian-Pilot* (January 23, 1994).

18. Ibid.

19. Mark O'Keefe, "More Heads Roll at Robertson's Regent University," Religious News Service (May 25, 1994).

9

Closing Thoughts

"We can put together right now a grassroots network that is unparalleled, but we're only a portion of the way there. We must complete the job in all fifty states. . . . We've got more work to do because I like 100 percent, not 60 or 70."
—Pat Robertson, 1995 "Road to Victory" conference

Many foolish things have been written about the Religious Right and the Christian Coalition over the years. While many reporters do an excellent job tracking this movement, others get in over their heads and jump to rash conclusions. Sadly, they end up misleading the public. An example of the latter occurred in *New York* magazine October 23, 1995. An article about the Christian Coalition and the general Religious Right referred to the movement as a "paper tiger" and asserted that it has no real political power and never will.[1]

Such a claim could not be more wrong and was, in fact, shown to be erroneous by events that were unfolding at the time it was written. Just before the article appeared, for example, every major Republican presidential contender except Senator

Arlen Specter (R-Pa.) addressed the Coalition's 1995 "Road to Victory" conference, all pledging fealty to the Coalition's goals. Speaker of the House Newt Gingrich and other prominent Republicans also addressed the organization. Thus, *New York* magazine may believe the Christian Coalition has no significance, but powerful Republicans—who now determine the agenda in Congress thanks to their control of that body—believe differently.

The Christian Coalition clearly has its eyes on the White House for 1996. And if the movement succeeds, it will give the country a show of just how powerful it is. Consider the Supreme Court, for example. Presidents Reagan and Bush tried to pack the federal courts with ultraconservatives who would turn back the clock on church-state matters and other social issues. This was done at the behest of assorted Religious Right groups, who demanded justices who would interpret the Constitution very narrowly. At the Supreme Court level, however, Bush made a fatal misstep when he appointed David Souter, who turned out to be a moderate and an advocate of church-state separation. Because of that error, the Court is now closely divided on church-state questions. Many decisions are 6 to 3 or 5 to 4. The next president, who will probably have the opportunity to name at least one justice, can shift the balance.

The right to legal abortion is hanging by a thin constitutional thread—one or two votes at most. The school prayer decisions and those striking down government aid to sectarian schools are similarly in danger. In fact, all of the Court's decisions on church and state could be overturned by an activist right wing court.

With so much at stake, are we to believe that a president backed by the Christian Coalition and put into office partly due to that group's votes will not put forth a Supreme Court candidate personally approved by the Religious Right? Be assured, that president's first appointee will not be a moderate along the lines of David Souter. He or she will be a Religious Right operative in the mode of Clarence Thomas. And once seated, this new court will begin to change things.

For too long too many Americans have believed the Religious Right will never achieve anything politically because the courts will always protect us. Some who oppose the Religious Right have even voted for candidates backed by the movement because they might agree with them on some secular issue, such as taxation or the national debt, all the while insisting that the courts will trim the far right's excesses.

This view is short-sighted and dangerous. If Religious Right candidates continue to win elections, sooner or later they will change the courts through appointments at all levels. (In states with elected judiciaries it can happen very quickly.) Obviously the courts cannot be a last line of defense against the Religious Right when the judges share the opinions of the movement.

Others have insisted that the Religious Right will never achieve power because the people win rise up and stop its excesses. Frankly, this is a lot to ask of the American people in the latter half of the twentieth century, and there is no guarantee it will happen. Americans have become notoriously apathetic about politics. Voter turnout, even in presidential elections, hovers at around 50 percent. For lower-level (state and local) races it can be much smaller. This power vacuum is just the opening for which extremists long. Will the average American rise up? I wouldn't bet my constitutional freedoms on that hope.

In Congress the situation is similarly dire. A survey undertaken by Americans United for Separation of Church and State and the Interfaith Alliance Foundation in 1995 found that nearly two hundred of Congress's 535 members voted with the Christian Coalition at least 83 percent of the time. Many members had 100 percent voting records in line with the Coalition. These members can and are advancing the Religious Right's agenda in Congress every day. Through its control of congressional committees and its ability to block legislation or amendments it dislikes, the Religious Right-influenced GOP is turning back the clock on civil liberties and working assiduously to rewrite the Bill of Rights. A major priority for the Religious Right is passage of a "Religious Equality Amendment" referred to in chapter 6 that would erase the church-state separation provisions from the First Amendment. Because of the supermajority requirement (two-thirds of each chamber must ratify), constitutional amendments are difficult to pass, but if the Christian Coalition continues sending its people to Congress, eventually the votes will be there to secure passage.

The Christian Coalition and other Religious Right groups have also made impressive gains in state and local politics. Operatives are pushing the groups' agenda—promandatory religion in public schools, provoucher, proreligious majoritarianism, procensorship, antipublic schools, antireproductive freedom—in the statehouses. At the local level, the Religious Right has succeeded in getting people elected to some community school and library boards, where they wreak havoc and work actively to undermine these important public institutions. Some boards—it is impossible to know how many—have been completely taken over by the Religious Right.

How can anyone seriously assert that the Christian Coalition has no real power? The group holds the country's majority political party in a headlock, yet we are to believe it is powerless? Pat Robertson oversees a multimillion-dollar broadcasting and political enterprise that sends orders daily to the Religious Right's activists, who stand ready to flood the Capitol Hill switchboard or flock to the polls on election day with "nonpartisan" voter guides in hand to pull levers for whomever Ralph Reed tells them to, yet the group has no power? Every major GOP presidential hopeful is tripping over himself to curry favor with Ralph Reed and Pat Robertson. One wonders why they waste their time on a paper tiger that is powerless.

From the jaws of defeat in the 1988 GOP primaries, Pat Robertson has snatched a great victory. His Christian Coalition, which grew out of that failed campaign, has been so successful that one is forced to wonder if the entire campaign wasn't merely a ruse to launch a political vehicle. It's true that the 1988 race cost Robertson a good deal of money, but he is an extremely wealthy man who can well afford it. The Christian

Coalition has already repaid Robertson—not in literal cash but in the other benefits he has received, chiefly, a greatly enhanced political stature, although the Coalition's power as a fundraising vehicle should not be dismissed. In 1988 Robertson was widely dismissed as a fringe candidate. Today he has top leaders of the Republican party hanging on his every word.

This book has been an attempt to explain not only how this deplorable state of affairs came about but why it must not be allowed to continue. Robertson's views are extreme, dangerous and, frankly, often bizarre. That such a figure is taken seriously on the political landscape today is a tragedy.

Americans should not be fooled by the mask of moderation worn by Ralph Reed. The Christian Coalition remains an extreme organization under the control of a man whose views on variety of subjects, from women's rights and religious freedom to democracy and church-state separation, are clearly out of the mainstream.

Robertson denies that he is an extremist, and Reed backs his boss up on this. To Americans wondering what the truth is about this increasingly powerful political preacher, I say, "Let them deny it. But be aware: Robertson's record speaks for itself."

Also, consider this: the resources I had at my disposal in preparing this book were vast, but not comprehensive. Robertson has been broadcasting since the 1960s, and much of that time has been blatantly political. Although several groups monitor Robertson today, as far as I know no one person or organization has videotaped, audiotaped, or written down everything he has said over the airwaves. No one has attempted to systematically go through everything he has written in books, magazines, pamphlets, CBN position papers, leaflets, and other forums to ferret out the extremism. Such a task is simply too daunting.

My point is that there may be a lot out there we still do not know about Robertson. No doubt I will hear from folks who want to fill me in on things I have missed or about which I ought to know.

My main concern here has been to prove Robertson's over-all extremism. I believe I have done this by examining his own words and actions. But in the end, the reader is left to synthesize and process this information. My belief is that Robertson is a dangerous menace whose political power must be checked. The influence and power of his Christian Coalition must be challenged by the facts and confronted with its own unreason. Exposing his radical agenda and unusual worldview is one of the most effective ways to begin that process.

I leave the reader with a few questions: Is Robertson the type of leader this country needs as we rush toward the twenty-first century? Is his agenda right for an America that is marked by expanding diversity and religious pluralism? Do his views truly reflect "traditional American values?"

I believe the answer to all of these questions is a clear no. And it is my fervent hope that enough Americans will wake up to the reality of the power Robertson wields, be alarmed by it and do what it takes politically, socially, and morally to pull America away from the precipice over which we as a nation may be about to tumble.

*　　*　　*

For more information about Pat Robertson and the Christian Coalition, contact Americans United for Separation of Church and State, 1816 Jefferson Place, N.W., Washington, D.C. 20036, (202) 466–3234. E-mail: AMERUNITED@AOL.COM. Website: http://www.netplexgroup.com/americansunited. Americans United publishes the monthly magazine *Church & State,* which regularly reports on Robertson's political activities.

Note

1. Jacob Weisburg, "The Religious Right Hype," *New York* (October 23, 1995).

Index

241